International Screen Industries

Series Editors:
Michael Curtin, University of California, Santa Barbara, USA
and Paul McDonald, King's College London, UK.

The International Screen Industries series offers original and probing analysis of media industries around the world, examining their working practices and the social contexts in which they operate. Each volume provides a concise guide to the key players and trends that are shaping today's film, television and digital media.

Published titles:
The American Comic Book Industry and Hollywood *Alisa Perren and Gregory Steirer*
The American Television Industry *Michael Curtin and Jane Shattuc*
Arab Television Industries *Marwan M. Kraidy and Joe F. Khalil*
The Chinese Television Industry *Michael Keane*
East Asian Screen Industries *Darrell Davis and Emilie Yueh-yu Yeh*
European Film Industries *Anne Jäckel*
European Television Industries *Petros Iosifidis, Jeanette Steemers and Mark Wheeler*
Global Television Marketplace *Timothy Havens*
Hollywood in the New Millennium *Tino Balio*
Latin American Film Industries *Tamara L. Falicov*
Latin American Television Industries *John Sinclair and Joseph D. Straubhaar*
Localising Hollywood *Courtney Brannon Donoghue*
Nollywood Central *Jade L. Miller*
Screen Industries in East-Central Europe *Petr Szczepanik*
Video and DVD Industries *Paul McDonald*
The Video Game Business *Randy Nichols*

The New Screen Ecology
in India

Smith Mehta

THE BRITISH FILM INSTITUTE
Bloomsbury Publishing Plc
50 Bedford Square, London, WC1B 3DP, UK
1385 Broadway, New York, NY 10018, USA
29 Earlsfort Terrace, Dublin 2, Ireland

BLOOMSBURY is a trademark of Bloomsbury Publishing Plc

First published in Great Britain 2023 by Bloomsbury on behalf of the
British Film Institute
21 Stephen Street, London W1T 1LN
www.bfi.org.uk

The BFI is the lead organization for film in the UK and the distributor of Lottery funds for film. Our mission is to ensure that film is central to our cultural life, in particular by supporting and nurturing the next generation of filmmakers and audiences. We serve a public role which covers the cultural, creative and economic aspects of film in the UK.

Copyright © Smith Mehta, 2023

Smith Mehta has asserted his right under the Copyright, Designs and Patents Act, 1988, to be identified as author of this work.

For legal purposes the Acknowledgements on p. viii constitute an extension of this copyright page.

Cover design: Louise Dugdale
Cover image: Little Things © Netflix / Courtesy: Everett Collection. Alamy Stock Photo.

This work is published open access subject to a Creative Commons Attribution-NonCommercial-NoDerivatives 4.0 International licence (CC BY-NC-ND 4.0, https://creativecommons.org/licenses/by-nc-nd/4.0/). You may re-use, distribute, and reproduce this work in any medium for non-commercial purposes, provided you give attribution to the copyright holder and the publisher and provide a link to the Creative Commons licence.

All rights reserved. No part of this publication may be reproduced or transmitted in any form or by any means, electronic or mechanical, including photocopying, recording, or any information storage or retrieval system, without prior permission in writing from the publishers.

Bloomsbury Publishing Plc does not have any control over, or responsibility for, any third-party websites referred to or in this book. All internet addresses given in this book were correct at the time of going to press. The author and publisher regret any inconvenience caused if addresses have changed or sites have ceased to exist, but can accept no responsibility for any such changes.

A catalogue record for this book is available from the British Library.

A catalog record for this book is available from the Library of Congress.

ISBN:	HB:	978-1-8390-2570-9
	PB:	978-1-8390-2571-6
	ePDF:	978-1-8390-2568-6
	eBook:	978-1-8390-2572-3

Series: International Screen Industries

Typeset by RefineCatch Limited, Bungay, Suffolk
Printed and bound in India

To find out more about our authors and books visit www.bloomsbury.com and sign up for our newsletters.

Contents

List of Illustrations   vi
About the Author   vii
Acknowledgements   viii

1   Studying the Indian New Screen Ecology   1
2   New Screen Ecology Narratives about Television   25
3   Mapping the Key Platforms and Portals   43
4   Indian Online Creator Culture   61
5   Regional and Localizing Online Content Practices   83
6   The Role of Intermediaries   99
7   Conclusion   119

Notes   135
References   137
Index   163

Illustrations

FIGURES

3.1	Photograph of YouTube Fanfest at Bandra Kurla Complex, Mumbai	47
4.1	Arré Facebook post promoting Voot content	69
5.1	Scheduled Indian languages in descending order based on the speaker's strength	87

TABLE

1.1	List of platforms/portals operating in India's new screen ecology	4

About the Author

Smith Mehta is an Assistant Professor at the Center for Media and Journalism Studies and Journalism, University of Groningen. He holds a Doctor of Philosophy in Creative Industries (2021) from the Queensland University of Technology, Australia, and specializes in media industries studies, creator cultures and production cultures. He has previously published in *Media, Culture and Society*, *The International Journal of Cultural Studies*, and other journals. Smith has previously worked in Viacom18 Media Pvt. Ltd as a content producer and was selected as a UNESCO Asia Pacific creative specialist in 2018-19.

Acknowledgements

This book is based on a PhD I began in 2017 at the Queensland University of Technology, Digital Media Research Centre, Australia. As someone who transitioned from industry to academia, it was not easy to imagine the task of carrying out a scholarly work of this scale in a different country. For this reason, I am supremely thankful to Stuart Cunningham, my PhD supervisor, and David Craig (Stuart's co-author of *Social Media Entertainment*, 2019). I am particularly grateful to Stuart for seeing in me what I did not and for taking me under his wing to build on his and David's stellar work on social media entertainment. I am equally beholden to my other PhD supervisor, Kevin Sanson, who continues to guide me since my PhD days. Thank you, Stuart and Kevin, for your unwavering support.

Even if the thoughts started taking the form of words in 2017, much of my knowledge in the working culture of the screen industries began developing in mid-2013, when I commenced working as a creative trainee at Viacom18 motion pictures. I am thankful to my mentors, Jyoti Kapur Das and Rukshana Tabassum, for patiently teaching me the art of evaluating scripts, responding to the calls of interest from filmmakers, but most importantly teaching me the art of diplomacy and networking.

Achieving this milestone was made easier due to the efforts of several academics and fellow students who have all played a significant role in shaping this work: Professors Amanda Lotz, Patrik Wikstrom, Michael Curtin, Aswin Punathambekar and Paul McDonald, Subin Paul, Jarrod Walczer, Guy Healy, Shanti Kumar, Elisabeth Prommer, Ashwin Nag, Akshaya Kumar, Rahul Mukherjee, Jean Burgess, Amit Rai, David Nieborg, Brendan Kreogh Sriram Mohan, Bondy Kaye, and other wonderful colleagues from the Digital Media Research Centre, Australia. All offered guidance and support in varying capacities. Special thanks to Adrian Athique and Sangeet Kumar for providing constructive feedback on my scholarship, my work would not be what it is today without their critique. Special thanks to my all-weather mentors, Ruchi Jaggi, Sarita Patil and Anshul Ailawadi, who continue to offer generous support whenever I ask for their help.

I owe huge debt to the University of Groningen for striving to make the monograph open-access. My gratitude to the entire Bloomsbury team, especially Rebecca Barden, Veidehi Hans, Merv Honeywood, Roza I.M. El-Eini and other for their prompt support throughout the publication process.

I am also thankful to the Center for Advanced Internet Studies (CAIS), Germany, which offered fellowship and generous funding support to continue my data collection on gendered production cultures. This study would not have been possible without the support of my industry colleagues and mentors, who offered to share their time and contacts during my fieldwork. Many thanks to my transcribers, Shivani Gera, Shilpa Talari and Pradyumna Kalagi, for assiduously transcribing the interviews within a short period of time. Many thanks also to my dear friends, Sohom Sengupta and Sumana Sengupta, who let me stay at their home during my fieldwork in Kolkata.

Sections of the book have been presented at conferences of the National Communication Association, International Communication Association, Digital Transactions in Asia, and European Communication Research and Education Association. Sections of the book have previously appeared in *Media, Culture and Society* (doi.org/10.1177/0163443719899804), *Convergence* (doi.org/10.1177/1354856519896167), *International Journal of Communication* (doi.org/10.1177/1367877919880304), *International Journal of Cultural Studies* (https://ijoc.org/index.php/ijoc/article/view/12577), *Feminist Media Studies* (doi.org/10.1080/14680777.2019.1667077), *Television and New Media* (doi.org/10.1177/1527476419861698; https://journals.sagepub.com/doi/10.1177/15274764221135798), *Communication, Cultural & Critique* (https://academic.oup.com/ccc/article-abstract/14/3/524/6307131), *Contemporary South Asia Journal* (https://doi.org/10.1080/09584935.2023.2203899).

This book is dedicated to my parents, Jyotsana Mehta and Nitin Mehta, my sister, Hiral Mehta, my partner, Magdalena Wischnewski, my brother-in-law, Jignesh Patel and my mother-in-law Karin Focke. I am indebted to them for embracing my failures and celebrating my successes. I am also thankful to my childhood friend, Ravi Ray, and Pooja Ray, for their unwavering backing. My deepest gratitude to my friends Zaher Auda, Vedran Tukera and Rucizka Tukera, for making Germany feel like home. As a first-generation doctorate, I am still trying to situate my place and contribution in academia but the endearing love and support of my near and dear ones keep me going.

This book has been published open access thanks to the financial support of the Open Access Book Fund of the University of Groningen.

1
Studying the Indian New Screen Ecology

Who would have imagined that the advent of internet-based content distribution services would render the Indian screen industries more informal than ever? The Indian production culture is witnessing an eclectic shift in creator cultures whereby writers become directors, talent agents become producers, stand-up comedians become writers or actors, vloggers become actors, intermediaries become producers and so on. The shift is principally aided by the advent of social media platforms that offer the infrastructure for media professionals to gain credability for creating content and producing talent without enduring the burden of distribution and marketing expenses that preface the film and television sector. The dynamic creator culture is a result of the advent of start-ups and emerging creators who, despite enduring the conditions of overwork, underpay and inequitable working conditions, are using platforms like YouTube and Facebook to build a career within close-knit and guarded Indian screen-industries communities by expanding their value propositions in the media-making processes.

Consider, for instance, the example of TVF's journey from social media entertainers to launching a subscription-based streaming services TVFPlay as well as creating and licensing content for other streaming services like Netflix, Amazon Prime Video, SonyLIV and ZEE5 (discussed in greater detail in Chapters 3 and 5). TVF's web series *Yeh Meri Family* (This is My Family, 2019) was licensed to Netflix (also available on its portal TVFPlay), while another web series, *ImMature*, was premiered at the Cannes film festival and is part of one of the largest Indian media network Times Internet's streaming service, MX player (Rajesh 2018). Similarly, media enterprise Arré (predominantly operating on social media; see Chapter 4) partnered with Times Internet's upcoming streaming service MxPlayer to create an original comedy web series *Tathastu* (So Be It!) (Rajesh 2018).

TVF's example is just one amongst a series of movements that emerging and existing media professionals are making based on their ability to attract internet audiences with their fictional content. Consider the profession of talent agents, who are typically known for identifying talent and helping them in career choices. The Indian talent agents such as Only Much Louder (OML), Kwan and Tulsea have used the digital transformation as an opportunity to diversify their business models by venturing into content production, distribution, marketing and syndication. As an example, OML produced stand-up shows on YouTube for their talent, Biswa Kalyan Rath and Zakir Khan, who are predominantly stand-up comedians. The success of their videos eventually helped the creators transition from performing stand-up comedy to writing web series for Amazon Prime Video, namely *Laakhon Mein Ek* (One in a Million) and *Hamare Chacha Vidhayak Hai* (My Uncle is a Legislator), respectively. Zakir Khan and Biswa Kalyan Rath both enjoy a massive following on YouTube, with subscriber bases of over two million (Khan 2011) and 0.5 million (Rath 2008). What makes these collaborations distinct is the trust of global streaming services such as Amazon Prime Video in providing the opportunity to creators who have been popular predominantly for their stand-up comedy to drive long-form narratives on the streaming service in the capacity of a writer – and, in Zakir Khan's case, also as an actor.

This book examines the ideologies, perceptions and the causes behind the shift in creator cultures. It focuses on the power dynamics between the key sets of media professionals such as streaming service executives, talent agents, creators (writers, directors, producers, vloggers, stand-up comedians), and non-television content curators (typically identified as Multi-Channel Networks, MCNs) to tell the story of the digital transformation of the Indian screen industries. I explore the media professionals' attempts to build social capital and distinct professional identities by adapting to the restructuring of the Indian screen industries. The central focus is on the internet-based content distribution services that not only comprise of social media platforms but also local and global streaming services operating in India. I define the tensions and the interdependent dynamics on the internet-based content distribution services between the key professionals as the 'New Screen Ecology' (NSE) as I argue that the metamorphic shifts in the production cultures would not be possible without the internet and the symbiotic relationship between these professionals. By tracing the digital transformation of the Indian screen industries since the launch of YouTube in 2008, and situating the social, cultural and economic changes within the historical formal and informal relations within the screen industries, this book offers an ethnographic perspective on the digital production cultures and its impact on the labour conditions in a post-colonial setting. I argue that the distinctiveness of the Indian New Screen Ecology arises from the platform–portal–film interdependencies enabled by the industrial practices of the creators, platform/portal executives and intermediaries, and the contrasting production cultures between television and the New Screen Ecology. This is despite the fact that televised content forms a major contributor of the broadcaster-owned streaming services.

The Indian Media and Entertainment industry is estimated to reach $55–70 billion by 2030 from its valuation of $27 billion in 2020 (Boston Consulting

Group 2021). Reports attribute this growth rate to the rise of internet-based content distribution services, commonly referred to as over-the-top (OTT) or streaming services, and the Gaming, Animation and Visual Effects (VFX) sectors. Although television continues to be the most viewed medium at 193 million homes with 878 million viewers in 2021, its viewership has gone down from 892 million viewers in 2019 (Kohli-Khandekar 2022). In comparison, India's streaming service viewership is estimated at 468 million (MICA 2022). Social media, entertainment and communications are, apparently, the three preferred activities of the 692 million active internet Indian users in 2022 (Mustaquim 2022).

The Indian online audio-visual entertainment, since the introduction of YouTube and Facebook in 2008–9, morphed into a hybrid space in which content produced by contemporary film and television industry professionals and professionalizing amateurs coexists. The participatory framework of platforms like YouTube and Facebook has changed the content production landscape in India (Kay 2018; Kumar 2016). According to an independent report by Oxford Economics, YouTube contributed approximately US$859 million and created 683,900 full-time jobs through its content-creation management system in 2020 (Shinde 2022).

The 40 platforms and portals operating in India as at early 2021 are listed in Table 1.1. The list is sourced from Rana (2022), MICA (2022) and Fitzgerald (2019).

Competing alongside social media platforms and broadcaster-led streaming media services are an eclectic mix of over 40+ digital native streaming services (Altbalaji, The Viral Fever (TVF)), global streaming services (Netflix, Amazon Prime, Spuul), language-specific streaming services (Hoichoi, Addatimes), and telecom provider-led streaming services (Jio). The growing interest in online video businesses is also fuelled by the availability of affordable internet-enabled multimedia devices, and reduced data charges (US8 cents per gigabyte) (BCG 2021). The new screen ecology mainly consists of players from six sectors: traditional broadcaster-led portals (Hotstar, Voot, SonyLIV); social media platforms (YouTube, Facebook); digital 'pure-play' native portals (Altbalaji, TVFPlay); global portals (Netflix, Amazon, Spuul); regional language-specific native portals (Hoichoi, Addatimes); and telecom portal JioOnDemand. I have restricted the scope of my study to two social media platforms (YouTube, Facebook) and eleven portals (ZEE5, Hoichoi, Addatimes, Netflix, Amazon Prime, Voot, Hotstar, Reliance Jio, Altbalaji, TVFPlay, Spuul) owing to their presence in hosting or commissioning original content. These are operating fully fledged businesses in the online content development and production space, either by facilitating talent on social media or commissioning original online audio-visual content. A

Table 1.1 List of platforms/portals operating in India's new screen ecology

Platform/Portal	Owner	Year
YouTube (platform)	Google	2008
Facebook (platform)	Facebook	2008
ErosNOW	Eros International Pvt. Ltd. company	2012
SonyLIV	Sony Pictures Network India	2013
Hotstar	Star India Pvt. Ltd.	2015
YuppTV	YuppTV	2015
SUNNXT	Sun TV Network Ltd.	2017
TVFPlay	The Viral Fever	2012 on YouTube. 2015 as a VoD platform
Netflix	Netflix	2016
Voot	Viacom18 Media Private Ltd.	2016
Viu	Vuclip	2016
JioOnDemand	Reliance Infocomm	2016
Amazon Prime	Amazon	2016
Altbalaji	Balaji Telefilms	2017
HOOQ	Sony Pictures Entertainment, Warner Media and Singtel	2017
Hoichoi	Shree Venkatesh Films	2017
ZEE5	Zee Entertainment Enterprises Ltd.	2017
MXPlayer	Times Internet (Times Group)	2019
Ullu	Ullu Digital Pvt. Ltd., a subsidiary of Jaypeeco Infotainment	2018
Shemaroome	Shemaroo Entertainment	2019
HungamaPlay	Hungama Digital media entertainment	2015
Flipkart	Flipkart	2019
Doordarshan	Doordarshan	2019
Aha!	Arha Media and Broadcasting Private Ltd.	2020
Firework (Platform)	Firework	2019
ShareChat (Platform)	Mohalla Tech Pvt. Ltd.	2015
ManoramaMax	Malayala Manorama Group	2019
Apple TV	Apple	2019
BigFlix	Reliance Entertainment	2008
CuriosityStream	CuriosityStream	2019
DocuBay	IN10 Media	2019

Veqta	Multimedia Group	2012
Koode	Studio Mojo	2020
Mubi	Mubi	2019
Stage	Vinay Sanghal, Shashank Vaishnav, Parveen Sanghal	2020
CityShor TV	CityShor.com	2020
Chaupal	Pitaara TV	2021
Planet Marathi	Akshay Bardapurkar	2021
Olly Plus	Subhrakant Sahoo	2020
Zomato Original	Zomato	2019

detailed clarification and analysis of respective categories is presented in Chapter 3, respectively.

Players such as Sony, Hotstar, Voot and Zee are typically categorized as traditional broadcaster-led portals due to their presence in the television industry. TVFPlay and Altbalaji's qualities as indigenous and digital-only content portals allow for their identification as digital 'pure-play' native portals. YouTube and Facebook are identified as social media platforms due to their social interface and free uploading of content characteristics that separate them from the rest. The specificity of the Bengali language allows Hoichoi and Addatimes to be different regional language-specific portals. Finally, the global online distribution networks of Amazon Prime, Netflix and Spuul qualify their distinction as global portals. Reliance JioOnDemand's distinct position as a telecom company-led portal reflects its categorization as a telecom and content venture.

The entry of Reliance Industries Limited (RIL) into the telecommunications sector in 2015 through Reliance Jio played a significant role in the roll-out of high-speed and low-cost internet to the masses. Reliance Jio's low-cost internet plans forced competitors like Vodafone and Airtel to follow suit (Mukherjee 2019). Besides investing US$42 billion in digital infrastructure, Jio scaled India's overall internet consumption by providing low-cost 4G internet rates and Jio smartphones. Athique and Parthasarathi's (2020) study of the political economy of the Indian platform articulates how the entry of Reliance Jio into the content and telecommunication sector through the introduction of Jio TV, Jio Music and Jio Chat offered the necessary means to expand its data services – a strategy that telecom competitors like Vodafone and Airtel adopted to explore multiple ways through which consumer data metrics could be captured through connectivity. I only map one telecom provider. Reliance Jio's content and pricing strategy (in Chapter 2), as my research is concerned explicitly with original content commissioning strategies, not all content acquisition strategies.

Four revenue models dominate the Indian NSE. The first model is referred to as Advertising Video-on-Demand (AVoD). It is characterized by singular dependence on advertisements as a source of revenue. YouTube and Facebook are clear examples of NSE players that operate under this model. As can be observed from YouTube's and Facebook's massive online video consumption and Hotstar's and Voot's launch strategies, such a system works very well in India, where consumers are shy of paying for content and often resort to piracy. The second model, referred to as Subscription Video-on-Demand (SVoD), is characterized by charging a fee in exchange for its streaming services. ZEE5, Hoichoi and Netflix employ this model. The third system involves using a combination of AVoD and SVoD models and is commonly defined as the Freemium or hybrid model. The Freemium model keeps marquee content behind a paywall and offers the rest under the AVoD model. Both Hotstar and Voot have pivoted to a hybrid revenue strategy. Finally, the Transaction Video on Demand (TVoD) model can be witnessed on Google Play Movies and TV, and charges a fixed fee for every video content purchase.

The Indian Government expedited the process of 5G under the National Digital Communication Policy launched by TRAI as a part of its Digital India initiative ('TRAI Chief Sees New Govt' 2019). While analysing the Indian Government's transparency measures in governance, Singh and Ilarvasan (2016) articulate the Digital India programme initiatives such as Aadhar Card (a biometric system for identifying Indian citizens), the introduction of online and mobile government services and the launch of a Government portal for engaging with citizens on issues concerning education, employment and tourism as key to the development of digital growth in India. The Digital India programme also proposes to connect 0.25 million Indian villages with the National Optical Fiber Network (NOFN) (Narayan and Narayanan 2016). Through collaboration with the Indian Government, Google launched the Indian Language Internet Alliance (ILIA) to facilitate Hindi-language content availability. While examining the complexities between the Government, the market and the digital economy, Thomas (2019: 71) argues that the close relationship between the Indian Government and the multinational internet-based companies arises out of the Indian Government's plans to 'mobilize resources, know-how, and technology in the creation of 22 smart cities by the year 2022' as part of its ambitious Digital India project.

While outlining the distinctions of social media entertainment from the traditional media industries (film and television), Cunningham and Craig's (2019) study on the US-centred social media platform landscape delineates streaming media services such as Amazon and Netflix as 'close-ended' portals (a term coined by media industries scholar Amanda Lotz (2017) to identify broadcast and internet-based television from social media) and YouTube and Facebook as 'open-ended' social media platforms. In doing so, they differentiate creators on the social media platforms from portals. They define the creators on social media as social media entertainers who monetize content through various commercial strategies such as brand integrations, marketing, and advertising. They argue:

> YouTube was launched and quickly engaged in competing with Hollywood film and television for audiences and advertisers through a mix of professionally generated (PGC) and user-generated content (UGC) strategies. But YouTube encountered competition from emerging PGC video portals, like iTunes, Netflix, Amazon, and Hulu, and turned to fostering the rise of creators through partnership agreements and programmatic advertising.
>
> (Cunningham and Craig 2019: 37)

However, unlike the US, the diversity within the Indian platform–portal space has led to the emergence of a small but growing segment of professionalizing amateur production companies, such as The Viral Fever (TVF), All India Bakchod (AIB), Arré and Pocket Aces, that are collaborating across the platform–portal divide based on their social media popularity.

The Viral Fever (TVF) was India's first YouTube channel to reach a million subscribers in 2015 through original programming of web series and sketches. Its journey from social media entertainers to launching a portal, as well as becoming producers for other portals, exemplifies the interdependence of Indian social media entertainment and portals.

In arresting these dynamic synergies in the Indian NSE, I foreground the platform–portal interdependencies concerning the histories of Indian film and television industries to investigate the practices that led to the digital transformation of the Indian screen industries. I draw attention to the shifting creator dynamics in contemporary film and television production with the advent of platforms and portals. I explore how creators navigate these digital infrastructures and benefit from the lack of censorship to develop sociopolitical narratives and industrial practices distinct from film and television in approach, management and treatment. The details of the empirical investigation of this contemporary networked production dynamics reveal how PGC, not limited to legacy media companies, thrives alongside UGC on YouTube and Facebook as creators use the social media as the starting point for breaking into portals and films and launching their media careers to counter the culture of favouritism and content-saturation within traditional media.

Drawing on first-hand research with three categories of human agents: creators, platform and portal executives, and intermediaries (talent agents, multi-channel networks), I develop the concept of the 'new screen ecology' to show how the Indian screen industries are affected by social relations between these human agents and how their industrial practices blur the amateur–professional divide through creator and content interdependencies beyond the platform–portal divide. By juxtaposing the contemporary digital production cultures with existing traditional media structures, I show how the contemporary platform–portal linkages are rooted in the formal–informal exchanges within which the Indian film and television industries are situated.

At a macro-level, both platforms and portals offer viewership metrics. The algorithms that power the NSE back-end capture user details, real-time video viewing habits and offer content solutions from its catalogue to the viewer based on these data. However, from a creator perspective, platforms and portals differ because platforms offer greater transparency on viewership data than the portals (Cunningham and Craig 2019: 45). This is understandable as creators depend on YouTube and Facebook data for direct (paid directly by the platform or through programmatic advertising) or indirect (sponsorship through views) forms of monetization. In contrast, portals bear no liability for sharing their content catalogue's viewership metrics as the compensation is independent of the portal's performance.

Moreover, there is a stark difference between television and online content in India. I argue that Indian television's regressive programming practices and over-reliance on soap operas also significantly motivate creators to use social media platforms such as YouTube and Facebook to express their creativity. Through the content-creation practices on social media, these creators build a distinct following for themselves through followers and subscribers – evidence of their ability to access the perceived 'professionally generated' spaces of films and portals. The portals also serve as another outlet for independent filmmakers and digital media companies who do not have the wherewithal to bear the enormous marketing and distribution expenses associated with theatrical releases (KPMG 2020).

Despite fostering the commercially sustainable practices of innovative multi-platform practices of creators, the Indian NSE has also induced new forms of precarious labour and reinforced gendered structural inequalities prevalent in India's media industries. While emerging digital media companies and social media platforms increasingly rely on newcomers and their multiskilled labour in writing, acting and production departments to offset their expenses, global portals dedicate their energies towards chasing established film professionals and those that acquire popularity on social media.

The lack of secure income afforded to the creators due to algorithmic uncertainty of social media platforms and the unpredictable decision-making of portals has led them to continuously look for opportunities across film and streaming media services. Owing to this, creators are working more than usual to cope with the demands of multimedia labour. The anxieties arising from insecurity, gender inequalities and overwork provide an analytical balance against the opportunities for creators in the Indian NSE, as discussed further in Chapter 5.

Moreover, a multilingual Indian audience within and beyond India creates a significant local and transnational demand for multiple Indian media markets. The demand for Bengali language content in several Indian states such as West Bengal and Maharashtra and countries like the US and Bangladesh is an example of language's potential to create market opportunity. While analysing the political economy of Indian media culture, Parthasarathi, Chitrapu and Elavarthi (2020) rightly signal that the linguistic organization of Indian states presents a critical opportunity for 'different historical, political and economic trajectories for media markets in particular geographies'. India's plurality of languages offers a distinct economic opportunity for media producers to target audiences defined by language, resulting in multiple and overlapping media markets. Parthasarathi (2017: 13) reminds us of the challenges that come with studying 'market power in a media economy characterized by multiple and overlapping "cultural markets"' in his investigation on the market dynamics of the Indian media economy. The drawing of Indian state boundaries based on language by no means bound the language-specific audience to a particular territory – an opportunity that is tapped by online regional (Bengali and Marathi) creators and producers as they challenge the monopoly of television distribution and use platforms like YouTube and portals like Netflix to pursue transnational careers, as will be further highlighted in Chapter 5.

Equally significant to the platform–portal–creator axis in the NSE is the dynamism of intermediaries such as talent agents and third-party service providers such as Multi-Channel Networks (MCNs), which, by executing functions of producers, media managers and talent managers, have exercised a strong influence over the content strategies of the Indian NSE. I limit the scope of intermediaries to MCNs and talent agents by building on previous scholarship on intermediaries concerning the digital transformation by Raymond Boyle (2018), Cunningham and Craig (2019) and Mohan and Punathambekar (2019). These influential scholarships have systematically foregrounded the significance of talent agents and MCNs in shaping digital production cultures in the UK, US and India.

My work on Indian intermediaries bears stark resemblances to Raymond Boyle's (2018) investigation of the UK talent industry grappling with the advent of streaming services. Based on interviews with commissioning editors, broadcasters and talent agents, Boyle (2018) unfolds how talent in the UK has been historically interpreted and constructed to underline the shifting roles of broadcasters, commissioning editors, producers, platform operators, talent agencies and public relations firms in identifying, valuing and managing talent in the digital age. In articulating the differing business models of intermediaries in Chapter 7, I borrow Boyle's (2018: 132) conceptualization and understanding of the MCNs as follows:

> The term multi-channel network (MCN) has been around since the mid-2000s and was used to describe networks of online content clustered under a brand mostly curating short-form non-television content. Such is the pace of change that while the phrase still exists its meaning is shifting and moving from aggregators of online content and numerous online channels, to a sense that generating and curating your own content and brand is becoming more important, not least as that age-old debate between content producers and platforms (and where the power lies) remains unresolved.

Much like Boyle's (2018) assertion on the shifting role of MCNs, my research on Indian MCNs such as Culture Machine, One Digital, Silly Monks and Qyuki Media adopted a platform-agnostic approach by functioning as a producer, organizing a creator network and localizing its services for platforms, portals, films and television producers.

RESEARCH OBJECTIVES

My study explores and analyses the networked production cultures between platforms, portals, creators, talent agents and multi-channel networks by focusing on three areas:

1. ownership structures and value propositions of the diverse streaming media services operating in India;
2. quotidian practices and motivation of content creators in relation to platforms and portals;
3. the role of intermediaries such as talent agents and multi-channel networks in the Indian new screen ecology.

Herbert, Lotz and Punathambekar (2020: 15) argue how different levels of inquiry can offer 'differing vantage points' for researching by eliciting how 'the surface of the earth appears differently from space, from a jet at 30,000 feet, a helicopter, a tall building, or when standing on the ground'. Building on this multiscalar perspective, I map the Indian digital production culture from three epitomized vantage points by choosing the objects of study at the macro (platforms and portals), meso (intermediaries), and micro levels within the NSE.

These objectives are meant to encourage inquiry into the everyday lives of media practitioners that use digital/social media to sustain the production, management, and circulation of online content that eventually impacts the way screen industries operate in India. Three frameworks underpin my understanding of the NSE, as discussed below.

KEY FRAMEWORKS

The first framework borrows from Cunningham and Craig (2019) and Lotz (2019) to distinguish the NSE into platforms and portals. The second framework uses the works of Sundaram (2009), Lobato and Thomas (2018) and Athique (2020) to situate the Indian NSE as a link between the formal–informal media economy. The third and final framework uses the CMIS approach to explore the multiscalar nature of the Indian NSE. These frameworks, together, propose the argument that given the historically intimate relationship between the Indian formal and informal media economy, it would be inaccurate to dismiss social media platforms from the study on Indian digital production cultures. I clarify these frameworks in the sections below.

Platforms and portals

The rapid uptake of technology by creators has produced remarkable changes in intellectual property management and funding structures. Holt and Sanson (2013) define this phenomenon as 'connected viewing', where the media companies employing multiplatform strategies and entrepreneurs with their start-ups are vying for attention from the audiences by employing innovative business models. In so far as the contemporary debates concerning the digital transformation of the audio-visual industries are concerned, there is a tendency to focus in the production culture on portals (see Bouquillon 2020; Fitzgerald 2019; Lotz 2017, 2018). This is because platforms are typically understood as 'user-generated content' (UGC) sites that do not contribute directly to the media industries – creators are not employed directly by the platforms, and the platforms do not provide data on either the creators they remunerate or the total amount that they spend on remuneration. It is not easy to reconcile the total economic value that these sites generate. Moreover, the vast scale and diversity of UGC content make it difficult to ascertain the originality of the content.

Equally confusing is the bifurcation between UGC and PGC. Note that the understanding of UGC from a labour relations perspective is users who fall outside the scope of professionally generated content (PGC) sites such as the film and television industries and portals, also at times referred to as 'low' or 'mediocre' (Keen 2007: 2–3). As van Djick (2009: 49) highlights, UGC creators are those who:

> contribute creative efforts 'outside' of professional routines and practices. Terms such as 'hobbyists,' 'amateurs,' 'unpaid labourers' and 'volunteers' often applied to internet contributors, contrast with the words 'professionals,' 'stars,' 'paid experts' and 'employees' commonly attributed to people producing traditional television content.

Amanda Lotz's (2014, 2017, 2018) formative scholarship on digital transformations within the US screen industry provides a comprehensive understanding of the changes brought about by portals like Netflix and HBO, which Lotz identifies as 'internet-distribution television', and sites for 'professionally produced content circulated and consumed through websites, online services, platforms, and apps, rather than through broadcast, cable or satellite systems'. Until the existence of PGC content on YouTube is acknowledged, the term is restricted to incumbent media companies that use YouTube services for promotion, distribution and marketing purposes (see Kim 2012). However, India offers a different NSE model than the US-centric one in that there lies a strong porosity between social media platforms, portals and the film industries.

Understanding the digital production cultures by delineating platforms from portals or the Indian NSE from the broadcast and film sector limits our ability to understand how Indian creators operate beyond the platform–portal–film divide and use it as a conduit for developing symbiotic relationships within the media industries. In contextualizing the interrelationships between platforms, portals, television and films in relation to the Indian online media landscape, I emphasize that the online content-creation cultures cannot be studied by isolating a single platform or portal.

This is because, in India's case, YouTube has emerged as a site that, besides hosting other non-commercial and homemade videos, is an alternative destination for web series, stand-up comedy videos and diverse genres that the Indian television industry could not appreciate due to its rigid industrial and cultural logics. Having arrived later than YouTube and Facebook, portals like Netflix, Amazon Prime and SonyLIV look to collaborate with individuals and digital media companies that have discovered success on social media through content and talent-led ventures to secure sustainable income from social media entertainment. As I show in this book, the success of media enterprises and creators specializing in and commercializing online content-creation practices paved the way for the portals to borrow the expertise of successful social media creator labour to develop their content slate. The focus on the Indian NSE is also driven by the creators' perception of platforms and portals and how these perceptions influence their NSE content creation practices.

Formality and informality

I build on the previous body of literature (Lobato and Thomas 2018; Rai 2019; Athique 2020), articulating the contribution of the informal economy in the Indian media industries to show how the contemporary platform–portal linkages are rooted in the informal–formal exchanges within which the Indian film and television industries are situated. Media scholars Ramon Lobato and Julian Thomas define the informal economy 'as an analytical concept that refers to a range of activities and processes occurring outside the official, authorized spaces of the economy' (Lobato and Thomas 2018: 7). The Indian NSE assumes an ambivalent site whereby it, at one time, adheres to the gatekeeping and gendered social hierarchies but at other times also challenges the nepotistic closed-network circuits amongst family-owned production houses and distributors by becoming a distribution outlet for independent talent and content. The NSE becomes a space that facilitates a relative diffusion of alternate voices and content that would otherwise struggle for attention on traditional mediums.

From this perspective, NSE embraces and epitomizes Amit Rai's (2019) articulation of the 'jugaad' culture in India. In his ethnography of mobile phone ecologies in Mumbai and Delhi between 2009 and 2017, Rai (2019: 6) defines 'jugaad' as:

> an everyday practice that potentializes relations that are external to their terms, opening different domains of action and power to experimentation, sometimes resulting in an easily valorized workaround, sometimes producing space-times that momentarily exit from the debilitating regimes of universal capital.

Building on Rai (2019), the NSE operates as a site fraught with frugal innovations and questionable work ethics, and a place that embodies resistance at various levels but also reinforces class and gender-based inequities. As an example, content that is prohibited on film and television, and which is restricted owing to the industry lore of film and television producers as well as professionalizing amateur talent without strong familial connections, are 'formalized' by the platforms and portals operating as aggregators and producers, respectively. At the same time, precarity arising from unreliable work opportunities and unsafe working conditions for women exemplify the continuation of endemic informalities. I argue the formal–informal links are crucial in establishing the link between the NSE as well as a distinction between the NSE and the film and television industries.

A brief look at the history of India's film and broadcasting media can also help us contextualize the vital formal and informal industrial practices that shaped these sectors and eventually paved the way for the Indian NSE. I narrow the Indian film sector's history to the Hindi film industry (Bollywood) as my scholarship principally focuses on the links between Bollywood and NSE.

The Bollywood (Hindi) film industry, in particular, was notorious for financing 40 per cent of the films during the 1990s through informal means (Athique 2012). Through a local and global network of informal distribution (local shops, pavement traders) and the use of technology in the form of Audio Cassettes, Compact Discs (CDs) and Digital Video Disc (DVD), 'entrepreneurs' and mafia indulged in the sale of pirated films to the South Asian communities in the West, Pakistan, Bangladesh and the Gulf (Athique 2012).

In order to curb the menace of crime and money-laundering and exploit Bollywood's local and global economic potential, the Indian Government accorded it the 'industry status' in 1998 (Govil 2013). With this status and the liberalization policy in effect, the industry could now seek local and overseas institutional finance funding. The industry profitability improved significantly with overseas box office collections, music and broadcast rights (Athique 2012). In many ways, the scale of the informal film economy alerted the Indian Government to Bollywood's economic potential. As observed later in the section on NSE, the emergence of NSE shows similar patterns of informality between platforms and portals in that the UGC-led platforms link with portals by emulating content and creator mobilization strategies.

Post-industrialization, Bollywood also witnessed a co-existence between 'Hollywood style corporatization' led by the entry of multinational companies Sony, Disney and Viacom and family-run media houses Dharma Productions, Yash Raj Films and Balaji Telefilms (Punathambekar 2013). However, despite this phenomenon, Lorenzen and Taeube (2010) highlight how film businesses are driven mainly by kinship and social relations, social structures determine the work opportunities within Bollywood. The industry's suspicion of the corporate culture arises due to their insistence on formal procedures. Lorenzen and Taeube (2010) unfold these tensions in their study:

> The corporate way of insisting on elaborate contracts tends to crowd out informal relations, and producers employed in the corporations are new to Bollywood and do not get many chances of building personal relations to star actors, directors and other Bollywood personalities, as they are shifted between projects and are subject to organisational changes in the corporation.

As I highlight in Chapter 4, instead of enforcing corporatization, multinational companies have conformed to the informality by either hiring industry insiders as top executives or giving undue preferences to the socially elite film professionals. Thus, social media platforms become passive conduits for pursuing a filmmaking career in such a scenario. Just as the film sector's finances came from sources outside the formal structures, the creators who participated in the digital transformation of Indian media industries came from the UGC sites – outside the 'formal PGC' networks.

Like Bollywood, the Indian television industry grew due to informal practices in its production, distribution, consumption, and non-transparent television measurement system. While analysing Indian television's post-liberalization business practices, Kohli-Khandekar (2010) argues that India's urban middle class had already transitioned to cable TV (television) systems since the 1980s, albeit illegally, to escape the state developmentalist programming of Doordarshan. While analysing the cable industry in Mumbai post-1990, Naregal (2000) highlights the underlying nexus between politicians, cable operators, broadcasting entities, police, government officials and corporates and the ensuing power struggle to control larger cable-distribution territories for revenue share.

The US broadcaster Cable News Network's (CNN) telecast of the Gulf War in 1991 paved the way for India's mushrooming of cable connections. All the cable operators had to do was invest in Dish Antenna, pick the signal and transmit the connections through the already connected households' wires. The spurt in television consumption, driven by the informal distribution network, attracted the attention of investors like Star TV, Zee and Tamil-language television channels Sun TV and JJTV. By 1995, a slew of South Indian regional networks such as AsiaNet, Eenadu TV and Udaya TV was launched to cater to South Indian languages (Tamil, Telugu, Kannada, Malayalam), resulting in 'the freeing of television from the Hindi-centric policies of state broadcasting' (Athique 2012: 59).

While the growth in television penetration is also a result of successive governmental interventions in the form of the Cable Television Network (Regulation) Act (1995), and the New Telecom Policy (NTP) (1999) to facilitate transparent and competitive space, questions still remain on the Government's considered policy silence over the issue of untransparent ownership of the television distribution business and cable distribution nexus between the politicians and businessmen (Parthasarathi and Srinivas 2022).

Thus, I argue that India's film and television histories remind us of the significance of informal and formal practices that need to be considered when studying India's digital transformation of the screen industries and therefore emphasize the inclusion of social media platforms alongside portals as an effective framework for studying digital production culture.

Critical media industries studies

Timothy Havens, Amanda D. Lotz and Serra Tinic (2009) outlined that Critical Media Industries Studies (CMIS) has its roots in cultural studies and operates within the broader contours of media studies. The framework promotes 'critical analysis of how individuals, institutions, and industries produce and circulate cultural forms in historically and geographically contextualized ways' (Herbert, Lotz and Punathambekar 2020: 11). It was constituted to address the lopsided attention given to media texts and audiences and explore how power operates within local, regional, national and global settings, media industries, and labour communities. I argue that CMIS's focus on creator-labour conditions offers the most appropriate framework for studying the micropolitics of labour in the Indian NSE. Besides the multiscalar approach, the CMIS's focus on the domain of power relating to creator autonomy and working conditions distinguishes it from other significant approaches used to study the Indian media economy. Compared to the other approaches, CMIS offers a theoretical background to investigate and assess the power dynamics concerning creator-labour conditions. The book's focus on the professional identities and the everyday schedules of creator labour responds to the growing calls by media industry scholars, for example see Kevin Sanson (2021), to examine the consequences of structural changes on the working conditions of labour.

CMIS allows multiscalar perspectives to analyse digital transformation in the Indian screen industry, focusing on creator careers. The CMIS approach also offers a mid-level framework to capture the micropolitics between organizational practices and production practices beyond the platform–portal divide. This is particularly useful as India's distinct NSE model is characterized by strong porosity between social media platforms, portals and the film industries. This cross-pollination has been led by next-generation SME talent largely excluded from the establishment film and television industry due to nepotistic reliance on family and friend circles, rather than trained professionals, and the extreme dominance of traditional soap operas on television (Mehta 2012).

The platforms and portals, in sum, adorn a distinct site of disjuncture as well as continuity – they are part of the screen industries but are diversifying far more in content, talent and genre sources. The term 'industry' is indicative of the set of 'social and textual arrangements, sites of enactment, and other dramaturgies of interaction, reflection, and reflexivity' that media scholar Nitin Govil (2013: 176) urges us to consider while exploring the factors that contribute to the production of a media industry. Similarly, a mid-level approach is crucial to understanding the varied relations that key human agents form within a production culture. I borrow from Govil's (2013) critical commentary to argue that the social and economic exchanges between the creators, platform, portals and intermediaries in the data metrics of viewership and subscription, content and talent are strong indicators of industrial practices. Building on Govil (2013), I argue that a critical aspect of media industry studies is to study industrial practices of social media platforms that are opaque due to lack of data and yet interact with industrial objects (film, television, portals) to develop content for popular cultural consumption.

In approaching the book from a CMIS framework, my work contributes to a small but significant corpus of work on creator labour within the Indian context (Booth 2008; Ganti 2012; Chitrapu 2017). Within India, very few studies have focused on labour itself (Chitrapu 2017; Mazumdar 2015). While investigating the inequities within Indian Film and Television production networks Chitrapu (2017) researches film and television labour unions to offer rich insights into the institutionalized gender discriminatory practices at play. Chitrapu (2013: 161) highlights how 'very few women are members of these unions and fewer still serve on committees of the unions'. Chitrapu (2013: 163) argues that the practice of privileging family and friend circles within the Indian film industry fosters:

> inequality of access to work between workers at the centre of the networks and workers at the periphery of the networks, thereby excluding women, minorities, and many others who lack privilege or connections in various forms.

Within the film industries, marginalization of creator labour occurs at the expense of privileging family and close friends in matters related to film financing, distribution and casting, as pointed out by Lorenzen and Täube (2008, 2010) in exploring the congested network of overlapping business and family relationships within the Hindi film industry. These networks' very selective preferential treatments reduce the Indian screen industries to a prism that refracts a spectrum of social and economic inequalities and renders certain jobs invisible. The prosaic nature of these divides is a reflection of India's deeply hierarchical class and caste-based society, and the digital infrastructures are no exception to this rule. Prominent SVoD portals, as I detail in Chapter 2, skew towards recruiting established film professionals alongside breakout social media celebrities and occasionally commissioning shows to digital media production companies that have a noteworthy following on social media. As I argue, this is because access to social capital is more valued than subscriber numbers.

An important point to mention here is that the omission of caste-based politics within the NSE ecology in this book is down to the fact that my book focuses on the motivations of creators for creating content on platforms and portals and the various social and material relationships that the creators derive with platforms, portals and intermediaries to pursue a creative career. For this reason, while any specific observations on a creator's caste in benefitting his/her career within the Indian NSE will be superficial as far as the book objectives and findings are concerned, I do acknowledge that the majority of the cohort of creators I interviewed as well as considered for the book belong to the educated middle class or upper-middle class. This is to acknowledge the fact that despite the increase in internet usage and decrease in data costs, the lopsided socioeconomic growth of India shows that creators with educated and cosmopolitan viewership are privileged over others when it comes to forging a career across platforms, portals and films. Moreover, the varying degrees of resistance women face in working within the Indian NSE are discussed at length in Chapter 5.

Thus, while analysing the influence of caste in the NSE is beyond the scope of this book, the book must be read with the caveat that the influence of gender and class does privilege certain creators over others. Nevertheless, this acknowledgement does not dilute the argument in the book that the NSE offers a glimpse of opportunity for individuals and organizations that are not intrinsically linked to the media industries. As I argue in this book, the metrics of viewership and subscriber data have enabled the so-called 'outsiders' to use the data for social and material gains and challenge the close networked structure of the traditional media industries. This structure was responsible for protecting a network of family and friends with repeated opportunities irrespective of economic failures.

The rise of the NSE created a space for emerging creators to show their talent against the backdrop of the closely guarded film and television industry. I argue that the sudden popularity and success of early social media creators like AIB, TVF and many other actors and above-the-line workers (whom I discuss throughout the book) and content created on both social media platforms as well as portals have led these industries to reflect on the need for innovation in talent and content whilst also reinforcing gender and algorithmic precarity.

DEFINING INDIA'S NEW SCREEN ECOLOGY

I examine the term 'new screen ecology' to explore its connotations regarding the Indian media landscape, its use and its limitations. 'New Screen Ecology' symbolizes the political, social, cultural and economic exchanges that creators, platform and portal executives, talent agents and multi-channel intermediaries negotiate in developing visual content for platforms or portals. Despite the content's intended delivery on digital-delivery distribution infrastructures, the transactions that facilitate the production have effects beyond the platform–portal divide and on the film and television landscape. The term 'New Screen Ecology' explores the effects and the nature of these manifold directions by using digital delivery as the layered site of production.

A broader and related understanding of the term 'ecology' can be traced to media scholar Baltruschat's work on the effects of digital transformation in the production and audience in Europe and North America. Baltruschat (2010: 18) uses the term 'media production ecology' to explore the close circuit of relationships between:

> producers, broadcasters, advertisers, sponsors, funding agents, cultural policy analysts, and—in regards to multiplatform media—digital content developers, telecommunications service providers, and interactive media …

Rahul Mukherjee's (2020) exploration of the effects of media coverage surrounding cell towers and nuclear reactors reminds us how an ecological approach to media infrastructures can be useful in exploring the politics of mediation. The use of ecology in my work is symbolized by the focus on mediatization of cultural production by specific human agents. It implies a web of complex, networked and inter-related relationships between platforms, producers, creators and intermediaries. As media scholar Debashree Mukherjee (2020) remarks in the Acknowledgements section of her influential monograph of the Bombay cinema in the period 1929–42, 'an ecological view of film production acknowledges that all acts of creation happen within a network of relations'. Taking a 'cine-ecological' approach to offer a distinctive histography of early filmmaking practices 'from financial speculation and screenwriting to dialogue delivery and stunt work', Mukherjee's (2020: 2) towering work is useful in defining the factors that stimulate the production site.

In making a case for studying the media as ecology, I also build on the previous studies (Cunningham 2015; Cunningham, Craig and Silver 2016) that have afforded similar distinctions while studying the scale and the impact of the growth of platforms and portals on the notions of media globalization. Cunningham and Craig (2019: 13) argue that an ecological approach implies,

> investigating the interdependencies amongst its elements: mapping the platforms and affordances, content innovation and creative labour, monetization and management, new forms of media globalization, and critical cultural concerns raised by this nascent media industry.

Two key differences underpin the difference in applying the term 'ecology' between Cunningham and Craig (2019) and my work. First, in contrast to Cunningham and Craig, my work highlights the dynamism between platforms and portals in shaping the social and economic transactions within NSE and not just social media platforms. Second, the Indian NSE projects a more dynamic relationship with the film and television industries. Its growth is rooted in the formal–informal exchanges like the latter but shares more commonality with the film industry in creator exchanges and production culture compared to the television industry.

My ecological and multiscalar approach is further informed by Athique, Parthasarathi and Srinivas' (2017) edited volumes on the Indian media economy that explore the interdependency between media businesses and economic sectors. In the second volume, Parthasarathi (2017: 2) stresses the need for an ecological approach to studying the 'burgeoning, complex relationships between the media sector and other social, symbolic, and financial structures'. Parthasarathi argues that the distinctive nature of the Indian media economy arises from the rich and varied degree of interdependences between media and other markets where media serves the role of logistics or service. For these reasons, contrary to a medium-by-medium approach, an analysis of these interdependences requires accommodating varied transactional processes of creators as they navigate between the mediums to build sustainable careers. Therefore, while it is not possible to parse out all the complexities arising out of multilevel interdependencies, the process of digital transformation can nonetheless be understood by determining the participants such as the platforms, portals, intermediaries and creators.

In exploring the meaning-making practices of the creators within the media industries, I situate my study within the broader production studies literature and have concentrated on the power struggle between creators, platforms, portals and intermediaries. This means that I have not focused in-depth on relevant aspects of the NSE in general, such as algorithmic culture, platform/portal infrastructure, the impact of advertising in financing the content of social media creators, and the new screen ecology audience as they are not a central part of my analysis.

METHOD

I have studied the Indian NSE through a combination of semi-structured interviews with media practitioners, discourse analysis of interviews, textual evidence of select online media texts, and analysis of trade press literature and industry reports.

The 90 interviewees can be subdivided into the following groups:

- *creators* (n=67) who have practised online content creation in the capacity of vlogger, writer, stand-up comedian, director, producer, actor, and founders of media companies operating on platforms and portals;

- *intermediaries* (n=9), such as talent agents, casting agents, and multi-channel networks operating within the Indian new screen ecology;
- *platform and portal executives* (n=14), such as chief operating officers, chief executive officers, content heads, and creative producers.

Apart from the Hindi and English language content creators, my cohort also includes respondents who create content in diverse languages such as Marathi, Bengali, Gujarati and Tamil. I kept the cohort diverse by conducting interviews with respondents from diverse spatial locations like Kolkata, Delhi, Chennai and Ahmedabad. This range of interviewees is consistent with my objectives and has enabled me to better understand the extent of the mutability of the NSE roles. While gender diversity within the Indian media industries remains a constant concern (see Chapter 5), I have tried my best to boost the sample size of female respondents (n=35) for the study.

I used a combination of purposive and snowball sampling to constitute the interview cohort. As I developed my understanding of the NSE, it became clear that I needed to interview representatives of the key components of the NSE, such as creators, intermediaries and platform/portal executives. This was easier said than done because the NSE respondents were difficult to interview, given the lack of reciprocity between academia and the industry. There was little or no perceived benefit for the highly entrepreneurial creators and intermediaries working on platforms/portals (Cunningham and Craig 2019), as well as the privacy-driven portal executives, who were unwilling to share their strategies due to a fear of giving data to competitors. My prior experience as a media practitioner for three years with Viacom18 Media, a joint venture between Reliance Industries and Viacom, was influential in identifying some of the micro-media industry transformations and finding respondents for the study.

The interviews were conducted in four waves. In the first wave, I conducted three semi-structured interviews in Mumbai and Ahmedabad and one interview over WhatsApp, as creator Sorabh Pant was on tour. WhatsApp was selected for convenience, as it is widely used in India. It also allowed Sorabh Pant to respond at his convenience. In the second wave, 15 email interviews with online creators and platform/portal executives from Mumbai, Bhopal, Ahmedabad and Delhi were conducted from Brisbane between October 2017 and January 2018. During fieldwork in Mumbai and Kolkata between March 2018 and August 2018, 48 semi-structured interviews were conducted, except for one email interview conducted in January 2019 with an MCN executive. Conducting email interviews before in-depth interviews helped map emerging trends and frame interview questions with precision. Finally, the remaining interviews, with the exception of two telephone interviews to examine women's working conditions in the streaming services, were conducted over Zoom in the fourth wave. Due to the sensitivity of the issue, I have anonymized their names. The four-wave approach helped me to cover gaps and get close to a good purposive sample. Most semi-structured interviews lasted between 60 and 90 minutes. All interviews were recorded, transcribed and then analysed along with email interviews using NVivo software. A combination of open coding aimed at 'delineating concepts' from raw data and axial coding to identify 'crosscutting or relating concepts' was used to develop themes for data analysis (Corbin and Strauss 2008: 195).

Long-form popular content on online media such as TVF Pitchers, Permanent Roommates and Little Things is used as textual evidence to compare its formal and aesthetical storytelling techniques with popular television fiction content. The textual evidence is based on a study of some of the most notable features of TV-style and narrative construction and comparing themes in soap operas and online series. I note the detailed studies of such textual aspects in Chapter 2. However, my primary focus is on the industrial and cultural logic that drives storytelling in both formats. I draw on textual evidence to support the creators' understanding of each medium's industrial and cultural limitations and affordances. I have also relied on popular press articles from *The Economic Times*, *The Financial Times*, *Huffington Post*, *Quint* and *Caravan* to track events in the Indian screen industry. Alongside these articles, media and entertainment industry reports were sought to track the industry size and viewership numbers.

Much of the Hindi film industry's data in trade magazines lack accurate statistics, owing to the lack of a 'centralized tracking agency' (Ganti 2012: 37), and the NSE fares no better in its comparison, for similar reasons. Like the Indian film industries, the NSE lacks a central body that can account for the size and scale of the ecology and provide numbers on the performance of platforms and portals. Even in cases where industry reports have circulated data on platform–portal viewership data, the figures have been sourced from third-party research companies. As Govil (2016) concludes from his investigation of the first Indian media and entertainment report in 2000, consultancy reports on media in India project optimism to promote a vision for the future. A characteristic of these reports is the aesthetical visualization of data, which depicts India's readiness to compete and complement global media economies (Govil 2016). These reasons have limited my ability to offer a more thorough comparison of platforms/portals on size, scale and performance criteria.

BOOK STRUCTURE

This study investigates the rapid growth of the Indian NSE populated by over 40 platforms and portals in India – a much larger figure than in most other countries, which provide the production milieu for new as well as existing voices and assist in producing new content/formats for a previously underserved, growing demographic – mostly male, predominantly urbanist, cosmopolitan and educated – under conditions of production and regulation that allow for greater freedom to experiment. I approach the study by applying a multiscalar critical media industries studies framework that emphasizes on analysing production cultures at macro- (platform/portal), meso- (intermediary) and micro- (creator) perspectives to parse out the underlying power struggles between media practitioners at varying levels of production and circulation of culture.

Chapter 2 critically analyses the various issues that have prompted select creators to focus their creative energies on NSE content. The chapter shows that because a growing segment of Indian content creators is disillusioned by television's programming and industrial practices, they increasingly embrace NSE as the preferred outlet for their creative expression. The chapter examines the everyday practices of the television industry and compares the formal and aesthetic qualities of their textual artefacts with the NSE, as these professionals navigate the larger structural tensions between television and digital media in India. Investigating this issue is significant for my book, as the internet came when television was already available to audio-visual content creators as a medium for expressing their creativity. Therefore, it is critical to analyse the factors that prompted the shift of talent from television to the online medium and, at the same time, made it more appealing for emerging creators.

Chapter 3 maps the market dynamics of diverse streaming media services in India concerning the value propositions of platforms and portals. By analysing the various content strategies, distribution mechanisms, ownership patterns and revenue models, this chapter offers a descriptive overview of the platform economy and the distinct value propositions offered by each of these platforms in shaping the contours of the Indian NSE. In particular, this chapter focuses on the industrial practices of thirteen dominant local, transnational and global streaming platforms and portals and their relationship with content creators, whose origins and practices form a critical base for analysis in future chapters. I explore the digital infrastructures and market forces that are determining the platform economy in India.

Chapter 4 demonstrates evidence of creator mobility from social media to films and portals. I articulate the porosity in creator labour and production culture practices between social media platforms (YouTube, Facebook), content, portals and films. This chapter also discusses how creators deal with precarity. I highlight the multimedia labour approach of Indian online creators to discuss the various ways in which the creators perform agentic subjectivity and embrace precarity. At the same time, I analyse the social conditions of their work to highlight the precarious conditions that force them to adopt multiplatform labour. Overall, the chapter offers insights on the key aspects that demonstrate how the NSE has influenced the Indian media landscape by opening new avenues and opportunities for emerging creators facing a backlash from traditional media industries over creative hegemony, censorship and nepotistic practices. Discussion themes include quotidian practices, identity construction of creators, non-hierarchical corporate structures, and localization practices, forming the basis for discussion in future chapters. Issues concerning NSE, such as censorship and treatment of women creators, are raised.

Chapter 5 expands on Chapter 4's theme of regionalization and localization practices within Indian NSE. In this chapter, I discuss the emergence of multilingual online content and its creation practices by regional online content creators, platforms and portals that go beyond the established practices of traditional regional media industries and the notion of 'catch-up television'. In this chapter, I foreground the growing popularity of the original multilingual Indian enterprises in the Indian NSE since 2017. In doing so, I show how the 'localization' strategy of platforms/portals as well as the 'translocal' diasporic consumption (Athique 2005) is strongly influenced by the creators emanating from regional spaces and creating content in their native languages. Through a primary focus on online content-creation practices in Bengali and Marathi languages, I explore their 'local', 'regional', 'transnational' and 'global' appeal, and the subsequent blurring of boundaries between 'regionalization' and 'localization' as they imagine communities beyond national or regionally drawn borders.

In Chapter 6, I show how intermediaries are increasingly gaining more prominence as architects of the NSE owing to their ability to first spot, represent and assist talent in building a career trajectory using social media affordances, and second, use online popularity as a means to secure deals with local and global streaming platforms such as Hotstar and Amazon Prime. The popularity of online content creators, platforms and portals among audiences has also led intermediaries to reassess their responsibilities and business models to widen their commercial opportunities (Boyle 2018) by operating as producers and diversifying their investments in media and talent-related ventures. Buoyed by the increase in the creation and consumption of online content, MCNs and talent agents have restructured their value propositions to function as a one-stop-shop for talent scouting, content production and other media and talent-related management activities.

In closing, this book addresses gaps in the media industry studies literature on the dynamics of digital transformation in the screen industries in a region-specific context and contributes to a body of literature on Indian production cultures and creator cultures.

2

New Screen Ecology Narratives about Television

This chapter argues that the economic imperatives of broadcast television engender very formulaic programming that is aimed at the general household audience, especially at those who use television as a companion to other activities in the domestic space. On the other hand, the New Screen Ecology (NSE) exploited new technologies and industrial models that allowed the targeting of different audiences in different locations, resulting in the production of more diverse and sometimes experimental content. It marshals evidence to suggest that the television industry's production culture discourages creators from seeking meaningful work and instead look for opportunities on the NSE.

An investigation that compares television with the NSE is also critical as the internet came at a time when television was already available to content creators as the prime medium for expressing their creativity. Therefore, it is critical to analyse the factors that have prompted the shift of talent from television to the NSE, keeping with the emphasis on interdependency – broadcaster-led portals' reliance on broadcaster content and the preference towards NSE from film and television creator labour – embodied in the concept of the NSE.

As established in Chapter 1, Indian television still holds high viewership across India. However, what I unfold in this chapter are creator narratives that have contributed to the increase of 39 per cent digital video consumption in 2020 in comparison to 9 per cent in 2014 (BCG 2021). Using a production culture perspective, I argue that the internet has offered greater freedom and less 'circumscribed agency' to creators instead of television. The chapter presents evidence to suggest that the television industry's production culture limits creators' ability to express themselves, which means they are unable to fulfil their aspirations of working in films and on portals. Instead, creators look for opportunities in the NSE (across platforms and portals) due to its production culture and its social proximity (exchange of personnel) with the film industry. By television's 'production culture', I refer to Indian television's over-reliance on soap operas and the industrial and cultural logic behind the construction of soap operas, which creators believe limits their chances of building a portfolio to fulfilling their career aspirations.

An argument based on a comparatively more creator-friendly NSE ecology is a result of the greater autonomy in the NSE that led creators to develop content to establish their identity. Outside the gatekeeping and hegemonic programming practices of Indian television, creators have exercised greater autonomy and become part of YouTube's participatory culture (Kay 2018; Kumar 2016). Some of the television's gatekeeping and hegemonic programming practices that I highlight in this chapter include monopoly of select producers across General Entertainment Channels (GEC) for creating fiction content, unruly control of broadcasters over producers due to access of flawed Television Ratings Points (TRP), and privileging producers to service social relations. While hierarchies always existed in the areas of creative production between and within above-the-line (ATL) workers (producer, director, writer) and below-the-line workers (stunt workers, make-up artists, stylists, cameramen) (see Curtin and Sanson 2017: 14), the power dynamics between broadcasters and ATL, access to TRP ratings and the desire to retain informal social elite relations resulted in the overall undermining of creators, creativity and innovation.

In contrast, beginning with YouTube, NSE promised international exposure and an emerging alternative to those with little or no social circle in the film and television industry. Moreover, unlike television, the NSE's non-linear programming meant that the platform and portal creators had no pressure to fill its daily programming schedule. By adopting motley strategies such as facilitation, aggregation, acquisition and commissioning of diverse content forms and genres (see Chapter 2), NSE offered a wider array of creativity and innovative content to choose from. These factors contributed to the slow rise of NSE viewing.

In what follows, I trace how the proliferation of television channels' demand to fill inventory space has had direct implications for television content, and thereby creative practices; this has marginalized the work of creative professionals. Second, I chart the industrial practices in the television industry that affect creative potential. To update and focus on the hegemonic practices of broadcasters identified previously by Kay (2018), Kumar (2016) and Mehta (2012), I draw extensively on fieldwork interviews with my cohort of creators. These creators can be classified into three categories: television renegades, creators such as stand-up comedians; 'above the line' practitioners working on platforms and portals; and media professionals working across the film, platform, and portal sectors. Third, I compare the textual features of Indian television and NSE.

TELEVISION'S INDUSTRIAL AND CULTURAL LOGICS

An overwhelming majority of at least 50 of the 66 respondents interviewed for this book pointed out the television industry's over-reliance on soap operas, rating systems and production culture as the main factors for dissatisfaction. Alienation from dominant television content and its craft made the medium unappealing for these media practitioners. KPMG reported that Hindi-language General Entertainment Channel (GEC) content dominated television viewership in the first quarter of 2018 (KPMG 2018: 36). The majority of GEC inventory consists of soap operas and reality shows (Jaggi 2011). Previous studies (Munshi 2012; Pant 2014) also established that soap operas drive maximum viewership and, therefore, occupy most of India's television programming slots.

The television industry post-liberalization was confronted by the growth of television channels which struggled to meet the demand to fill inventory. Figures from 2018 show that Indian television has 866 channels, with 60 per cent of its revenue coming from advertisers (Kathuria, Kedia and Sekhani 2019) compared to 70 per cent in 2012 (Mehta 2012). Co-founder of YouTube channel AIB Rohan Joshi (2018) claimed:

> As there was such a huge inventory demand, our country became used to the idea of daily programming. There was not enough talent and creativity to meet that demand. This led to a bureaucratic system where one player took control over everything. Balaji (telefilms) saw the opportunity and grabbed it.

Joshi's claims are not entirely wrong, given that between 2000 and 2008, Balaji Telefilms produced three high-rated soap operas, *Kyunki Saas Bhi Kabhi Bahu This* (Because the Mother-in-Law was Also Once a Daughter-in-Law), *Kahaani Ghar Ghar Kii* (The Story of Every Home) and *Kasautii Zindagi Kay* (The Trials of Life) (Munshi 2012: 4). Moreover, the fact that the GEC channels only produce 3.5 per day hours of original content on average (with the remaining 20.5 hours being reruns) (KPMG 2018: 36) also limits the possibility of engaging more storytellers who are looking for an opportunity as well as genre diversity – hence the examination of soap opera as a representation of the Indian television industry's production culture.

While discussing the television industry's fundamental challenges, Nalin Mehta (2012) argues that the industry suffers from a *severe* dearth of talent. The then head of Star TV, Uday Shankar, lamented the lack of talent development and training measures as crucial factors affecting television's content quality. Amrit Gupta, the head of online media company TVF vertical Screenpatti, who had earlier worked in television on a general entertainment programme, described its industrial practices as a 'factory' that indulged in creating homogenous mass production. Gupta (2018) exposes the 'ghostwriting' practice that exists within the television industry:

> Multiple writers work for a TV show, but credits are only given to one popular writer. The rest of them (writers) remain unknown but quite known within the industry as ghostwriters. The main writer is supposed to get the work done from these writers, but the main writer usually does not have the time to invest in teaching or keeping a check, which leads to a decrease in the quality of content being produced.

Gupta's exposition of the phenomenon of 'ghostwriting' is similar to the observations made by Gulati (2016) in her interviews with 'above the line' television workers. These experiences indicate the marginalization of creators and reflect the poor industrial practices that are symptomatic of the quality of contemporary television production.

Inherent in these critical accounts are the gruelling production schedules that require television to serve content daily. Indranil Chakraborty (2018), CEO of production company Big Synergy, which has produced over 4,500 hours of content across nine languages on television and portals,[1] remarked, 'Actually, they do not get time to do anything. The time constraint will not allow you to do anything else. You have to reach the set at 7 am, and you are stuck till 10 pm.' Chakraborty shares the structural limitations that restrict the television industry from innovation as well as from nurturing talent.

The media system is shaped in such a way that it allows very little room for even the existing professionals to demonstrate their creativity, as was expressed by Rasika Dugal, an actress who has appeared in critically acclaimed television shows such as *Powder* and *POW – Bandi Yuddh Ke* (Prisoners [Women] of War). Besides television, she has also acted in several Bollywood films and Netflix and TVF web series. Dugal (2018) elaborated on her preference to stay away from a 'certain' type of television content despite facing financial issues at one point:

> One does not require brains while doing these kinds [soap operas] of television shows. There is no script or character treatment. Most people care only about competing the shooting on time and nothing else. They work for 18 hours straight.

As she highlights, these factors limit the scripts' creativity and also the characters' and forces them to look for other media to fulfil their creative aspirations.

In 2016, the popular cultural magazine *Caravan* published a detailed analysis of how Indian television soap operas are created by writers who run their plots based on Television Rating Points and themes that are designed to appeal to the audience's superstitions and regressive practices (Gulati 2016). Sarcastically titled 'Lather, Rinse, Repeat', the article uses interviews with television writers and content analysis of popular soap operas to expose the rampant malpractices within the industry, such as ghostwriting, a lack of creator agency and monopolization of creative output by a few dozen individuals. Delivering a scathing summary of television's most-watched general entertainment programmes, Gulati (2016) observed:

> The most successful shows across Hindi general entertainment channels, or GECs, have a variety of supernatural elements: black magic, evil spirits, witchcraft and – perhaps the most popular of them all – the mythical Ichchhadhari Naagin, a shape-shifting snake-woman. Obsessed with these tropes, television creates a bizarre alternate reality. In one show, a seemingly innocuous daughter-in-law turns out to be a venomous, shape-shifting snake. On another, the greatest challenge in a woman IPS (Indian Police Service) officer's life is to save her husband and his family from dark powers. And in period dramas, historical figures such as Ashoka and Akbar ward off seductive *naagins* (snake-women) while ruling their kingdoms. With more than 50 soap operas being aired across four big networks that run GECs, competition in the industry is fierce. Each time a new idea works, producers descend on it like vultures.

It is pertinent to note that my objective is not to critique soap operas or their melodramatic tone. The objective is to show the broadcasters' lazy and cost-saving production culture practices that imagine their television audience as passive viewers who would be happy with whatever is produced. This understanding of broadcasters has alienated my cohort of creators (who are predominantly urban, educated and influenced by international content and the internet audience) from the television. Previous studies (Jaggi 2011; Munshi 2012; Rao 2001) have already highlighted the distinctiveness of Indian soap operas for their 'larger than life' sequences featuring overtly melodramatic narratives rendered possible by almost exclusive reliance on 'flashback' and 'close-up' sequences. The tacit understanding of the industry gatekeepers who assume that this audience would only be able to understand a 'certain type and construction of melodrama' has had a cascading effect on the professional lives of creators who, based on the evidence I have gathered, feel that their creativity could be utilized more effectively.

Similarly, the academic literature that I examined (Kay 2018; Kumar 2016; Mehta 2012; Rao 2001) alongside my empirical findings illustrates the growing disenchantment that exists among creators due to television's industrial practices, which are motivated largely by economic reasons. I regard these practices as 'regressive', not because they are soap operas but because it is overkill and results in a lack of diversity in fictional content across the GEC channels. Implicit in this understanding is the failure of Indian soap operas to represent the growing reality of 'modern' and 'urban middle-class' families – especially Indian women who situate themselves between traditional values and a modern outlook (Rao 2001: 3). At the same time, the 'hypersensitive' approach to television rating points arising from the dependence on an advertising revenue model has affected television's ability to produce innovative programming and nurture talent (Mehta 2012).

Industry lore

Mehta (2012: 616) states that a lack of talent is one reason for average content marked by 'low levels of innovation in programming and constant repetition of anything that seemed to work'. Vivid examples can be drawn from the aesthetics of Indian soap operas that occupy the majority of the inventory of Indian fiction programming (Jaggi 2011). Based on extensive interviews with a diverse group of Indian television producers, writers, broadcasters and television audience measurement (TAM) executives, as well as textual analysis of five highly rated soap operas between 2000 and 2010, self-confessed soap opera viewer and media researcher Munshi (2012: 210) found that:

> Various techniques of representation such as the swish pan shot, thrice repeated, in different colors, at various climactic moments; the 'recap–precap' procedure; and the return from the 'dead' . . . which, in Indian soaps, includes plastic surgery to keep pace with new actors entering the show, or the same actors returning with makeovers.

Dorothy Hobson (2003: 67) observes that for most of the time in British soap operas, actors are required to 'produce performances that are understated and low-key, always less than "actorly", for it is their job to create the illusion of the ordinary'. Indian soap operas, on the other hand, are overly melodramatic, with several close-up shots that often limit the ability of the actors to deliver quality performances (Munshi 2012: 91).

As someone who interned as an entertainment reporter during his master's course, I recall visiting a set of a high-rated television show, *Uttaran*, in 2014. A dual-camera set-up was organized for one scene, only to take close-ups from different angles of an actress looking at the moon through a sieve, celebrating the Hindu festival of 'Karva Chauth', a custom practised by women for their husbands' wellbeing. Throughout the two hours or so that I spent on the set to cover the update of the show, all I witnessed was the same scene being enacted with close-ups of different emotions and slight modification of postures, offering a glimpse of the repetitive narrative identified by Munshi (2012) and Mehta (2012). Munshi (2012) also discussed the career trajectories of key television actors to highlight how the melodramatic overtones of Indian soap operas often led them to be typecast, affecting their ability to seek roles outside the television industry, as argued in an interview by actor, writer and producer Ranganathan Madhavan.

Madhavan was one of the first 'mainstream' (film) actors to appear in the web series space in a critically acclaimed eight-episode Amazon Prime Original series titled *Breathe*. Madhavan (2018) drew on the example of actor Sumeet Vyas (a former television actor who became popular after acting and writing TVF web series), who drew a large following among young audiences after shifting to NSE work, to argue that the industrial logic of the television industry deterred actors from pursuing their craft. Summing up the technical practices characteristic of the television industry, Madhavan (2018) asserted: 'television is basically a medium of close-ups. All the drama on television is in the close-ups; acting does not really matter.' Other than money, these creators can rarely leverage the 'cultural capital' accumulated by working in Indian soap operas across the Indian media and industry landscape. The lack of genre diversification (Mehta 2012) and over-reliance on overt drama and close-up shots affect their chances of seeking more creative work.

However, it was not just the writers but several professionals from other video-making departments who believed that their careers had been stymied in television. Gupta (2018) recounted a story of his friend who worked on a crime investigation show to give an account of the poor treatment meted out to the television writers:

> One of my colleagues, who used to work for television and write crime investigation shows, was given just seven days to write a 40 minutes episode. He was given crime-related cases of just five to six lines and told to create a fictitious story around it. While the entire media industry works on writing software like *Celtx* and *Final Draft* for scripts, my colleague was specifically asked to change the script format to a Word document.

The television industry's failure to adapt to the adherence of professional standards suggests a lack of recognition towards the contribution of its writers. It also indicates an apathetic attitude towards the development of its writers, who are expected to turn out scripts in a short amount of time with little or no supervision. In her ethnographic fieldwork on television industry professionals, Munshi (2012: 50, 58) repeatedly notes that the producers and broadcasters often feed off each other's 'instincts' and 'gut feelings' to decide 'what will work'. These practices marginalize the contributions of creative professionals, who are trained for a specific task.

Consider the work of casting agents, who identify and prepare characters for their roles. Their services are generally utilized for their ability to spot these characters' descriptions through auditions. They also conduct a series of workshops for featured casts to prepare them for the role. Comparing his experience of casting in television as opposed to the film and online mediums, Indian Casting Company co-founder Trishaan Sarkar (whose company has been responsible for casting in Bollywood and Hollywood films, and web series on platform and portals) posited that their company generally abstains from casting in television shows as their methods are often driven by quantity over quality. Sarkar (2018), who has graduated from acting school and often takes up acting roles, observed:

> Television depends more on coordinators than casting directors. Coordinators are people who will find a catalogue of actors for the audition of a role as opposed to the casting director, who will shortlist five faces as per the brief given to him.

Discussing his personal experience of casting for a television show, *Life OK*, Sarkar added:

> We kept auditioning for 20 days for casting three characters and ultimately chose the actor that the director had mentioned on the first day. The other two were my choices. Typically, they [producers/broadcasters] have a habit of going through hundreds of auditions before selecting an actor. They are not comfortable if they are shown only three faces and are told to choose from that.

Sarkar's frustration with the television industry arises from the fact that there is a lack of trust in the work of a casting director, thereby leading to doubt about the quality of their work, which involves 'casting' the right actor for the role. Sarkar also highlights the vague selection methods that value quantity over quality, noting that the actors contacting him are often reluctant to take up acting roles in television, building on the popular self-theorized fear that they will be 'treated like a prop on television where there is one wide shot and countless close-ups', providing little scope to demonstrate their talent (Sarkar 2018).

In contrast, creators on platforms/portals rely on the expertise of the casting agent, who has know-how about conducting auditions and identifying actors following the needs of the script. Explaining this to me was the co-founder of Casting Bay, Abhishek Banerjee. Casting Bay is one of the earliest casting agents to have ventured into casting for online content. Abhishek started as a theatre artist in Delhi. He took up the job of a casting assistant in a feature film, *Dev D*, where over time he developed passion and acumen for his job; this eventually led him to start his venture in 2015, along with his colleague Anmol Ahuja (Banerjee

2018). Banerjee and Ahuja have become prominent in the casting industry due to their experience in casting for feature films and web series.[2] Within the NSE, the duo has worked on most of TVF's web series, including *Permanent Roommates* (2014), *Tripling* (2016) and *Yeh Meri Family* (This is My Family) (2018). They also partnered with Amazon Prime for casting in web series such as *Mirzapur*, *Hamare Chacha Vidhayak hain* (My Uncle is a Legislator) and *Inside Edge*. While illustrating the influence of the casting agents in web series, Banerjee (2018) emphasized that the casting directors 'come into the scene' even before the script is written. Banerjee's testimony suggests an increasing involvement from creators in the internet production culture as opposed to television.

While describing television's casting practices in his industry lore, he highlights that:

> Casting Bay has never even considered casting for television as they are not looking for actors. They are merely looking for faces who will connect with a housewife sitting in Kanpur [a Tier 2 Indian city] or a man in Ranchi [another Tier 2 Indian city] as it is a general entertainment channel. The problem here is that anyone who has a decent talent for delivering a line and looks decent enough on camera can become an Actor in television. One does not need to drill himself with workshops, training or voice modulations. I have had previous experience in television where actors used to get the script on the morning of the shoot. Television does not need 'Casting Bay'; they need people who can just provide pretty faces and not creative expertise.
>
> (Banerjee 2018)

The perception of their work, and therefore their classification as mere 'coordinators', has also rendered the services of casting agents invisible, further discrediting their line of work. These reasons have pushed casting agents to look for new challenges, and they have focused their services towards online media and films, where their skills are more valued.

Jyoti Kapur Das, who has worked across the film, television and digital mediums as a writer and director, reflected on her experience of working with a regional GEC television channel, Star Pravaha (Marathi language). Kapur Das (2018) said that her main motivation for working on television was the huge 'pay-cheque' at the end of the month. She narrated how 'film technicians used to, and even now, look down at working in television'. The creators' perception of television suggests a lack of any motivation other than the economic benefits. The disregard for other creative forces in the engineering of these shows has thus affected the ability of workers to engage creatively. However, it is equally important to note that the business model of television broadcasters has heavily influenced their production practices.

Economic base for industrial and cultural logics

The Indian television channels are heavily dependent on advertisements (which now represent 60 per cent of revenue) compared with a subscription fee, contrary to most developed television industries in the United States, United Kingdom and Europe (Mehta 2012). This makes the broadcasters very sensitive to television ratings. As Mehta (2012: 620) notes, 'the structural economy of television forces many channels to focus on content with the lowest common denominator that will register on television rating panels'. Good ratings mean that the producers/broadcasters are keen to stretch the storyline on the same constructed sets to save costs, even at the expense of creative fatigue. Connecting the dots between the demography of the audience and television programming, Sidharth Ravindran (2018), Marketing Manager at Netflix and a former MTV marketer, observed:

> Television works on the advertiser's money. If one looks at its relevant audience today, one has to look where the ratings come in from. They come from smaller towns and rural areas, which means that the storytelling has to be simple enough for them to understand. How this has impacted the content on television is that they have dumbed down their narrative, over-explained the situations (through the narrative), and overall spent a lot of time to seize the situation rather than the reaction of the character.

This explains the deployment of close-ups and taking up screen time in employing 'swish-pan' shots, as these strategies make up the episodic duration and the series can be stretched as far as possible. As Ravindran (2018) quips, 'Television has always been about economies of scale. What I mean is it has always tried to churn out the maximum number of episodes at the best cost possible.' By indulging in these industrial practices, the broadcasters can shoot many episodes on a single set. This helps them reduce their production costs while also benefiting from the everyday viewing of the audience, who are heavily invested in the character and do not mind the stretched narrative. At the same time, Ravindran's industry lore of the television audience as 'rural' and Mehta's (2012) view of them as the 'lowest common denominator' warrant further attention.

Owing to the digital and urban–rural divide in India, there is a populist perception that television is construed as a medium for the masses as opposed to individuals. It is a 'collectivist' escape medium that encourages family viewing (Mankekar 1998), given that most houses in India own only a single television set (KPMG 2018). Thus, broadcasters make systematic attempts to create soap operas that are universal and family-friendly. Even socially, most states in India still follow a patriarchal system whereby men go out to work and women are expected to take care of the family for various reasons such as family expectations, social stigma, male domination or literacy (see Jensen 2012; Jayachandran 2015; Klasen and Pieters 2015; McKelway 2019). While this may not be true in all urban and developed metropolitan cities, large swathes of rural areas are closed to different philosophies, owing to a lack of exposure to the internet, education and, more importantly, resources that allow for reflection beyond survival and maintenance of a standard of living.

There are strong reasons for the rural focus, even though the treatment (lack of talent and content development measures) may not be justified. First, as we discussed earlier, 70 per cent of the Indian population still resides in rural areas with a lack of digital infrastructure, leading them to depend on television as their single source of entertainment. Partho Dasgupta, the CEO of the Broadcast Research Council of India (hereafter, BARC), the nodal agency for issuing television ratings, highlighted two of the pertinent rural India practices that complement the current television industry's focus on rural audiences. As Dasgupta (2017) observes:

> [About] 96.5 per cent of the total of 183 million television-viewing households are single-TV households. This suggests that affluence may have led to the purchase of other consumer durables than opting to purchase a second television. The unique Indian habit of the entire family sitting together prevails. Urban India may have 84 million of the total 183 million television households, with penetration of close to 87 per cent. But rural India has overtaken it with 99 million television households, even as television penetration remains 52 per cent.

Television's obsession with the television rating points system often comes at the expense of creative inputs of 'above the line' workers who feel marginalized by its creation practices. This has led broadcasters to react in quite a sinister way, adopting 'lazy programming and taking short cuts to register high on the ratings, somehow, anyhow – whatever the cost' (Mehta 2012: 621). The cost was losing talent, as television now has a direct competitor on the internet. At the same time, enough empirical and academic evidence exists to suggest the gendered notion of television consumption. As Kumar's key analysis of Indian television programming post-1990 argues, the content across television channels was constructed to evoke an identity of post-colonial 'nationalism' that drew upon a 'collective sense of familial and cultural heritage' (Kumar 2010: 178). The concept of familial values, however, is deeply rooted in the patriarchal history of India, and it has contributed to creating a certain type of content that alienated the creators even further.

Gendered perception of television

While analysing soap operas produced in 2017, a journalist observed that 'Women in television serials are either black-magic performing witches, docile daughters-in-law or exist only to protect or take care of another character' (Nair 2017). In analysing the construction of identities and the portrayal of sociocultural aspects of television soap operas post-2008, feminist media scholar Ruchi Jaggi (2011: 146) notes that the media texts 'provide a lot of opportunities to include ritualistic and religious elements to construct stereotypical, traditional narratives'. Malhotra and Rogers (2000) concur in their study of ten top-rated television programmes in 1997 that while women assumed greater visibility and had an increased screen presence, an abysmal 10 per cent of women characters worked outside the home as opposed to 95 per cent of men characters, indicating characterizations conforming to patriarchal and national interests. In her critical commentary on an Indian soap opera, *Kyunki Saas Bhi Kabhi Bahu Thi* (Because the Mother-in-law was Also Once a Daughter-in-Law), Fazal (2009) notes that television has failed to mediate the lives of urban middle-class families, modern Indian women and their lived experiences. Moorti (2007: 13) corroborates this analysis in her study of prime-time programming on Indian television: 'Independent women are presented as those requiring regulation and by the narrative's end revert to being doormats or shadows.' These shreds of evidence reflect television's failure to imagine an urban Indian community and an industry blinded to the sociocultural reality of working women and the nuclear family.

Despite a celebratory account of soap operas, Munshi (2012) notes that the shows revolve around the conflicts between the 'mother-in-law' and 'daughter-in-law' and the latter's idealistic portrayal to impress the former. The story is unveiled in the post-marital home, where the couple live with the husband's entire family in a traditional joint family arrangement. The narratives are strategically targeted at Indian households with a patriarchal structure, where it is common for married women to stay at home while their husbands go to work. While it is not unusual for children to live with their parents after marriage, these shows indulge in objectification and vilification of some characters – in most cases, women. Soap operas consistently reinforce the patriarchal value system by demonstrating that it is only women's self-sacrificing nature that helps them overcome conflict situations. These conflicts are mostly planted inside homes, overtly posturing towards women's role as a homemaker. At the same time, from a production perspective, an indoor shoot will always cost less.

At the same time, shooting episodes with sluggish narratives featuring women protagonists is another example of catering to a skewed female audience. This was alluded to by TVF Creative Director Nidhi Bisht (2018):

The narrative of these shows is usually structured in such a way that the housewives can watch these shows while cooking or other everyday household activities. For instance, the narrative is deliberately sluggish to allow them to catch up even if they are caught up doing their household activities.

Bisht highlights the deep-rooted patriarchy in which women are expected to take care of household chores. Jain and Pareek (2018) note from their study of gender portrayal on thirty family soap operas from 1990 to 2016 that females are often relegated to perform domestic chores as opposed to men. Thus, conforming to familial values that celebrate patriarchy continues to mediate television content right up to the present day, alienating young and urban audiences and creators.

The dual effect of antique industrial practices and regressive content has severely impacted the creative aspirations of creators as the differences between them and the broadcasters over what works and what does not keep growing. Dugal (2018) argued that:

> We [producers, television broadcasters] are not doing justice by bracketing our audience into several headings by saying that 'this audience is there on television and a particular type of audience is there on digital'. A person who watches '*saas-bahu*' saga [meaning family dramas around the mother-in-law and daughter-in-law relationship] shows can even watch *Powder*. It is not right to think that a person will watch only a particular type of content. Often, creators on television make shows that are path-breaking in terms of the content being created but then in the middle of these shows, the broadcasters get scared because of losing Television Rating Points (TRP) and try to 'switch' to make the content more commercialised. There is a kind of feudalism on this medium, where broadcasters try to dictate what will work.

Here Dugal refers to *Powder*, a limited-episode narrative that exposes the underbelly of the narcotics trade in Mumbai, which was discontinued on television due to low ratings. *Powder* was also recently acquired by Netflix for distribution on its platform.[3] Dugal's first-hand experience offers a clear account of the contemporary tensions between the creators and broadcasters over the preoccupation with television rating points, contributing to a history of scepticism about the television measurement system (Mehta 2012). These reasons have combined to contribute to the migration of talent to online media.

As has been evident from the creators' views, they continue to compare the production practices of soap operas with the work offered in the NSE to highlight the distinctive work opportunities available. Often, these discourses refer to fiction storytelling on the internet, such as sketches and web series as the basis for distinction. In order to analyse these distinctions in detail, the next section will focus on the gratification that the creators seek in working on the internet. Similarly, select media texts created by digital media companies are analysed to unpack the contextual differences in the portrayal of content. Findings suggest that repetitive and regressive content programming on television has served as a creative counterpoint for NSE creators. The cinematic techniques employed in Indian soap operas, such as the 'swish-pan shot', the endless frames and generation-leaps, are popularly deployed as objects of humour, parody and satire on the internet.

MOVING TOWARDS NSE

Contrary to soap operas, Indian web series come with a limited length of 10 to 15 episodes. Some of the most popular soap operas have run into more than a thousand episodes (Munshi 2012). Web series on streaming media services such as *Pitchers* (TVF and YouTube), *Breathe* (Amazon Prime), *Sacred Games* (Netflix), *Chukyagiri* (Arré), *Tripling* (TVF and YouTube) and *Humorously Yours* (TVF and YouTube) have all had single-digit episodic runs. Long-form internet web series like *Pitchers* and *Permanent Roommates*, among many others, tackle issues of start-up enthusiasts and live-in relationships, which find greater resonance among the young audiences and creators than the stories about family sagas that are more common to television. The internet is the medium of convenience for creators and audiences and forms part of the realities and identities of young urban Indians, with its selection of stories. For most of these individuals, the stories of live-in relationships and entrepreneurs are cathartic and represent 'their' everyday stories of struggle, choices and aspirations.

As an example, the first Indian web series was *Permanent Roommates*, produced by TVF in 2015. *Permanent Roommates* traces the story of a couple (Mikesh and Tanya) in a three-year long-term relationship, wanting to get married. Mikesh's insistence on marriage and Tanya's subsequent reluctance lead them to a compromise where both agree to a live-in relationship as a testing period for marriage. The first season ends with a fallout between the two. The second season begins with a run-up to their marriage, where Tanya's and Mikesh's families meet. However, things take a surprising turn as Tanya finds out she is pregnant. The series tackles live-in relationships and premarital pregnancy issues, both of which are common for urban middle-class audiences and would not be aired on television. The content on the online medium has also received a favourable response from Indian millennials and cosmopolitan audiences who relate to this content as opposed to television soap operas (Kay 2018: 4).

The writers of the web shows identify with these young audiences and possess 'lived experiences' that are relatable. Writer/director/actor Dhruv Sehgal – who works for digital media company Pocket Aces Pvt. Ltd., which produces sketches and web series on its multiple YouTube channels as well as for Netflix – argued that while writing, 'he wants his craft to be as close to reality as possible' (Sehgal 2018), so he 'writes stories by keeping in mind the characteristics of people he lives with'. The company's founders encouraged Sehgal to come up with 'relatable content'. Having shifted to Mumbai from Delhi, he came up with the story of 'a Delhi boy, living in Mumbai', which eventually culminated in a popular web series, *Little Things* on YouTube,[4] with an average viewership of five million. *Little Things* essentially chronicles the story of the everyday life of a young couple in a live-in relationship in Mumbai. The primary characters, a PhD student played by Sehgal and a sales executive played by Mithila Palkar, reflect the lifestyle and choices of young, educated, urban Indians. It highlights the everyday anxieties associated with careers and relationships and how the characters deal with them.

It is difficult to raise these issues on television, which still depicts the customs and traditions of traditional India in its prime-time fiction programming. Ekta Kapoor, the co-founder of Balaji Entertainment Pvt. Ltd., confessed in an interview:

> The internet is your new private life. Putting content on TV [meant for the internet] is actually saying, 'You now watch it here, with your family.' And, the families are not ready for it. I do not think things will change on TV because the youth and the people, who want more individualistic stories, will walk away from the medium.
> (Pathak 2017)

For Kapoor and several channel programmers and television producers, television is primarily a medium for the family, and the internet is for the youth. The narrative of Mikesh and Tanya, while being watched online by new audiences, is not perceived to be palatable for family audiences. It is almost as if both the mediums are portraying different 'realities' of modern India.

Sehgal (2018) further explained how he kept the conversations real and grounded. For instance, from his own experience, he elaborated how migration from Delhi to Mumbai could lead to different pronunciations and further provide depth to the character and the story setting:

> As I belong to Delhi, my pronunciation is different for certain words. I cannot pronounce the word 'Panda' correctly. So, when I was making a web series in which one of the characters was also from Delhi, I intentionally used the wrong pronunciation of the word 'Panda'. However, I do believe that it is good to commit mistakes as the internet is not supposed to be 'pretty', but is supposed to be 'real'.

The online creator culture allows Sehgal to use his experience in writing for the internet (YouTube, Netflix). He argued that the online medium 'offered more opportunities for experimentation' (Sehgal 2018). Actor Naveen Kasturia, who has acted in Hindi feature films as well as short films, sketches and web series on YouTube, ZEE5, Altbalaji and Voot,[5] acknowledged that the success of TVF *Pitchers* (2015) made him 'a known face within the Indian screen industry' (Kasturia 2018).

According to Arunabh Kumar, the founder of The Viral Fever (a YouTube channel and now a portal), the lack of enthusiasm shown by television channels for a parody show prompted him and his friends to launch their TVF (The Viral Fever) YouTube channel. TVF is India's first YouTube channel to have acquired a million subscribers in 2015 based on original content. Arunabh elaborated in an interview that youth television channel MTV and several media conglomerate broadcasters had rejected his ideas for spoofs and parodies around popular Indian youth shows (Dwivedi 2013). However, the availability of an open-access platform like YouTube allowed creators like Kumar to give expression to his creative vision. Kumar joined the bandwagon of online content creators who have been disappointed by the rigid operational practices of Indian broadcasters, whom they believe are averse to experimentation and have a limited view of what works on television. With the advent of digital media, the creators did not have to rely on the mercy of traditional mediums to exercise their vision for the first time. In many ways, TVF has forged a unique place for itself. The success of its shows has prompted the team to launch a new portal, TVFPlay (see Chapter 3). Interestingly, as I entered the TVF office, I was greeted by the self-explanatory TVF logo, 'It's not on TV, it's on TVF', similar to HBO's 'It's not TV, its HBO'.

Television actress Chhavi Mittal left her long, illustrious television career to run a digital media company named Shitty Ideas Trending (SIT), along with ex-television actor Mohit Hussein. SIT operates predominantly on social media platforms such as YouTube, Instagram and Facebook, where they create sketches and web series for an online audience. Reflecting on her transition from television to the internet, Mittal (2018) said:

> Television is catering to a certain section of society who expect the shows to be a family drama, melodramatic and all that. I was kind of bored of doing all that. I have done stuff on Shitty Ideas (SIT) that I never thought I could do in life or that I was capable of doing in my life. In my previous experience, I only used to act. I was given a script in hand, and I was expected to deliver those lines as per the character's demand. I was good at that, but I did not know that I could be a writer or producer. With SIT, I have done sound engineering too.

For Chhavi Mittal, the NSE allowed her to foster her creativity by reprising 'exciting' roles, exploring 'newer forms of storytelling' and, more importantly, challenging herself to 'try her hand' at other departments of filmmaking without conforming to stereotypes.

The participatory culture of YouTube allowed Mittal and her husband, actor Mohit Hussein, to quit their television careers and create a YouTube content channel. What started as a hobby soon developed into a fully fledged digital media entity as SIT developed sketches and web shows in collaboration with brands on YouTube. Mittal's career trajectory, along with Chakraborty's, shows how television's rigid industrial conventions and 'high-risk' factors associated with mass viewing make it difficult for television workers to experiment in multiple departments. At the same time, having a self-funded YouTube channel also means that one has to be good at multitasking to cut costs. For creators like Mittal, Hussein and Sehgal, digital media offers greater agency and experimentation, even at the risk of financial precarity.

Madhavan argued that the preparation for films was on par with NSE content, where the performances and treatment were superior due to the fixed number of episodes and fast-paced treatment. Madhavan's testimony is particularly evident in a case where popular Hindi film actor Rajkumar Rao shaved half his head to look like the real-life character of freedom fighter Netaji Subhas Chandra Bose in Altbalaji's streaming media service historical drama web series *Bose: Dead or Alive* (2017).

The agency and the social and cultural capital that actors receive from the internet-based content owing to its relatable character graphs, witty dialogues and a fixed number of episodic shows make it a lucrative medium for expression. Unlike soap operas, internet dramas offer a time-bound commitment and do not tie actors down to a never-ending saga that restricts them from taking other roles. The absence of genre diversity on television has also contributed to the fatigue of actors.

CONCLUSION

These narratives are not meant to create an impression that NSE does not facilitate regressive content. However, Indian NSE's diversity in talent and content, and its competition with the global video production cultures, supersede television's generalized and saturated narrative of the Indian viewer and especially its lazy production practices. The diverse voices of the creator labour such as casting agents, actors, writers, producers and directors expose how the fractured cultural and industrial logics and practices of television broadcasters emanate from its economic factors. These voices have shared similar apprehensions about what television has come to be, but more importantly, how the industrial logics of NSE are supposedly different and, therefore, more appealing compared with television.

While, in some cases, incumbent television actors from the television industry have protested against doing the 'same kind' of shows, the dip in ratings for 'supernatural' genre shows such as *Vish ya Amrit* (Poison or Nectar) and *Tantra* (Magic) hoping to follow the success of *Naagin* (Snake Woman) have forced the television broadcasters to shut these shows down and rethink their content strategies ('Supernatural Genre is Fading Away' 2019). The 2018 FICCI-EY report noted that: 'While Indian broadcasters produce over 100,000 hours of content annually across languages and formats, newer players (portals) are investing higher amounts per episode (albeit for much smaller quantities of content) and are taking up with leading talent.'

My cohort was relentless in critiquing television's industrial practices – so it did not come as a surprise when Sidharth Anand (2018), Vice President (Films and TV) for Saregama, claimed:

> I have been working in the television industry for 15 years as a professional before joining Saregama (Music Label and content production company). It is a place where creativity dies. I think that it is very unhealthy for the creative soul of our country. As an insider in the business, I also know that broadcasters are scared because talent does not want to work with them. The best talent wants to work on web series or feature films.

From the perspective of my interview cohort, television broadcasters have grown comfortable with offering a similar type of content to an audience, which has been limited by viewing choices and restricted by the infrastructure to explore alternative options. With the increase of internet penetration across the country and increasingly affordable internet prices – as highlighted in Chapter 1 and this chapter – audiences will be exposed to diverse genres and content styles and will therefore be more discerning in their choice of consumption. This may lead to a major restructuring of the television industry, where both the programming and the creative practices might be reconfigured to address the pressing concerns of talent and audience migration. This has also allowed for more experimentation, which has led the NSE to flourish in India and establish itself as a competitive medium within the screen culture that complements and challenges the commanding influence of film and television mediums.

In the next chapter, I will highlight the significant aspects of the industrial culture of online creators, such as their quotidian practices, working conditions, identity construction, non-hierarchical corporate structure, and localization practices. I will show how today's Indian creators are ambitious and more willing to produce content consumed globally. They believe that their content will reach beyond India and put them on a global stage alongside global media professionals.

3
Mapping the Key Platforms and Portals

In laying the ground for studying India's online creator culture, I begin my mapping exercise by diving deeper into the characteristics of eleven portals (Hotstar, Spuul, Hoichoi, Addatimes, TVFPlay, Reliance Jio, ZEE5, Voot, Netflix, Amazon Prime Video and Altbalaji) and two platforms (YouTube and Facebook). I study the value propositions that these streaming services offer to highlight the NSE diversity, the platform–portal interdependence and the NSE's interdependency with the film and television industries.

While a study of the Indian digital audience and its viewership behaviour is not central to this thesis, it is important to note that the advent of platforms and portals, combined with the decrease in the cost of mobile phones and internet usage, have transformed India's viewing habits. I attribute this causal relation to the price-sensitive nature of the Indian audience, which can now afford the cost of the internet and mobile phones to consume online content. At the same time, television continues to be the most viewed medium, owing to the extremely low cost of acquiring cable or Direct-to-Home (DTH) connections in India (Sharma 2020) and for as little as US$6 a month, an Indian television-owning household is likely to secure access to more than 260 television channels (including all television channels from legacy networks and sports to childrens' channels).

Compare this to Netflix's premium plan, which not only charges approximately US$10 a month for a maximum of four users but also does not provide live streaming of sports or news content. Add this to the internet's subsequent cost to consume Netflix and it raises the overall entertainment consumption cost. Thus, comparing the utility of linear television based on the affordability of price and audio-visual choices could triumph over any portal service. These reasons inform India's portal challenges in contrast to the single-screen viewing (family-viewing), price and choice-sensitive traits of Indian TV consumers. These very reasons prompted Netflix to introduce the mobile plan for US$3 per month in India in 2019 (Bhushan and Szalai 2020). It also explains why social media and AVoD platforms have emerged as substitutes and favoured business models for Indian online viewers who are hesitant to foot monthly portal subscription fees. Moreover, about 51 per cent of Indian viewers deem it okay to share their portal accounts (Jha 2022a).

Another distinguishing feature of digital content distribution is the cultural politics and geopolitics of catering to India. India's cultural diversity of 121 languages provides both challenges and opportunities to the platforms/portals that, unlike television, do not have to confine themselves to a particular language or category (such as general entertainment, news or sports). The transnational appeal of multilingual content also helps portals to service countries other than India. At the same time, the preference of the portals to create Hindi language content – a language spoken widely in North India and promoted religiously as an official language by the Indian Government as a part of the nation-building project (see Athique 2012) – places emerging NSE regional creators in a precarious position (see Chapter 4). Nevertheless, as I show in this chapter, the advent of language-specific portals like Hoichoi and Addatimes offers regional creators newer forms of resistance and opportunities.

Further to Chapter 1, where I offered a summary of the thirteen selected platforms and portals – broadcaster-led portals (Hotstar, Voot, ZEE5); digital 'pure-play' native portals (Altbalaji, TVFPlay); regional language-specific native portals (Hoichoi, Addatimes); global portals (Spuul, Netflix, Amazon); social media platforms (YouTube, Facebook); and telecom-led portal (Reliance Jio) – the origins of these enterprises offer the key to their distinctiveness.

TELECOM-LED PORTAL

Reliance Jio

As highlighted in Chapter 1, Reliance Jio Infocom's $42 billion investment in digital infrastructure, followed by its entry into the platform economy, has redefined the operating definition of telecom service providers. While analysing the enmeshment of infrastructure and platform-related discourses, Mukherjee (2019: 1) argues that: 'Jio made infrastructural investments (in the spectrum, cell towers and fibre-optics networks) to promote its suite of apps (JioTV, JioChat, and JioMoney).'

Rishi and co-workers (2018: 7) demonstrate how Reliance Jio schemes such as 'offering free sim cards with unlimited free high-speed 4G data, voice/video calls, instant messaging and numerous free applications that covered a range of services from news to entertainment to education' for a period of 90 days, which was subsequently extended to March 2017, enabled the company to amass a 50 million-strong subscriber base in just 83 days, a feat that existing telecom companies such as Airtel and Vodafone had taken 12 and 13 years respectively to achieve ('Reliance Jio crosses 50 million' 2016).

Soon after its launch, Reliance Jio introduced the Jio portal, JioOnDemand, which featured a host of diverse content offerings such as movies, television and short clips. JioOnDemand is part of a cluster of applications launched by the telecom service provider, including Jio Beats (music), Jio Play (live television) and a messaging service and cloud storage. The JioOnDemand content library does not boast any original content. It largely licenses content from its subsidiary, Network18, which it acquired in 2014 for US$619 million to signal its intent of venturing into the media and broadcast industry. By completing the takeover of Network18, the Reliance company also became the majority shareholder of Viacom18, a previous joint venture between Paramount Pictures Pvt. Ltd. and Network18, thus strengthening its presence in the television, film and digital offerings of Viacom18.

In 2017, Jio acquired a 24.9 per cent stake in popular television and digital production company Balaji Telefilms (Choudhary 2017b). Incidentally, Balaji Telefilms also owns Altbalaji, a recently launched subscription-based portal. Altbalaji is discussed in greater detail later in the chapter. Through its holdings in multiple media entities, acquisitions, sporadic productions by way of its subsidiary Jio studios and strategic aggregation deals with broadcasters and OTT services such as SonyLIV, ZEE5 and Disney+ Hotstar, Jio offers content solutions to essentially sustain its 'retail, telecom and data ecosystem' (Athique 2020: 39) and symbolizes the meta-market social, material and economic exchanges within the Indian media economy (Athique 2019: 432).

Among the many Jio service applications that it offers exclusively to Jio subscribers, the prominent ones are Jio TV, a catch-up destination of syndicated and aggregated television shows with episodes that have featured within the last seven days, and Jio Cinema, where Jio subscribers can watch beyond the seven-day history of television shows, together with movies, music videos, sketches and short films.

SOCIAL MEDIA PLATFORMS

YouTube

Since its launch in 2008 in India, YouTube has largely been responsible for spurring the growth of UGC content by facilitating uploading, sharing, and monetizing content across most regions of the globe (Burgess 2006). Based on the 2021 data, YouTube leads mobile consumption with an average of 425 million monthly active users (MICA 2022). As of 2021, 4,000 Indian creators have accumulated over a million subscribers (Oxford Economics 2021).

In order to mobilize creators and assist them with the production of content, YouTube has created ten YouTube Spaces globally, one of which is in Mumbai. Based on a 2015 partnership with Whistling Woods International, a media and communication institute, it has workshop training and offers studio and camera equipment to creators with a minimum of 1,000 subscribers. YouTube also initiated two 'YouTube Pop-up' spaces, dedicated three-day events in Hyderabad in

2017 and Delhi in 2018 ('First Ever YouTube Pop-up Space Delhi' 2018), where creators were given a chance to create content using YouTube's production equipment and further attend workshops and meet fellow creators for networking and collaboration.

Recalling the initiative, Jigisha Mistry (2018), Head of YouTube Space in Mumbai, stated:

> The first fanfest started four years ago. It was like a small community get-together between creators and fans that was aired in a small open-air theatre in Bandra, Mumbai. Over time the number of creators has grown all over India. We currently have over 330 channels that have crossed the million subscribers mark, and it is not just in Hindi and English but also in other regional languages.

In its fifth year in India, the Fanfest was held in the cities of Hyderabad, Delhi, Chennai, Bangalore and Mumbai to connect the fans with creators through live performances and meet-and-greet sessions. Such is the euphoria for YouTubers amongst the audience that in the YouTube Fanfest 2018, held in Mumbai, I found myself lost amongst millennials in huge queues at separate tents waiting to meet their favourite stars.

As can be observed from the onsite photos, children were accompanied by anxious parents who were trying their best to ensure that the kids do not get lost amongst the crowd. The Mumbai Fanfest was held on 23 March 2018 with a robust schedule of events like special performances from popular creators, meet and greet followed by a 'La Oscar' treatment where these creators walk through the red carpet with fans on either side, with the six-hour marathon event ending with live performances from select creators.

Multiple stages were erected to host 'YouTube stars' who were listed to perform their skits for the event. The glitz and glamour of the Fanfest marked similarity to the film industry awards shows where actors and actresses performed in-between award presentations, except that internet sensations had replaced film celebrities (Figure 3.1).

The popularity of these creators has enabled YouTube to organize events in Mumbai on a scale and demographics that could eclipse any Bollywood awards show. Nabh Gupta, Marketing Manager for Amazon Prime, noted how the YouTube Fanfest in Mumbai had metamorphosed from a small gathering of 100 people in Bandstand (Bandra) to a diversely demographic population with a turnout well enough to fill the 10,000-capacity Jio Garden, Bandra Kurla Complex in the city.

In order to compete with portals, YouTube introduced a freemium model and created a line-up of YouTube Originals in India in 2018 that was available only

Figure 3.1 Photograph of YouTube Fanfest at Bandra Kurla Complex, Mumbai (Mehta 2018).

to YouTube premium users. It commissioned the only Indian show, *Arrived*, an Indian singing reality talent show produced in partnership with MCN Qyuki (Jalan 2018) (see Chapter 5). However, the subsequent failure of its freemium model in 2019 led YouTube to allow all YouTube viewers to access original shows. In Chapter 5, I highlight how Marathi and Bengali social media creators construct everyday local identities on YouTube through sketches and web series to compete for attention against the backdrop of Hindi and English language content.

Facebook

In order to counter YouTube's dominance over video content, Facebook launched the 'Watch' video tab globally on its platform in August 2018 (Carey-Simos 2018). What began as a strictly controlled space for running video advertisements with selected publishers and celebrities, changed within a month (as of 16

December 2018) as more pages were allowed to run video advertisements for over three-minute content with data showing access to over 23,000 pages (Maheshwari 2018). Further, to position itself as a hybrid version of the platform and portal, it launched six original series (Kim 2018), out of which four originals were recommissioned for the second season (Shah 2018). With a repertoire of aggregated and user-generated content across news, entertainment and sports categories, Facebook commands a userbase of 447 million ('Meta's Facebook Growth Sees Woes in India' 2022).

In 2021, Facebook CEO Mark Zuckerberg rebranded the company Meta to reposition itself from a social networking company to an immersive virtual reality world (Ball 2022). Further, in June 2022, Zuckerberg announced the Facebook Reels Play Bonus Program in 150 countries. Under this program, creators who have developed more than five reels and have accumulated over 100,000 views in the last 30 days could be eligible for monetizing their Facebook Reels (Kar 2022).

Like YouTube, Facebook held creator camps across selected cities in India to mobilize and raise awareness of its localization practices in India. Creator Priyam Ghose (2018), who creates sketches and comedy videos through his Facebook page,[1] described the important events at the creator meet in Kolkata to which he was invited:

> At the camp, Facebook apprised us of the many features Facebook offers to creators to reach its audience. For example, Facebook analytics like the Publishing tool where you can create, delete, expire, and re-upload your post with a new date. Analytics help you keep an eye on your top videos, overall page reach and your fan base – be it the gender, age bracket, country and the city they are from.

To attract Indian creators to its platform and its subsidiary, Facebook announced a global licensing deal with Indian music label Saregama, making the label's music catalogue free to use for Facebook and Instagram creators. By introducing ad breaks in Hindi, Malayalam, Bengali, Tamil and English in 2018 ('Facebook Makes Ad Breaks Available' 2018), Facebook signalled its intention to promote regional and local advertisers through the ad breaks on its platform.

However, safety and privacy are the greatest concerns that Facebook faces in India with an internal research report admitting that Indian women were leaving Facebook because of objectionable content, unsolicited friend requests, messages and comments from strangers ('Meta's Facebook Growth Sees Woes in India' 2022).

BROADCASTER-OWNED PORTALS

Disney+ Hotstar

Hotstar was part of Rupert Murdoch's behemoth media corporation, 21st Century Fox, until Fox was brought over by the Walt Disney Company for US$71 billion, and renamed as Disney+ Hotstar. In June 2022, Disney+ Hotstar recorded a subscriber base of 50.1 million (Farooqui 2022). Apart from Disney's slate of original shows and television content from HBO and Showtime, Disney+ Hotstar also possesses content from Star India Network, a collection of over sixty Indian broadcasting channels across multiple Indian languages (such as Kannada, Malayalam, Telugu, Tamil, Hindi) and diverse genres such as general entertainment channels, news and sports. This gives Disney+ Hotstar (hereafter, Hotstar) the advantage of a strong library of content, extensive live sports programming and a ready-made audience, as opposed to Netflix and Amazon Prime. Hotstar's subscriber base as of 2022 is estimated to be 46 million in comparison to Amazon Prime (22 million) and Netflix (5 million) (Thakur 2022).

Launched in 2015, Hotstar offers its services through a 'freemium model' – a combination of free and premium service in which viewers are offered a portion of the content for free and must pay a subscription to access further content under this model. Like Netflix, Hotstar introduced a mobile-specific subscription plan at INR 499 (approx. US$6.25) in 2022 that supports single-screen 720 pixels high-definition viewing (Murdeshwar 2022).

Also setting Hotstar apart from its competitors in India is its aggressive investment in the sports genre. Hotstar's content strategy is reflected in its creation of marquee sports properties such as its indigenous intellectual sports property Pro-Kabaddi League, acquisition of broadcast rights for the much-celebrated Men's Indian Cricket Premier League, exclusive digital coverage of the English Football Premier League and Indian Football League, as well as live streaming of a total of fourteen local and international sporting activities that includes golf, badminton, hockey, athletics and horse racing.[2] Hotstar's investment in the sports (live) genre is a stark contrast to most portals, even at the global level, given that most Western SvoDs (Hulu, Netflix, Amazon Prime Video) have stayed away from the acquisition of sports telecast rights. In 2021, it commissioned eighteen titles comprising Hindi, Telugu and Tamil films and web series (Arora 2021). Further, in 2022, Hotstar partnered with popular YouTube creator Bhuvan Bam's production house BB Ki Vine Production to commission the web show *Taaza Khabar* (Fresh News), and another popular social media creator Dice Media for *Ghar Wapasi* (Returning Home), further signalling the close links between platform and portal talent (Jha 2022b).

Voot

Like Hotstar, Voot has the advantage of operating under the umbrella of a broadcaster. Viacom18 Media Pvt. Ltd. owns and gives the freemium portal ready-made content from the network's broadcaster channels such as MTV, Colors, Nickelodeon, VH1, Colors Bangla and Colors Kannada, highlighting its extensive mix of television broadcast content portfolio across genres and languages. As of July 2021, Voot claimed to attract 100 million active users (Farooqui 2022). As a freemium service, it offers two subscription options for its premium content, i.e Voot Select – INR 99 (US$1.2) monthly and INR 399 (US$5).

The Viacom18 network was founded in 2007. It owns 44 television channels and is broadcast in 80 countries. It is owned through a joint venture between TV18 Broadcast (51 per cent stake), a subsidiary of Reliance Jio Infocomm founder Mukesh Ambani, and the foreign conglomerate Viacom18. As well as its broadcasting business, the company has invested in digital (Voot), live events (Supersonic music festival), films (Viacom18 Motion Pictures) and merchandise (consumer products).

Both Voot and Hotstar offer direct access to their broadcast television channel subsidiaries. They thus have a diverse and robust library of television shows to function as a destination for 'catch-up' content and 'content around content', an analogy used to define the creation of exclusive online content around television shows. Further, Voot also benefits from its Motion Pictures division of Viacom18 Motion Pictures – similar to Fox Star Studio's affiliation with Hotstar – to add to its catalogue of films. While it is not as heavily invested in creating original content as Hotstar, or Netflix, in 2022 Voot acquired the digital rights for the period 2023–7 for the Indian Premier League for US$3.1 billion, thereby marking its entry into the sports sector that had been previously dominated by Sony and Star (Sanjai 2022). Further, Voot launched a two-minute short-video tab to drive its portal long-form content viewership (Chacko 2022).

Voot has managed to leverage its catalogue of television programmes to expand its portal viewership by creating online content alongside its reality shows such as *Big Boss* (Colors), *Splitsvilla* (MTV), *Roadies* (MTV) and *Khatron ke Khiladi* (MTV). Moreover, there has been a conscious attempt to extend television shows such as *Silsila* to Voot to translate the television viewership online (Mahendra 2022).

ZEE5

Alongside fellow legacy Indian broadcasters Star and Viacom18, Zee Entertainment Enterprises Ltd. (ZEEL) introduced its streaming media service, ZEE5, in February 2018. Interestingly, Zee is a late entrant because it was the first Hindi language satellite television in India. However, one might also argue that Zee had initially launched two streaming platforms: DittoTV in 2012 (EA

2012) and OZEE in February 2016 (Pai 2016). While DittoTV served as a destination for other live television channels streamed globally through its electronic programmatic guide, OZEE focused exclusively on streaming Zee's broadcast network content of 66 linear television channels.[3] In February 2018, Zee decided to subsume OZEE and ZEE5 services to incorporate and relaunch its streaming platform as ZEE5 (Ahluwalia 2018), which in addition to hosting its television network content, and its acquired and licensed film library and original shows, would also produce short films across multiple Indian languages, such as Marathi, Hindi, Tamil, Telugu and Gujarati.

Available in over 190 countries and 18 languages, ZEE5 amassed a viewership of 105 million monthly active users in 2021–2 (Ramachandran 2022). Maintaining its focus on tapping India's linguistic diversity, ZEE5 has managed to create original web shows in diverse languages such as Marathi (*Liftman*, *Date with Saie*, *Sex, Drugs and Theatre*), Bengali (*Sharate Aaj*, *Alarm*, *Kaali* ('ZEE5's Tejkaran Singh Bajaj Moves to Jio' 2018)), Telugu (*B.Tech*, *Nanna Koochi*, *Chitra Vichitram* ('Zee5 Launches Its Third Telugu Original' 2018)) and Tamil (*Kallachirruppu*, *America Mappillai*, *Alarm*). Because 22–25 per cent of its viewership came from the US, there has been a conscious attempt to cater to the South Asian international diaspora through 'local commissions, English- and Spanish-language dubbing and subtitling and reaching deep into the South Asian diaspora through grassroots promotions' (Ravichandran 2022).

In 2021, Zee and Sony signed agreements to merge into Sony Pictures Network India (SPNI) – a deal that would combine both their content libraries and synergies in fiction, non-fiction and sports programming (Frater and Ramachandran 2021).

'PURE PLAY' LOCAL PORTALS

TVFPlay

A rather disruptive player in the mix is TVF (The Viral Fever), which has been purely conceived out of the success of its social media channels on YouTube, Facebook and Instagram. TVF is the first entity to create the first-ever web series in India through YouTube (*Permanent Roommates* 2014). Since its debut on YouTube in 2012, TVF has transitioned from creating content on social media to launching a dedicated portal and a specialist online creator, operating as a producer on Netflix, Amazon Prime Video and SonyLIV by creating web series on their portals.

It is hard to map TVF's viewership engagement, given that its audience consumes content through its YouTube channels and the portal as its viewership is spread across the various social media channels it operates, the portals it produces for, and its own portal.

However, TVFPlay engaged 1.5 million monthly active users in June 2021(MICA 2022). To date, TVFPlay is the only portal to have originated from social media platforms. As I show in Chapter 5, there is a continuous exchange of media personnel from platforms to portals. However, despite the existence of its portal, TVF has continued to create short-form content on its social media properties. As of 8 August 2022, the TVF network comprises four YouTube channels – *The Viral Fever* (11 million subscribers), *The Screen Patti* (5.78 million subscribers), *The Timeliners* (7.08 million subscribers), and *Girliyapa* (4.61 million subscribers) – which have a dedicated team that creates content and collaborates with other YouTubers. This is largely due to their availability to promote and engage with their large online fan base while also using that data traffic to negotiate better with brands for placement opportunities.

The social capital derived from success on social media is used to develop web shows with other portals, such as Amazon Prime Video (*Kota Factory*, *Hostel Daze*), SonyLIV (*Gullak*), Netflix (*Yeh Meri Family*) and the recently launched MxPlayer (*Immature*). TVF's web series for MxPlayer (*Immature*) was India's first-ever and only nominated web series in CannesSeries at the 2018 Cannes Film Festival. In 2021, Netflix acquired and streamed the second season of *Kota Factory* whose first season received critical reviews and 58 million views on YouTube.

Explaining the rationale behind TVFPlay, its Associate Creative Director Nidhi Bisht (2018) said:

> YouTube was a mall, and my channels were shops in the mall. A mall naturally has more shops [owned] by other people. So, to have exclusivity, we made a showroom in the form of a portal where all the content that we make is available, and all the people who exclusively want to follow them can find them at a place called TVFPlay.

While the platform may not have excess capital to invest in the acquisition of global content or the legacy networks' vast content library, it has relied on its creativity, authenticity and loyal fan base to attract partnerships and audience.

In my analysis on NSE creator culture in Chapter 5, I highlight how such a level of success is not limited to TVF alone as, since the introduction of YouTube and Facebook in India, several companies – such as Dice Media, Arré, ScoopWhoop and Culture Machine – have coexisted on platforms and portals.

Altbalaji

Altbalaji debuted in April 2017 (Jha and Gupta 2017). It is a fully owned subsidiary of Balaji Telefilms Pvt. Ltd., a popular television production company, by Ekta Kapoor, who has previously produced successful television shows for Indian broadcasters like Star and Viacom18. Following its launch, Reliance Industries

Limited – which also owns telecom company Reliance Jio – bought a 25 per cent stake in Balaji Telefilms Pvt. Ltd. (Choudhary 2017b). This deal allowed Balaji Telefilms to further channel these funds to create content for Altbalaji in exchange for exclusive access to the platform's content for Jio telecom subscribers. Kapoor also produces Hindi films under the banner of Balaji Motion Pictures and is a familiar name in India's media and entertainment industry. Altbalaji attracted 2.1 million monthly active users in 2021 (MICA 2022). While discussing the reasons for introducing Altbalaji, the Chief Operating Officer, Sunil Nair, noted:

> Altbalaji's reason for existence is the fact that the Indian TV industry over the last 27 to 30 years has kind of morphed in a strange manner where the GECs caters to women and largely the rural audience.
>
> (Nair 2018)

That a leading television production house opened a separate vertical and named it Altbalaji, with the logo 'everything that's not TV', makes another distinction between television and internet content.

Altbalaji is a subsidiary of the popular television production house Balaji Telefilms, which has run a host of highly rated television shows. Ironically, Balaji Telefilms brought the 'saas-bahu' sagas to the fore; as already discussed, these shows have been widely critiqued for their creative and programming practices. Altbalaji's recent multi-seasonal television show *Naagin* (Snake Women), although performing excellently for the television channel due to high Television Rating Points, was berated for its regressive content and mediocre Computer-Generated Imagery (CGI) graphics.

Altbalaji offers 32 original web shows with a strong focus on Hindi language content. Furthermore, a cursory glance at its content slate also reveals how Altbalaji has interestingly roped in popular faces from television for its many shows, such as Poulomi Das, Sakshi Tanwar and Ram Kapoor (Suthar 2018). This is also because of Balaji Telefilms' closer association with television stars – although the portal's ability to permeate crossover of television celebrities is unique considering the overall general porosity between film and online creator labour (see Chapter 4).

That Altbalaji's male viewership is twice the female viewership should not come as a surprise since web series like *Gandi Baat* (Bad Conversations), a six-season-long web series, *XXX Uncensored*, *Who's Your Daddy* and *Virgin Bhaskar Bekaaboo* (Uncontrollable) provide a ready template to satisfy heterosexual fantasies. A former senior Altbalaji employee reveals how specific data points of high audience engagement are used as evidence to commission titillating content for heterosexual men.

LOCAL STRATEGIES OF GLOBAL PORTALS

Netflix and Amazon Prime Video

While Netflix boasts of successful global shows from its current library with its SVoD model, Amazon Prime Video also bundles the benefits of running an e-commerce website by offering purchase and delivery benefits along with content. One of the most significant comparisons relates to how these portals are priced. Netflix offers four plans, ranging from mobile-only INR 99 (US$1.24) to premium plan INR 899 (US$10) – the latter plan allows multiple user-viewing and screen-viewing, as well as viewing quality. In comparison, Amazon Prime offers three options – one can either opt to pay INR 129 (US$1.80) per month or INR 999 (US$14) per year or take a mobile plan for INR 89 (US$1.12). Interestingly, Amazon Prime Video, Disney+ Hotstar and Netflix charge the lowest subscription rates in India compared with rates in other countries (MICA 2022). While Amazon Prime Video amassed a 22 million subscriber base in 2022, Netflix has engaged only 5 million subscribers (Thakur 2022).

Ramon Lobato's book *Netflix Nations* (2019) explains how debates surrounding cultural and linguistic diversity, localization and platform imperialism can be addressed through an analysis of its content library. In his analysis, Lobato (2019: 185) highlights how most of Netflix's Indian library is reserved only for a smaller population of 'English speaking, tech-savvy and urban Indian elites', compared with the much wider socioeconomically diverse, multilingual, Indian NSE audience. However, given that Netflix has produced more than 90 titles since its launch in 2017 and invested about US$200 million in 2021 alone (S 2022), there are greater concerns than the lack of original content that is affecting the service's performance in India.

In an investor call in 2022, Netflix CEO Reed Hastings termed Netflix's low subscriber numbers in India as 'disappointing' (Thakur 2022). One of the obvious reasons is the inability to shed the image of an 'elite service'. The omission of the sports genre, especially cricket which is widely watched by the masses, and the lack of broadcast fiction and non-fiction dailies means that the original content productions and acquisitions need to develop a strong relationship with the audience. Netflix has been unable to develop that intimacy with its reviewers as reports claim that the Indian subscriber base still prefers its international originals over local titles. Furthermore, within four years, Netflix has seen three changes in content leadership in the form of Swati Shetty, Shrishti Behl Arya and the current head Monika Shergill. Unlike Netflix, Amazon Prime's content head Aparna Purohit has been with the company since its launch in 2016, thereby signalling much stronger stability and the desired time to underline Amazon Prime Video's brand identity. Moreover, Amazon Prime's strategy of bundling e-commerce with audio-visual offerings cannot be understated.

Media scholar Ishita Tiwary (2020) uses the framework 'eco-sphere' to articulate the integrated nature of Amazon's services. Tiwary (ibid., 88) underscores Amazon's strategy 'to enter the audio-visual space, not as a television provider per se, but as a seller of video products densely inter-linked to multisided markets in retail, advertising, music, data and finance'. Lotz's (2022: 12) defining work on the distinctions that characterize SVoD services identifies streaming services like Amazon Prime Video and Apple TV as 'corporate complements' because of their ability to measure success differently (e.g. Amazon Prime memberships) than subscriber count.

In comparison to Netflix, Amazon Prime Video has developed a successful collaboration with social media creators to produce their live shows and allow them to create web series through a strategic partnership with talent agents OML. I will discuss OML's role in detail in Chapter 7, where I articulate the intervention of intermediaries. Besides signing stand-up comedians with massive social media following, Amazon Prime commissioned TVF to produce two seasons of *Panchayat* as more evidence of the blurring of amateur–professional boundaries.

By roping in media practitioners from Hindi and regional film industries in original web series such as *Inside Edge* and *Breathe*, and recently released gangster dramas *Mirzapur*, *Vella Raja* (Tamil) and *Gangstars* (Telugu), it has also been able to leverage their fan following while appealing to a wider audience already known for its multilingual diversity. Amazon Prime Video's catalogue in India offers films that are available across nine spoken languages: English, Marathi, Bengali, Hindi, Tamil, Gujarati, Punjabi, Kannada and Telugu. Further, in its bid to increase the convenience of navigation for native Indian users, it has also introduced a Hindi language interface along with forthcoming application developments in Tamil and Telugu language interfaces, which highlights the importance it places on the South Indian diaspora (MICA 2022).

Amazon Prime Video Marketing Manager Nabh Gupta (2018) said these strategies were developed by keeping in mind the multicultural diversity of Indian audience as he remarked,

> Within every 10 kilometres in the Indian market, the culture and language changes. So, you want to cover all the customers, and secondly, it is purely around the scale. It is only once you make content available in the language and in preference which will cut across the urban cities or the quintessential top 10 towns that you will be able to penetrate within the local areas and get them to use technology.

Gupta's understanding highlights an interesting way of looking at Indian audiences: it does not segregate between Indian language content and further challenges the definition of 'regional language' to argue the heterogeneity that exists within Indian regions. I elaborate on the localization practices and cultural politics of platforms as well as creators in Chapter 6.

Spuul

While India is seeing a rise in streaming platforms that are increasingly localizing their content strategies by venturing into original production, Spuul, an SVoD platform with its headquarters in Singapore, functions purely through the acquisition and licensing of Indian television and film shows by brokering strategic partnerships with production houses and studios. It is a global streaming service that caters to the Indian diaspora around the world and those who are familiar with Indian content.

With over 47 million globally registered subscribers, Spuul's majority audience comes from the South and South-East Asian regions, North America, the United Kingdom, the Middle East, Australia and New Zealand, hinting at the two major audience sectors on which it is betting: the global Indian diaspora and the acclimatized audience of Indian television shows and films – especially Hindi films.

As Spuul's Head of Content Girish Dwibhashyam (2018) elaborated, the company's strategy was informed largely by the internal data and its target audience:

> When Spuul as a platform is acquiring or commissioning any content, language plays a role in taking a call on whether content should be acquired or not. Depending on the audience that they are targeting, the language of the content is decided. For example, if they want to target Canada and Australia, then the preferred language of the content will be Punjabi as a vast majority of Punjabi Indians live in that area. Also, another reason language is considered is that regional language content costs less than the content available in mass languages English and Hindi.

The SVoD portal's library hosts 10,000 hours of Indian content, including television shows and films from seven popular Indian languages: Hindi, Punjabi, Malayalam, Telugu, Bhojpuri, Bengali and Tamil. Spuul targets the Indian diaspora living in the US, UK and the United Arab Emirates. However, Spuul is also keen to expand 'its customer base by delivering global content to local consumers and local content to the global diaspora',[4] and offering content in 'non-English languages like Arabic, Korean, Chinese, Filipino, Thai, Bahasa and Spanish' (Dwibhashyam 2018). Spuul has also initiated the use of blockchain technology to launch 'Spokkz', an initial coin offering (ICO) through which it intends to develop a decentralized economy, whereby viewers will be rewarded for engaging via comments, reviews, shares and advertisement viewing; they will also be offered a chance to fund content projects of their choice ('Bollywood

Streaming Service Spuul Launches' 2018) further contributing to the NSE distinctiveness in content and business models. However, there have been no updates on Spuul's performance in the news reports since 2021. Spuul's social media assets, too, have been silent on the company's next steps.

LANGUAGE-SPECIFIC PORTALS

While this research focuses only on two Bengali-language-based portals such as Hoichoi and Addatimes, since 2017 there have been at least eight launches of language-specific portals in India. For example, portals like Talkies (Tulu, Konkani and Kannada languages), Oho Gujarati and CityShor TV (Gujarati language), Planet Marathi OTT (Marathi language), Olly Plus (Odia language), Aha (Telugu language), ManoramaMax (Malayalam language), Chaupal (Punjabi, Haryanvi and Bhojpuri), Koode (Malayalam) and SunNXT (Tamil, Telugu, Kannada, Malayalam, Bengali and Marathi) are all examples that specialize in creating non-Hindi and non-English Indian languages (Rana 2022).

Hoichoi

While the majority of the streaming platforms produce in Hindi, English or a mixture of the two, investors have also produced original regional content, as shown by Hotstar's investment in the Tamil language web series. However, it is one thing to have content diversification as a part of the portal strategy and another to conceive a portal that focuses solely on a specific language.

Based out of Kolkata, Hoichoi and Addatimes are two portals that specialize in developing Bengali-language content. With its subscription-based model, Hoichoi offers two subscription plans of INR 599 per year (US$7.59) and INR 899 (US$11.29) per year in India depending upon the number of users and screen-sharing options. Furthermore, it is also prevalent in other countries with Bengali-speaking audiences, such as Middle East countries, Bangladesh, the United Kingdom, the United States and Australia, with a country-specific pricing structure.

Launched in 2017, Hoichoi is owned by established media and entertainment company SVF Entertainment Pvt. Ltd., which has produced television shows and over 100 films in Bengali, making it one of the biggest production houses in Tollywood (Bengali cinema). It also owns four television channels: Sangeet Bangla, Music India, Music UK and Sangeet Bhojpuri. SVF Entertainment Pvt. Ltd. is engaged in multiple media businesses, such as production, distribution, exhibition, online video and online audio. It has also been popularly dubbed the Yashraj Films (a popular Bollywood production and distribution company in Mumbai) of the East (Roy 2014).

Due to its domination across the Bengali-language television and film industry, Hoichoi has emerged as one of the marquee destinations for Bengali entertainment, providing over 500 Bengali titles out of which 100 are self-produced (Rana 2022). However, Hoichoi is also planning to dub its titles in other languages such as Tamil, Arabic, Telugu and Hindi to diversify its audience ('Hoichoi Announces' 2018). According to Hoichoi, the portal serves 250 million subscribers and 30 per cent of its subscription revenue comes from the US, UK, Australia and Canada (S 2022).

Owing to its familiarity and success in Tollywood, Hoichoi has utilized Tollywood talents such as director Moinak Bhaumik and actress Priyanka Sarkar among many others, to produce its original web series and films. Moreover, to attract a Bangladesh online audience, it has teamed up with award-winning director Amitabh Reza Chaudhuri to produce the first Bengali web series, *Dhaka Metro* ('Hoichoi Announces' 2018). To strengthen its presence within the Bengali-speaking markets, Hoichoi has collaborated with telecom and broadband operators to license its content such as Link3 and Grameenphone in Bangladesh and JioFibre, Airtel XStream, Alliance, Wishnet, and Meghbela in India (S 2022).

Addatimes

Rajiv Mehra, the founder of Addatimes, is a veteran in the Bengali television industry, with over seventeen years of experience as a television producer. He pointed out his frustration with the television rating system and the attitude of Bengali-language television broadcasters as the prime reason for launching this Bengali language-specific portal (Mehra 2018). Like Hoichoi, Addatimes is an SVoD portal and offers two yearly subscription options – INR 399 (US$5) for single-user and single-screen viewing and INR 599 (US$7.52) for multimedia viewing (MICA 2022). It was launched in Bangladesh in 2020. Unfortunately, its viewership data is not available in industry reports.

Addatimes relies on these audience viewing habits to offer a repertoire of movies, original web series, music and sport from its collection. Under the sports category, it offers free live streaming of the Calcutta Football League.[5] Mehra (2018) added that a huge scope exists for regional online content creators, as streaming platforms are increasingly expanding their content portfolio in languages other than Hindi and English. For instance, he highlighted that one of the directors of the web series *Khyapa*, Korok Murmu (Mulchandani 2017), collaborated with ZEE5 to direct the portal's first Bengali language web series *Kaali* ('Zee5 Announces First Bengali Web Series' 2018).

Thus, portals like Hoichoi and Addatimes leverage their understanding of Bengali audiences to create language-specific content consumed in East India, Myanmar, Bangladesh, and diasporic Bengali-speaking audiences worldwide. These examples highlight how the globalization of technology and services has led a diverse country like India to think globally and act locally, opening doors for the new generation of regional, transnational storytellers.

CONCLUSION

The mapping of thirteen platforms/portals highlights three key factors: diversities, similarities, and interdependences in content, pricing, and creator strategies. India is one of the few countries that facilitates a culturally and industrially vibrant but unstable NSE with many platforms and portals experimenting with different value propositions while also proposing distinct business models and pricing to compete within the competitive Indian NSE. Specificity is achieved within the content by experimenting with genres, languages, and partnerships with established multimedia creators and film producers to leverage their popularity.

Four distinctive features shape the NSE content strategies. First, the excessive dependence on Bollywood, either through employing Bollywood practitioners or acquiring, licensing or commissioning Bollywood films, highlights a close relationship between Bollywood and the NSE. Second, there has been a systematic attempt to bank on social media creator labour for boosting portal viewership, as seen from the existing content strategies of SonyLIV, Hotstar, Netflix, Amazon Prime and ZEE5. Third, the help of intermediaries in developing localization strategies by global for portals like Netflix and Amazon Prime has paved the way for experimentation and the blurring of platform, portal and film-creator labour. Fourth, the portals are slowly realizing their brand identity in the market based on their viewership metrics. As an example, whereas most broadcaster-based portals are ramping up on their originals independent of their television programming, Voot is developing content around its television shows to replicate its television audience. Similarly, Netflix and Prime Video are diversifying their content productions and acquisitions into regional markets to localize their portal services.

In the next chapter, I focus on the creator labour perceptions towards the television and film sector to underline how their medium-based perceptions shape the New Screen Ecology's production culture.

4

Indian Online Creator Culture

This chapter explores the creator's contribution to the distinctiveness of the Indian NSE. I probe the reasons behind some Indian creators' preference for social media as a pathway into the professional industry in two ways. First, I highlight the multimodal practices of content creators, who typically use social media to promote their talent in stand-up comedy or acting or content genres such as sketches and web series. I trace the pathways of select online content creators to discuss the strategic ways in which creators organize themselves and use platforms as a calling card to demonstrate a range of creative work that serves as a skills-based portfolio for seeking projects (McRobbie 2002) in screen industries. Second, I discuss the everyday practices of creators who co-produce content on platforms to seek status among social media communities and develop sustainable enterprises. Building commercial and social capital helps the Indian creators to deal with precarity and negotiate relationships as they navigate the hierarchical structures of India's media industries.

By commercial capital, I allude to the revenue gathered from creator labour on platforms and portals. While working on platforms, creators aspire to build relationships with advertisers and audiences alike. Monetization opportunities accrued from sponsorships, advertorials and subscriptions are direct means of earning revenues from platforms. Social capital is one of the byproducts of social media in that the popularity of creators on social media gives opportunities for monetization on films and portals. The creators use their social media portfolio to partner with film and portal practitioners. In this way, the creators use their success to transcend from UGC to PGC set-ups and navigate the entry barriers to films and portals. Such an understanding of social capital is borrowed from Bourdieu's (1985: 248) definition of social capital that recognizes its intangibility and defines it as the 'aggregate of the actual or potential resources which are linked to possession of a durable network of more or less institutionalized relationships of mutual acquaintance or recognition'. I argue that many creators would prefer to deal with precarious creativity on social media platforms than to deal with the hegemonic production practices and closed-door networks of Indian traditional media. The approach to platforms and eventually portals is one pathway for both individuals and institutions, as it allows them to navigate the informality of traditional media industries while also embracing the precarity of algorithmic culture. I show this by highlighting through varied examples how this manifests among my cohort of interlocutors. Instead of attempting to break into socially elite circuits, creators take up less remunerative and more labour-intensive works on social media in the hope of gaining popularity.

As I will show, the multitasking characteristic of social media, which is essentially a method of keeping the costs of production low, also serves as a useful exercise in skill-building and a demonstration of adaptable talent. In doing so, I balance Chapter 3's top-down emphasis on platform/portal centricity with a bottom-up focus on the centricity of creators and highlight the precariousness induced by globalization on local creator labour practices (see Curtin and Sanson 2016).

PRECARIOUS CREATIVITY IN THE INDIAN SCREEN INDUSTRIES

Media scholar Sangeet Kumar (2016) discusses the precarious creativity of Indian online creator labour through his study of five creative entrepreneurs from diverse genres, including vlogging, cooking and fashion blogging. Kumar argues how these entrepreneurs are finding it difficult to achieve sustainability owing to YouTube's changing algorithm and growing competition. It is no surprise that YouTube's algorithms are not designed to reward merit or quality, and the successes are less frequent than the failures. In acknowledging Kumar's findings regarding the precarity of the new screen ecology, my analysis shows how both individuals and firms develop strategies that allow them to move back and forth across various components of the ecology to establish a career pathway towards success. Therefore, while the term 'precarious' may be useful for foregrounding our understanding of the political economy of the NSE, there are inherent complexities that are distinct to the Indian screen industries that need to be contextualized to understand the creator's preference for the NSE.

As a producer within the content development team of a corporate, creative set-up (Viacom18) across films and online vertical for three years, we often profiled screen incumbents (writers, actors, directors, independent producers, stand-up comedians) based on their prior experience, even before they had pitched their ideas. The risk-taking quotients in genres, as well as new voices, were extremely rare. Often the same traditional media professionals would get work opportunities due to being part of privileged creator and producer circuits. Their requests for collaboration are often prioritized over any of the newcomers. This practice contrasts with the NSE where, as Viacom18's (Voot's) digital content producers, we proactively sought meetings with popular social media creators and intermediaries (see Chapter 7) who managed social media creators.

As discussed in Chapter 2, the industrial practices in the overall Indian film and television industry have a well-documented history of being 'hegemonic', with broadcasters and studio executives having the final say on every creative decision (Kay 2018; Kumar 2016). Similarly, I have raised the issue of how the general entertainment television channels only produce an average of 3–3.5 hours of original content per day (FICCI-EY 2018: 36), a task often handed out to the same producers regularly. Third, censorship on television remains an obstacle for creators, who are looking to the NSE as a 'dynamic outlet in which discourses of the nation, identity, censorship, feminism and representation' are undertaken (Kay 2018: 1). A relative lack of governmental regulations and a lesser degree of circumscribed agency compared with the television industry has helped the NSE facilitate an emerging pool of creators (see Chapter 1) who are looking to experiment with diverse forms of storytelling.

The creators discussed here have medium-agnostic creator aspirations but are not part of the elite cultural hierarchy and are precarious due to their exclusion from the Indian screen industries. By negotiating their creativity on social media, creators – as well as media enterprises specializing in online creation – are gaining wider acceptance from the online audience for their creativity and then using it as a form of currency for circulation within the overall Indian screen industry. At the same time, the intelligence of creators in negotiating the algorithmic capitalistic logics of the social media platforms (as distinct from traditional media's capitalistic logics), and materializing their aspirations, places them on the same side of the equation as the powerful platform/portals in the digitized economy.

In other words, they deal with precarity by serving and supporting capitalist structures that reproduce the same inequalities they are meant to address (Herman and McChesney 2003). However, the availability of social, economic and cultural capital derived by serving in the digitized economy still offers a better chance of building a meaningful career as an outsider because social media affordances provide newcomers with a chance to express themselves.

At the same time, it is useful to note that the findings do not negate Sangeet Kumar's (2016) critical intervention concerning the precarious nature of India's social media creators. As pointed out by my respondents, the precarity at an everyday level arises from various factors such as consistency of content creation, choosing a topic for creation, imagining a community in terms of relevance, searching for brand partnerships, networking for collaboration with fellow social media creators and offline networking with industry practitioners, to list a few. The uncertainties of work in the digital media economy are too obvious to be overlooked; however, the preference for dealing with this kind of precarity instead of waiting for traditional media to spot one's talent makes the NSE distinctive. This is because the hope of building on the fame and creativity produced on social media as a calling card for gathering work of preferred choice across the Indian media entertainment landscape overrides the precarity that creators experience on social media platforms. Additionally, while the precarity of the new screen ecology seems paler in comparison to the gatekeeping practices of the traditional media, it also faces imminent challenges in the form of censorship and unsafe working conditions for women. Before highlighting these challenges, I will first analyse the business practices of the new media ecology.

NEW BUSINESS PRACTICES

In adopting a bottom-up approach ('ground level') and building upon the 'helicopter' level mapping of the platforms and portals (see Chapter 3), I asked online creators to elucidate their daily content creation practices to highlight the distinct emerging practices within the new screen ecology. As I argue, these online practices enable them to survive within the Indian screen industries.

Strategic approaches to labour

I call these practices 'strategic approaches to labour'; in turn, they influence how creators construct their identity and the 'non-hierarchical corporate structures' within which they interact, as evidenced by brand partnerships and organizational practices. By non-hierarchical corporate structures, I mean organizational structures similar to those of corporations but which operate with greater agency. The strategies creators adopt concerning their creative labour reflect the multifarious nature of labour in the online content creation space. Few of my cohort (n=12) stated that their creative online labour was spread across various digital platforms, indicating no strong preference for one platform over another. When asked about the different approaches to publishing content across various platforms, comedian Sorabh Pant replied that, 'Everything is almost becoming each other . . . it is all merging into one' (Pant 2017). As platforms add new features, such as Facebook's live video or YouTube's status update features, creators are becoming more platform-agnostic, preferring to increase their presence across a spectrum of digital platforms and cross-posting certain content. As Cunningham and Craig (2019) note, while multimodal practices help to mitigate risks, they also increase the burden of extra labour as different platforms require different content presentations.

Frugality is also vital to sustainability and success with short-form content, as Anirudh Pandita (2018), co-founder of Pocket Aces, explained: 'In the short form you are watching for five minutes, having a laugh and sharing it with your friends and going back to what you were doing. That is the method of consumption.' Pocket Aces is a digital entertainment company that runs three YouTube channels, which produce sketches and web series. Collectively, the three channels have amassed over one million YouTube subscribers. Pandita (2018) was also quick to point out how Pocket Aces deploys meme culture to attract audience attention, 'Our Content team creates content quickly through memes ... we use [memes] as an experiment ... does this joke work?' By strategically posting content at specific times and across specific platforms, the Pocket Aces team can capitalize on the fast-moving format of memes without needing to invest significant time for maximum audience traction.

As Pandita further explained, popular memes, sketches and on-screen cast member dynamics are repeated in a broader context through web series. In this way, Pandita and Pocket Aces can minimize risks by recreating successful ideas or jokes with different characters. This strategic use of short-form content illustrates a dynamic approach to testing for popularity and ascertaining the viability of longer format content. Creators must also be strategic when competing for attention online. They must be cognizant of viewers and create content that can quickly be circulated through different communities. According to Pandita (2018), the first step is to understand how each of these platforms helps to reach viewers and then to devise a multiplatform strategy:

> We came in when YouTube had several channels offering diverse content with a strong subscriber base. So, we thought, if I put a video up on YouTube, how will I get it to count? How do I get it to be discovered? So, the actual discovery was done on Facebook and not YouTube ... We went for Facebook first ... And the sharing started getting us the initial virality.

Online creators are not only using a combination of platforms to extend reach but are also prioritizing them depending on the life-cycle of their content or channel. As a platform, Facebook is more conducive to creating communities, whereas YouTube promises remuneration but may limit the prospect for discovery (due to the concentration of content). The creators distinguish between YouTube and Facebook as they seek to commercialize their practices across these platforms. As observed in previous instances, the digital media economy not only enables a participatory framework (Jenkins 2008) but also encourages opportunities for self-employment (Ross 2013) and self-branding (Gandini 2016), which can be used as a currency for circulation, collaboration and monetization.

As creators navigate the uncertainties surrounding the economic outcome of social media, the creators' understanding of platforms and knowledge of platform-specific audiences enables them to produce different values from their usage of each social media platform (Scolere et al. 2018). Rather than using each of these platforms simply as distribution models, their use is determined by their perceived prime value: Facebook for community building and YouTube for monetizing.

Ultimately, the brands are attracted to the Facebook community base and are used as proof of popularity with the audience to attract more revenue. By applying these learnings, the content creators can sustain, engage and multiply their audiences, attracting advertisers and multimedia platforms for collaboration in the process.

Social media also provide more avenues for additional revenue through creative labour. The five stand-up comedians I interviewed each mentioned the additional writing work they do to supplement their incomes. Translating content, writing copy and cross-platform integration offer opportunities for more revenue streams, but at the cost of dividing creators' attention and time that could otherwise be spent on other professional work. The second theme developed through interviewees' repeated insistence that they were not 'just YouTubers' focuses on the professional identity of these creators.

Professional identity

In addition to strategic approaches to their labour, the independent content creators wanted to cultivate a specific professional identity. Interviewees again pointed to the utility of platforms when building their online identities because, as Aditi Mittal (2017) explained, 'social identity is a new currency'. Specific creators I interviewed wanted audiences to sample their work via social media to further explore their more substantial bodies of work. These findings challenge Cunningham and Craig's (2019) assertion that social media represent a repository for nonlinear open sharing of amateur content creation while digital media (portals) remain the hub for professionally generated content.

Showcasing art does, in many cases, lead to potentially lucrative opportunities, as demonstrated by Aditi Mittal, who released a Netflix comedy special in 2017. She explained, 'I have got tons of work because of the stuff that I have put online ... it is kind of a CV, a glorified video CV, on things that I have been doing for the past seven years.' Comedian Atul Khatri (2017) described these 'digital calling cards' as tools to reach out and boost ticket sales for his live comedy shows. Such an approach helps the creators to embrace the precarity of social media platforms.

Vaibhav Sethia (2018), a former architect and a stand-up comedian with 170,113 subscribers on YouTube and 11,446,517 cumulative views from uploading seven stand-up comedy videos as of June 2019, identified YouTube as a platform 'for reaching a larger audience'. Sethia uses many social media platforms to reach his audience, specifically: 'YouTube to upload videos of my work. Facebook, Instagram, Twitter, and Snapchat to publicize shows and for personal use.' This is akin to Burgess and Green's (2018: 84) articulation of 'cross-platform' strategies of creators. So, while an increase in viewership on YouTube does earn revenue for him, his low uploading count in the last two years shows his dependence on YouTube is for popularity and promotion rather than monetization. Sethia also identifies himself as a 'stand-up comedian' rather than a 'YouTuber', crediting YouTube with 'establishing stand-up [comedy] as a full-time career choice in India'.

Before stand-up comedy, Sethia tried a variety of jobs from architect to assistant director in Bengali films. Eventually realizing his passion for stand-up comedy, Sethia, from Kolkata, began performing stand-up shows in 2012 but struggled for paid gigs as the stand-up comedy scene was not particularly developed – especially in Kolkata. However, as Kay (2018: 15) notes in her study of Indian internet comedy, the advent of YouTube led to a demand for, and the popularity of, stand-up comedy as a form of entertainment. This resulted in a growing number of stand-up comedians who eventually used social media platforms to build a fan base in the hope that some viewers would eventually turn up for their live events. Their social media following was also used as evidence to convince comedy clubs to hire them. Popular stand-up comedian Kunal Kamra noted that 'Tickets would not sell if comics were not promoting themselves online' (Mishra 2019). Sethia's popularity on social media platforms also led Amazon Prime to sign him for a stand-up comedy special show, *Don't*, in 2018. Today, online creators are becoming increasingly aware of the motivations behind their use of social media, whether it is for self-expression, promotion or commerce.

Non-hierarchical corporate structures

Another marker of the increasing means to battle precarity is what I term 'non-hierarchical corporate structures', a flatter and more democratic working culture adopted by online media companies to combat the demand for content and audience retention to retain social media relevance and algorithmic uncertainty.

Companies such as TVF, AIB and Pocket Aces have grown through content creation on YouTube and are now functioning as fully fledged production houses. Their expertise in social media content creation offers competitive advantages over independent creators in online screen media markets and provides more security to the executives working in these companies. Associate Creative Director for TVF, Nidhi Bisht (2018), highlights TVF's non-hierarchical corporate structure, which he terms a 'creative corporate structure' deployed to pitch and develop ideas:

> We have a creative corporate structure. Let us say I have an idea which I think has the potential, the first thing I will do is ... bounce it in the room, and there would be like-minded people who think that the idea has the potential. So, as we bounce the

idea and ten jokes come up, and we see writers getting excited for this . . . then we say, yes, something can be done on this . . .

This distinctly non-hierarchical corporate culture echoes an attempt to decentralize the traditional corporate hierarchy and change how ideas are pitched and developed in the Indian film and TV industries. An open corporate environment that emphasizes sharing ideas from all levels is reflected in the corporate culture of another digital media company, Pocket Aces, as co-founder Anirudh Pandita (2018) noted:

The company is actually based on some of our core beliefs of the culture. So, we always put culture above everything else. You saw the office; it is pretty open. There is no cubicle, so it is a free atmosphere. Because there is much belief that interdepartmental disciplinary skills will bring out content and ideas.

Moreover, the popularity of original content creations and a nuanced understanding of audiences can also assist companies to function as a traditional production company and pitch their 'portfolios' (Scholere 2019) to portals; this is a strategy practised by Arré, a digital entertainment content company established by UDigital content in 2016. Founded by a team of media professionals, Ronnie Screwvala, Ajay Chacko and B Sai Kumar, the company leadership changed hands with Ronnie Screwvala exiting as an investor in place of Sanjay Rai Chaudhari (Bhattacharyya 2016). In 2016, the company received an undisclosed amount of funding from Enam Holdings, an investment group, to further its business plans and content offerings (Johari 2016). With a workforce of fifty media professionals, Arré operates across social media verticals such as YouTube, Facebook and Instagram, while also serving as a producer, marketer and distributor to television and streaming platforms.

Arré's Vice President, Product and Business Development, Niyati Merchant, elaborated on the company's genre and format-agnostic content strategy to discuss how Arré, since its inception in 2016, has produced sketches, web series, documentaries, editorials and podcasts across comedy, thriller, food, travel and adventure, and music segments. Arré has also distributed content to portals such as Ola Play, Jio, SonyLIV, Yupp TV and TataSky. As of June 2022, it has over 1.8 million subscribers on YouTube (UDigital 2021) and 1.7 million likes on its Facebook page (UDigital n.d.). The popularity of Arré's content on social media ultimately served as the calling card, as portal Times MXPlayer commissioned Arré's to produce a popular six-episode web series sitcom on Indian start-up culture, titled *Tathastu* ('Curated by Arré' 2019). Naturally, its social media library of sketches and web series also shows the ability of its production team to mount short- and long-form narratives.

Figure 4.1 Arré Facebook post promoting Voot content (Facebook 2018).

Arré's strong audience metrics of subscribers, views and fan engagement on social media also serve as a strong portfolio for engaging in business practices with brands and NSE enterprises looking to target Indian online viewers. Figure 4.1 shows Arré managing Viacom18's portal, Voot's, social media promotion on Facebook.

Non-hierarchical corporate structures on social media help launch careers, develop and execute innovative ideas, and deliver high-quality content. Creators use these structures, in conjunction with strategic approaches to labour and carefully crafted professional identities, to take full advantage of the new creative affordances of digital media platforms.

Building a media career from social media

A new generation of Indian creators and media entrepreneurs are experiencing the freedom of creative expression through social media creation, attaining popularity and using it to achieve career aspirations. For instance, consider the case of Bhuvan Bam, who won Global Entertainer of the Year at Cannes 2019, principally for his YouTube channel BB ki Vines. Bhuvan Bam exemplifies content creators who began their careers on social media. BB ki Vines is focused primarily on creating vlogs, sketches and short comedy videos and had over 12 million subscribers (Bam 2016) as of June 2019. While discussing his online creative work in an interview, Bam described practising as a singer, songwriter and guitarist before becoming a YouTuber, 'After my 12th boards (final exams), a guy offered me to sing in a restaurant. Till my second year of college, I used to perform at a Delhi restaurant. Then I started writing my own songs' (Arora 2016). In this manner, Bam, a musician, could create a popular satirical channel by conjuring multiple imaginary narratives laced with humour. The 'vernacular creativity' (Burgess 2006) on the internet is a result of the social media affordances that empower creators to engage in multiple genres of entertainment and forge their career trajectories, as evidenced by Bam's social media performance as an actor, vlogger, writer and editor.

Online creators such as Bam are not afraid to innovate with their roles – Bam has appeared as an actor in multiple web series, commissioned on YouTube channel Happii Fi (owned by television network Sri Adhikari Brothers Television Network Ltd.) and TVF (owned by Contagious Online Media Pvt. Ltd.), respectively. In late 2018, Bam became the first Indian online content creator to reach 10 million subscribers (Bhattacharya 2018). Bam teamed up with Guneet Monga, a well-known producer of films including *The LunchBox*, *Gangs of Wasseypur* and *Masaan*, to star in a short film titled *Plus Minus* ('Plus Minus' 2018). It was written and directed by Jyoti Kapur Das, whose previous short film, *Chutney*, was also released on YouTube, where it received 135 million views (Largeshort Films 2016). In *Plus Minus*, Bam plays the role of a 22-year-old Indian army soldier, which required him to prove a high level of acting – marking a dramatic shift from his previous narratives of satire and humour. The film has received widespread praise from critics and internet audiences alike, receiving 28 million views as of August 2022 (BB ki Vines 2018).

Das's prior experience as a media practitioner spans Indian television, film and NSE, taking on the roles of writer, producer and director. The acceptance of Das from both the audience and skilled film professionals suggests an opportunity for online creators who are keen to work beyond the platform–portal–film divide. Bollywood film producers are not shy about investing in an online content creator simply because of the creator's YouTube origins. On the contrary, by releasing the short film on his YouTube channel, the producers and the director managed to use Bam's popularity to gather a ready-made audience (Das 2018). Bam's case study exemplifies how film professionals trusted his acting prowess based on his portfolio of low-budget vlogs and sketches.

Bam's popularity among his subscriber base led him to become the brand ambassador for Mivi, an electronics brand that also co-sponsored *Chutney*. Moreover, the engagement between India's YouTube sensations and successful film industry professionals for the short film also meant a flurry of articles covering the news about the short film, creating a buzz around the film. At the same time, creators can balance out the tensions between authenticity and commerce (Cunningham and Craig 2017) as they professionalize their content-creation practices. In 2018, Bam also performed a sketch with mainstream Bollywood actor Shah Rukh Khan (Bam 2018), who came to promote his film *Zero* on Bam's channel, further strengthening Bam's popularity as an 'influencer' (Abidin 2015) and Bollywood's need to include promotions on online content creators' channels as a part of its film marketing strategy.

The intermingling of social media labour with film industry professionals is another example of the power dynamics emerging between Bollywood and internet creator culture. The NSE, therefore, consists of content creators who can use networked technologies to their advantage. Bam's case study is meant to highlight how a commoner hailing from a middle-class Delhi household with no connections to the film or television industry used social media to carve an identity for himself within the media industry landscape. It also exemplifies how earnings from social media are simply not enough to sustain a media career. Building connections with established traditional media circuits can help the creator navigate the structural tensions that arise from each medium – social media's uncertainty and the nepotistic tendencies of traditional media.

Siddharth Alambayan, Creative Head at Times Internet Ltd., the digital venture of the legacy media company The Times of India, one of India's largest media enterprises, commented on the seamless nature of online content creators concerning securing future projects. While discussing the movement of creator labour in the NSE, Alambayan (2017) argued:

> It has become a society that lives by the osmosis of creators. Zakir Khan (comedian) can have his own (YouTube) channel, market small snippet videos on Facebook, and appear in *AIB* (YouTube channel) sketch with ease. Devika Vatsa (actress) can be in a Hewlett Packard advertisement and a *Timeliners* (TVF vertical) sketch. Shibani Bedi, who works on Times Internet's social media vertical, iDiva, a women's lifestyle channel, is seen in a YouTube ad by Horlicks (hot milk drink) because she attained her screen fame on the internet via ScoopWhoop (she was previously working with ScoopWhoop) and then a facelift from iDiva.

In highlighting these examples, Alambayan exemplifies the fluidity and commerciality of vloggers, actors and stand-up comedians with social media presence in negotiating their popularity across multiple media. As Baym (2015: 4) notes, 'the ability for individuals to communicate and produce mediated content on a mass scale has led to opportunities for fame that were not available outside of the established culture industries before'. Actor Naveen Kasturia, who has appeared in critically acclaimed Hindi feature films like *Shanghai* and *Sulemaani Keeda*, as well as scripted web series on multiple portals such as TVFPlay and ZEE5, noted that he received a lot more offers after the success of the TVF web series *Pitchers*, where he played the role of one of the four protagonists: 'It changed many things. I also started getting more money on commercials' (Kasturia 2018). For NSE creators, social media is not so much a destination as it is a way to further their sustainability and commerciality within the media industries.

However, the constant hustling across mediums is also a key strategy for alleviating risks arising from the volatilities of dealing with social media. While social media affordances allow for creator videos to feature on the social media feeds and timelines of subscribers, the lack of transparency and unpredicted changes to the systems act as a deterrent for creators as well as companies who are investing all their time, energy and finances on these platforms to build their brands. At the same time, these platforms are increasingly populated by a range of players competing for attention across multiple disciplines, mediums and genres.

In such a scenario, it is difficult for less successful and less economically privileged creators to attract attention and practise their craft as a full-time job, as noted by Priyam Ghose (2018), an emerging regional online creator from Kolkata who specializes in creating Bengali language content. As well as producing sketches on his social media channels, Ghose holds a full-time job in the social media vertical of Bengali-specific portal Hoichoi (see Chapters 3 and 6). Reducing social media dependency is thus one way for online creators to build their career paths, so they are less precarious. I discuss precarity and the opportunities for regional online creators in Chapter 6.

Entrepreneurial labour

My creator cohort (n=45) in India revealed that the 'entrepreneurial' nature of the job allowed creators an opportunity to build their brand, which eventually paved the way for opportunities to achieve fame and money. As online content creators continue to struggle with social media algorithms and metrics, they are constantly adopting new creative and cost-effective measures to produce content that attracts the most views. One of the ways to achieve this is by employing creators who can do multiple tasks within the media-creation process, such as writing, acting and editing.

Nidhi Bisht (2019), Creative Director of TVF, argued that TVF encouraged a multitasking environment where 'the one who wrote also had the leverage to act or direct'. However, creators confessed that these prudent measures afforded them greater agency, increasing their involvement in and passion for their work. Creators also see multitasking as improving online visibility and creating more chances of securing work on portals and from Bollywood.

Dhruv Sehgal, a senior content creator of Pocket Aces, a digital media company specializing in creating content on social media, argued that 'writing and acting for Dice Media (YouTube verticals) led him to receive several offers from media companies'. Multitasking is also a regular occurrence for online content creators who prefer to stay behind the camera. Sehgal also recalled his impromptu acting debut: 'We were making a video for Dice Media [Pocket Aces' long-form content YouTube channel], and one of the actors did not turn up, and hence I was asked to do the role instead' (Sehgal 2018). The ability of firms to take risks and engage their workforce on-screen is precarious, emancipatory and cost-efficient. Shifting roles allows creators to attend to audience preferences and capitalize on unexpected opportunities for creative labour. Sehgal, a Delhi-based media graduate, shifted to Mumbai to take up his first job as one of the original employees of Pocket Aces in 2016. Having worked earlier on a documentary and short film as an associate director and actor, the founders encouraged Sehgal to explore writing.

Sehgal developed a show for Pocket Aces based on his own life experiences, called *A Delhi Boy, Now Living in Mumbai*. A couple of Sehgal's sketches on YouTube, where he acted alongside Mithila Parkar, went viral. However, his biggest writing/acting success came in the form of *Little Things* (2016) – a five-episode web series on Pocket Aces' YouTube vertical Dice Media, which was a sensation among Indian digital audiences, grossing an average of approximately eight million views (average viewership of all shows). *Little Things* loosely follows the everyday life of a couple living in Mumbai. As discussed in Chapter 4, stories like these reflect the aesthetics of online content as a storyteller's medium. Sehgal's approach to online content as a storyteller's medium illustrates creators' liberty to express their identities realistically online.

The success of *Little Things* is not limited to YouTube alone. Its second season was acquired by Netflix (Bhattacharya 2018), and a *Little Things* book was contracted to be published by Penguin Random House India (Vikas 2018). The streaming of the series on Netflix (*Little Things* 2018) offered Sehgal a chance to showcase his talent across 190 countries.

Sehgal's popularity eventually earned him opportunities for brand endorsements, with Anirudh Pandita, the co-founder of Dice Media, even acknowledging that Sehgal had 'received an offer for a feature film' (Pandita 2018).

Pandita's revelation is not surprising, given that since *Little Things*, Sehgal's co-star, Mithila Parkar, has appeared in the Marathi-language feature film *Muramba* (2017), the Bollywood film *Karwaan* (2017) and the Netflix feature film *Chopsticks* (2018) (Sharma 2019). The 'multitasking' labour approach of these media companies not only makes their content cost-effective but also rewards the investment in energy and time by employees.

The greater degree of dependence on talent among digital media companies and within the overall media industries helps them overcome the venture labour critique that Neff (2012) offers in her study of Silicon Valley entrepreneurs. The varying degrees of success enjoyed by independent content creators and the show *Little Things* exemplify the power of online content to derive new meanings from identity, help creators cross over to other platforms and reward the individuals involved.

FUTURE CHALLENGES

While the previous sections focused on the agency of creators in traversing new avenues to create new forms and business practices, my cohort pointed to three ongoing challenges that continue to plague the new screen ecology in India: censorship, gender inequality and the #MeToo movement.

Censorship

Despite the success stories described above, our interviewees were wary of the persistent spectre of censorship in India. Comedian Pant (2017) cautions, 'You have to toe the line a little bit more in India than you would ordinarily in the West' (Pant 2017). Online creators in India are in a unique position regarding government censorship compared with their film or TV counterparts. Films in India must be certified by the Censor Board of Film Certification (CBFC), and television content is subject to retrospective censorship (after telecast) by the Broadcasting Content Complaints Council (BCCC), set up by the Indian Broadcasting Foundation.

However, the principle of the uncensored web in India may be short-lived, as the Bombay High Court recently sought advice from the Ministry of Information and Broadcasting, Ministry of Home Affairs and the Ministry of Electronics and Information Technology against public interest litigation (PIL) filed over 'obscene and vulgar' representation in content being streamed on the Netflix and Altbalaji portals (Mangure 2018: 1). These developments have also triggered concerns about the relatively lawless ambit under which these platforms and portals operate compared with the film and television industry.

In September 2019, the state of Maharashtra's regional party, Shiv Sena, filed a police complaint against Netflix for 'defaming the country' through its various shows, such as *Sacred Games*, *Leila*, *Ghoul* and *Patriot Act* ('Complaint against Netflix' 2019). In alignment with their right-wing counterpart, extreme right-wing Hindu outfits Rashtriya Swayam Sevak (RSS) and Vishwa Hindu Parishad (Worldwide Hindu Foundation, VHP) were quick to voice their support for digital media censorship (Malhotra 2019). Following the calls for regulation and Supreme Court notice, the Internet and Mobile Association of India (IAMAI) developed a code of best practices for online content, which was signed by fifteen major streaming services such as Hotstar, Netflix, Amazon Prime, SonyLIV, ZEE5 and Jio (Deep 2020). The practices discussed in the code include some standard practices, such as an age-categorization system to classify content into distinct viewing categories.

However, the code also prohibits exhibiting content that represents children in sexual acts, content that has been previously banned by Indian Courts of Justice, or is malicious to India's national interests, the latter being vaguely defined and broadly open to interpretation (Singh 2019). Furthermore, the code proposes a 'complaints redressal system' that addresses user complaints while acknowledging intervention from the Ministry of Information and Broadcasting in cases where the Government receives complaints directly.

In 2021, the Indian Government introduced the 'Information Technology (Intermediary Guidelines and Digital Media Ethics Code) Rules 2021' to regulate digital media companies as a part of the current regime to enforce censorship of the internet (Ministry of Electronics and Information Technology 2021). This enforcement comes against the backdrop of the Information and Broadcasting Ministry's demand for censoring an Amazon Prime web series, *Tandav*, under the pretext of communal threat. The Information Technology Rules, 2021, proposed that digital media companies follow a three-tier grievance redressal system to ensure against the misuse of internet services, the final tier of which would be overseen by the Government. The proposed rules are being contested through seventeen petitions filed across the various Indian States by individuals and organizations alike (Ahooja and Sarkar 2021). However, in 2022, the draft was amended. Under the new draft, digital media companies are to form a Grievance Appellate Committee (GAC), the constitution of whose members would be presided over by the Central Government (Rudra 2022). These proposed rules threaten the autonomy of the streaming services to enable freedom of expression and prohibit the ability of the Internet to facilitate alternative voices that are already censored on film and television.

At the same time, the Government's silence on the threats made by right-wing extremist forces in enforcing censorship has raised serious concerns among netizens and industry insiders regarding the medium's ability to encourage freedom of expression and foster depictions of complex social issues – especially in a country such as India, where the platforms and portals serve as an alternative to the closely scrutinized film and television medium (Kay 2018). Another reason to fear the Government's control is the relentless blocking of internet services under the pretext of preserving communal harmony and countering terrorism. According to multiple reports, India leads other countries in enforcing the most number of internet lockdowns – between 2012 and 2022, 665 lockdowns have been imposed on mobile, dial-up, wired and wireless broadband internet services (Singh 2022). At a time when artists and artworks are living under the constant threat of being attacked by the Government or its allied groups, the idea of leaving internet censorship to the Government's control is indeed scary. The proposed state interventions to curb the only remaining mass medium that has so far allowed largely unrestrained free expression shows that India may be post-colonial by definition but still retains its colonial legacy in its political mindset.

Beyond the nation-state control, one interviewee pointed to cases where she self-imposed censorship to avoid cultural taboos or controversial topics. Aditi Mittal (2017) recounted instances when she was wary of telling jokes that might portray her family or parents negatively and attract an outpouring of the kinds of negative and abusive comments posted to a video in which she joked about feminine hygiene products. In both cases, her material would not be removed for contravening any censorship laws, but it would still be cut to avoid toxic audience backlash: 'You will receive death threats to say what is wrong with you, so you have to be very careful' (Mittal 2017). This leads to the second critical challenge facing the Indian new screen ecology: gender inequality.

Gender inequality

Mittal (2017) asserts that: 'Most trending content right now is just misogynistic bullshit ... and I have no idea what that shit is, but still, it is trending.' In her view, the internet audience in India consists largely of boys and young men, which explains why sexist content performs so strongly while female creators are frequently disparaged and attacked online. Aditi Mittal uses her content and comedy to address a highly under-served population of Indian women. Mittal's assertion highlights the struggle of female content creators working as 'aspirational labourers', characterized as those who produce 'authentic' content built on relationships and entrepreneurship, yet receive disproportionate compensation while also conforming to gender stereotypes and social inequality in the online media industry (Duffy and Hund 2015: 9).

Sexism online is not unique to India; however, cultural taboos (women perceived as a burden for the family) and norms (patriarchy) have prevented messages of gender equality and empowerment from entering the mainstream until recently. According to Kay (2018: 37), 'Internet comedy has come to be a social imperative by a generation of Indians, which speaks to a wider project of challenging Bollywood and the emerging discourses around gender, discrimination, politics and the media as pressing and pertinent.' Aditi Mittal's comments reaffirm this important point. Mallika Dua, who rose to fame as a vlogger, actor and writer, accused talent agency Only Much Louder (OML) of under-negotiating her deal with Star TV for the comedy show *The Great Indian Laughter Challenge*. Dua argued that her male counterpart Zakir Khan, also managed by OML, was paid twice the amount she was offered ('Mallika Dua Says Zakir Khan' 2019). In another interview, Dua lamented that women comedians in India are often identified by their gender as 'female stand-up comedians', while also pointing out the deep-rooted gender disparity and pay structure across the Indian media industry landscape ('I Have Never Evaluated Myself' 2018).

Providing further evidence for this claim, ex-Buzzfeed video producer Sumedh Natu and stand-up comedian Aayushi Jagad created a YouTube video highlighting systematic under-representation of female characters by popular YouTube creator team AIB (Kanchwala 2018). Natu and Jagad's (2017) textual analysis of previous AIB videos demonstrated how, even in the fewer roles offered to women, they were merely utilized as 'feminists or plot devices' (Natu and Jagad 2017). They claimed that AIB only used women in videos as objects to maintain 'feminist creators' image within their social networks. However, the systemic exclusion of women is not restricted to local practices, as even global portals such as Amazon Prime, with their Western and seemingly progressive ideals, have been accused of propagating an identical philosophy.

In 2017, film critic Anupama Chopra ironically invited five male comedians and just one female comedian to discuss prevalent sexism within the Indian comedy circuit for her YouTube channel Film Companion against the backdrop of Amazon Prime's signing of only male stand-up comedians as a part of their India launch (Manral 2017). To add to the irony, when Chopra asked whether there was an inherent 'bro-culture' within the comedy industry, all the male comedians emphatically denied in unison, thereby conveniently forgetting Aditi Mittal's presence.

The various endemic issues concerning women in the NSE are emblematic of broader gender politics in the Indian screen industries. The roots of such notions are often seeded at the educational level, as was highlighted by actress Rasika Dugal. Dugal's disturbing experience at the Film and Television Institute of India (FTII), an apex film school ('Entertainment Education Report' 2018), provides an informative insight into how the culture of toxic masculinity propagated within media industries is also a result of systemized gender discrimination practices in reputed media institutions. While discussing the pervading sexist environment within FTII, Dugal observed:

Even though more women had applied for specialisation in [FTII's] acting course, only five girls and 15 boys were selected for the same. I find it shocking how, in every field, this ratio is skewed. Unknowingly, we are fighting so many battles, and I was unaware that the situation was becoming difficult. That is the problem with gender discrimination: it is so well-embedded that we are not even aware that we are dealing with something like this.

(Dugal 2018)

Dugal's reflections demonstrate how deeply rooted and culturally embedded these issues are – and for some, they begin even before they get their first work. Indrani Biswas, the creator of YouTube comedy channel Wonder Munna and winner of YouTube Nextup 2018, casually remarked that she did not find any female creators on YouTube in Kolkata when she started making videos (Biswas 2018). At the same time, these issues seem universal as Burgess and Green's formative scholarship on YouTube articulates how most of the top 30 homegrown YouTube channels belong to male talent (Burgess and Green 2018: 90). Despite the preliminary evidence promoting the NSE as a safe space for the empowerment of alternative voices, female creators continue to struggle for compensation and screen space compared with their male counterparts.

As I discuss below, the #MeToo movement in India laid bare the implications of this pervasive gender inequality and destroyed the businesses and careers of several online media practitioners.

The #MeToo movement and the Indian NSE

The emergence of the #MeToo movement in the Indian media industry laid bare the fallacy of the public as well as private institutions in checking the power and abuse of privileged men, in particular the Indian online video industry that has been otherwise valorized for giving opportunities to new voices and newer expressions. The movement has manifested itself in different ways, traversing regional film industries and entrepreneurial sectors. While actress Tanushree Dutta's allegations about the harassment she faced from the senior actor Nana Patekar on the sets of the film *Horn Ok Pleassss* (2008) triggered the #metoo movement in the Indian Hindi film industry in 2018, the actress received very little support from the industry. However, similar allegations were made against All India Bakchod (AIB) team members, one of India's most popular and earliest online YouTube channels, leading to its shutdown (Pathak 2019).

The severity of the movement had a tremendous effect on its relationship with its streaming services, such as Amazon Prime, Hotstar and Netflix, who pulled the plug on their partnership – prominent amongst them being AIB's US$4 million financed debut indie feature film *Chintu ka Birthday* (Chintu's birthday) that was to be acquired directly by Netflix but was cancelled (Pathak 2019b) and was eventually developed by ZEE5. Questions concerning the efficacy of the Sexual Harassment Act, the Internal Complaints Committee, and the management policies of entertainment companies were raised. More importantly, these acts exposed the rooted gender bias and misuse of power that these internet-based companies claimed to address through their production cultures.

The #MeToo movement's impact on digital production culture has been, at times, gendered and, at other times, reactionary. While there has been a tendency to be dismissive of the movement altogether or rehabilitate the accused for financial reasons, there have been cases where the services and production houses, because of their financial interests, have fired the accused and put sexual harassment policies in place. However, many of these policies are designed to safeguard the producers' interests.

Producers who worked with Netflix and Netflix executives highlighted how Netflix carries out a 'Respect' workshop before going on to production. In this workshop, Netflix executives run a Powerpoint presentation where the cast and crew are shown instances that could count as harassment and as well as rules, regulations, and ways of conducting themselves on the set. However, as our cohort highlighted, in most cases, accountability is a significant concern as there is no clarity about to whom harrassment cases should be reported, whether it be the producer, supervisor, director, or the streaming service. Especially, there is a lack of clarity on what legal and general support options the streaming service provides to the survivors to protect their identity. Also, how does one navigate the economic implications of replacing a harasser who has completed a significant part of the project?

Moreover, most of the accused wield enough power within their kinship networks to go scot-free and find work, and the streaming services are wary of upsetting the prevailing power of the social and kinship networks of the Hindi film industry. As an example, actor Alok Nath, accused of rape and sexual harrassment by multiple women, continues to find work in films and Netflix commercials despite the fact that writer-director Vinta Nanda accused him of sexual harassment in 2004–5 in an interview that was covered on the front page of the *Bombay Times* – an English-language daily newspaper *Times of India* supplement that principally covers celebrity news (Anjum 2022). The libraries of major streaming services such as Netflix, Amazon Prime, Disney+Hotstar and ZEE5 continue to show Alok Nath's films even as Nanda was ostracized and had to pick up piecemeal professional opportunities.

In 2018, at the same time as the #MeToo movement started gaining momentum in India, Nanda filed a police complaint against Nath and revealed her alleged experiences in a Facebook post. However, just as in 2005, Nanda lost work opportunities in studios and production houses due to her complaint. Vinta Nanda's survival story is just one of many examples that proliferate in the Indian media industries, where the accused are rehabilitated with opportunities, and the survivors are left with blame and losses of all kinds. Thus, the streaming services' loyalty to the film elites is rewarded with access to wider social capital in Indian audio-visual industries that are notorious for their informal hiring practices.

Despite a general consensus about increased awareness and open conversations about the #MeToo movement both on set and in media companies, the mechanisms and procedures to check sexual harassment cases are lacking. Daria (name changed), who worked in the production department of Only Much Louder (OML), a media production-cum-talent management company, for over a year and a half, highlights how despite OML being caught up in the #MeToo allegations and having joined OML post-#MeToo, no one apprised her about the ICC or of the procedure in case of sexual harassment. Sexual harassment cases are even worse for employees who belong to the LGBTQ+ community. Samar (name changed) was subjected to sexual harassment from his immediate boss. Having sought psychological help to recover from the stress of the harrowing process, Samar recalls,

> I face harassment based on my sexuality in my office by my manager, and I have to raise a harassment case, and we don't have any laws supporting us. POSH is only for women. There is no POSH for us! So, it (the case) went really long. I was asked to provide proof. How do I prove things that happened with a very casual attitude? Also, it is illegal to record things.[1]

In her analysis of the media's role in anti-rape and sexual harassment cases, feminist media scholar Pallavi Guha (2021: 10) notes that: '99% of rapes and sexual harassment incidents go unreported'. The many reasons, as Guha points out, include the stigmatization of the survivors by the media and the objectification of their bodies. I build on Guha's intervention to argue that survivors experience the strongest stigmatization by patriarchal and privileged power structures that directly impede survivors' chances to mobilize support. Neetha (name changed), who accused a prominent Bollywood actor and filed legal proceedings alleging sexual harassment, highlights how one of the female senior media executives she bumped into mocked her,

> Guess what? The joke around the industry among men is now 'you too.' Those (men) left out from being named are feeling excluded.[2]

The passive aggression that the survivors have to face contributes to the efficacy of the movement in supporting their voices. Asha (name changed) feels that the post-#MeToo era saw the industry eliminating work opportunities for women under the guise of reducing the chances where harassment could happen. Web-series writers like Vahini (name changed) and Sharmila (name changed) revealed that women had been systematically excluded post-#MeToo from both casual get-togethers in academia and after-work parties – crucial for networking and scoping future opportunities – due to the fear of accusation.

Post-#MeToo, as a producer recalls, there were 'concerns' about hiring women for outdoor shoots. The strategy to evade responsibility to prevent possible lapses meant that women were not invited or actively encouraged to come to after-work parties – depriving them of the networking opportunities for scoping future projects.

CONCLUSION

Precarious creativity in the NSE context is realized by harbouring promises of equal opportunity and freedom of expression for creators looking to pursue a career in the media, with piecemeal measures to tackle unsafe and insecure working conditions that exposes the limitations of NSE in offering an ever-inclusive space for progressive cultural politics. Precarious creativity thus assumes ambivalence, offering grounds for linguistic and cultural diversity (see Chapter 5) but also denying those who do not conform to a capitalistic logic by rewarding select creators.

The purpose of this chapter has not been to valorize the NSE; rather, it should be viewed as an attempt to highlight how distinct kinds of online creators derive value on social media through their sense-making as they deal with precarious creativity. Because the economic and social transactions within the traditional media are unapproachable to the newcomers, despite offering value propositions, social media have been able to create a perception of a more equitable site for creating content as well as for reaching the audience. That social media creators do not have to deal with gatekeepers before creation and can create content that is true to their perceptions also propagates a sense of belief that the inequities of traditional media are dealt with, or at least lessened to a certain extent, by creating on and not for platforms. This belief is strengthened by working on more individualistic motives entrenched within the capitalist logic.

Moreover, this chapter offers fresh insights into creators' ability to negotiate content clutter and position themselves in competition with local and international 'legacy' media. I have introduced seven themes concerning NSE production culture that contribute to a better understanding of content creators' daily practices, new affordances and looming challenges. The principal contribution in highlighting these content creation themes is to foreground the content creators themselves, as opposed to the platforms and portals for which they create content. The inroads they have made through open-ended platforms like YouTube and Facebook to close-ended platforms like Netflix and Hotstar signify a platform agnosticism, which is supported by the fact that many do not wish to be labelled based on one particular platform, such as being known as 'YouTubers' or 'Instagrammers'.

In the next chapter, I focus on the two key aspects of this ecology by first outlining the unprecedented growth of regional online content creators and their influence in shaping platform/portal content strategies. Finally, I look at the emergence of new facets of celebrity and fandom practices arising from the popularity of regional creators defying the otherwise dominant paradigm of popularity afforded to film and television personalities.

5
Regional and Localizing Online Content Practices

Building on India's region-specific context in Chapters 1 and 2, it is pertinent to note that India uses more than 104 languages for broadcasting on the radio, 87 for the print medium, 67 languages for primary school syllabuses and another 104 languages in the adult learning curriculums (Mohanty 2010). I draw attention to the fact that even within India, on average, there is only a 36 per cent chance that two Indians can communicate with each other (Kawoosa 2018). Thus, India's population is so diverse that even Indians from different regions find it difficult to interact in one common language. Given the complexity of India's multilingual diversity, catering to native Indian languages is a critical step in NSE localization practices to appeal to a larger Indian audience, as was readily conceded in Chapter 3 through the analysis of platforms and portals.

In this chapter, I show how the unprecedented creation of regional online content on YouTube since 2017 (KPMG 2018) has led the NSE to focus on localization strategies marked by three practices: the mobilization of popular regional social media creators by platforms and portals; the emergence of language-specific portals (Hoichoi and Addatimes, as introduced in Chapter 3); and the commissioning of regional content that has a 'local', 'transnational' and 'global appeal'. In 2021, 47 per cent of web series and 69 per cent of films released on portals were in non-Hindi and non-English languages (FICCI-EY 2022: 56).

Through a primary focus on online content-creation practices in the Bengali and Marathi languages, this chapter explores their 'local', 'regional', 'transnational' and 'global' appeal and subsequent blurring of boundaries between 'regionalization' and 'localization'. The focus on Marathi and Bengali language content-creation practices is a significant intervention in that it departs from the previous scholarship that has either focused on South Indian languages (see Mohan and Punathambekar 2019; Srinivas et al. 2018) or upon languages (see Tripathy 2013; Kumar 2014 on Bhojpuri language content) that have lacked state formation. Moreover, a recent industry report states that the majority of the portal viewership originates from Hindi, Marathi, Bengali, Kannada, Tamil, Telugu and Malayalam languages (FICCI-EY 2022: 63).

This is not to suggest that regional content on YouTube never existed before 2017. Previous studies (Punathambekar 2008; Srinivas et al. 2018) have articulated the participatory culture of online media in mobilizing the excesses of regional cinema, whether it be through content or creators. Punathambekar (2008) highlights the participatory culture of A. R. Rahman's fans on various online spaces to show how the internet serves as a site of sociality for sustaining fan culture. Following Punathambekar (2008), Srinivas and colleagues (2018) trace the migration of big-budget Tamil and Telugu films from single-screen cinemas to YouTube. In particular, Srinivas et al. (2018: 246) show how regional blockbusters are dubbed in Hindi and Bhojpuri languages to argue 'the decoupling of regional cinema from both language as well as location of production' and as means to expand the regional audience base to include Hindi- and Bhojpuri-speaking audiences.

The focus, instead, is on the active creator mobilization strategies of platforms and portals upon realization of the role that regional online creators – who appeared first on YouTube – can play in expanding social media consumption practices beyond states and nations. Building on original content and native social media creators is critical since social media platforms reluctantly serve as spaces for exhibiting pirated and copyright-infringing content. By banking on the success and entrepreneurial abilities of native-to-internet regional creators, social media platforms can reduce their dependency on aggregated content and project themselves as an aspirational hub for developing 'homegrown' creators. Furthermore, the relatively 'seamless' trans-border flow of regional content due to the cultural politics of select languages (such as Hindi, Bengali and Marathi) and the 'boundary-less' feature of digital infrastructure (see Kumar 2021) also help the NSE expand its value propositions beyond one country and to sustain its business.

Despite the digital divide, India has the world's cheapest data prices, with a gigabyte of mobile data costing US$0.83, compared to a global average of US$8.53 (Roy 2019). This has also amplified the possibility of the economic viability of accessing the internet across different strata of Indian society. India has the second largest smartphone userbase at 503 million (FICCI-EY 2022: 59). As of September 2021, 834 million Indians have internet subscriptions (FICCI-EY 2022: 56).

This is not to say that the demand for and circulation of regional online content never existed previously. Within the global media landscape, the circulation of pirated copies, licensed and unlicensed DVD and VCDs of regional films at grocery stores and video rental stores, constituted an important source of consumption for the Indian South Asian diaspora that had migrated across North America and to the United Kingdom and Australia in 1990 (Athique 2006). As Mitra (2006: 53) argues in her study of online content from the Indian diaspora situated in the West, the internet helps manage 'the tensions produced by movement and the loss of the sense of familiarity and security related to a "place of origin"'. I argue that the regional creators combine the cultural politics of language, region and identity to create their distinct online viewership.

REGIONAL CONTENT AS A DISTINCTIVE FEATURE OF THE INDIAN NSE

One of the fundamental insights of my book has been revealing how platforms and portals expand the scope of regional content through the facilitation or production of original web shows, short films and full-length films. This chapter analyses how regional creators capitalize on YouTube's and Facebook's affordances to distribute their content and forge collaborations within and outside the NSE based on their social media success. The access to viewer data also helps both creators and portals/platforms accurately trace the content consumption of local and global audiences. YouTube (Ganguly 2018b) and Facebook (Laghate 2018) have also held creator camps for regional language content creators to expand their content database beyond the Hindi and English languages. The courting of non-English speaking YouTubers offers significant viewership potential, given that 93 per cent of the Indian YouTube viewers consume content in Hindi or other Indian languages (Tewari 2022: 63).

While describing the impact of video cassette distribution on the Indian film industry, Athique (2009: 704) notes that:

> The ability of VCR technology to match viewers with content, regardless of how dispersed or fragmented an audience was, marked the end of the broadcasting paradigm and the rise of the niche audience as the dominant model of media reception.

Similar to Athique's observation about the use of technology to meet viewer demands and address audience fragmentation, I argue that the NSE offers compelling evidence for the benefits of technological innovation in creating social and economic affordances for creators as well as portals/platforms to reach their target audience. Buoyed by the popularity of regional content creation and consumption on YouTube, local and global portals such as Viu, Altbalaji, Netflix and Amazon Prime have commissioned original content in Indian regional languages (Farooqui 2018) to cater to the non-Hindi and non-English Indian diaspora. This corresponds directly to the focal argument of the book claiming greater interdependence between the Indian platforms and portals as a distinctive aspect of the Indian NSE. The diversification into regional content is part of the technical affordance of the streaming media services, which, unlike television channels, do not have to confine their content to a single language. Further, language-specific portals such as Hoichoi and Addatimes, and regional online creators Bengali and Marathi, self-limit content creation in a specific language strategically to capitalize on the portal/creator's expertise, as well as to maintain their niche audience base.

Mohan and Punathambekar's (2019) influential study on YouTube's localization practices in India highlights the 'regional' and 'local' content strategies by analysing popular multi-channel network (MCN) Culture Machine's YouTube channel, Put Chutney. The authors discuss Put Chutney's use of the 'Tamil' language and sociopolitical commentary in this language, which is specific to the southern Indian peninsula, to connect with the Tamil-speaking diaspora. Further, through close readings of cultural exchanges on YouTube within the southern peninsula and India and Pakistan, Kumar, Mohan and Punathambekar (2021) articulate how the cultural lens of 'region' offers a stronger description of the way platforms shape online creator culture, time and space. In doing so, the authors (ibid., 237) argue 'how new patterns of cultural production and circulation emerge when these technological features militate against established regulatory structures such as the nation state'.

I build on this literature to further my inquiry on NSE distinctiveness in two ways. First, I extend the scope of 'localization' practices within the NSE by demonstrating the content strategies of local and global platforms/portals such as YouTube, Facebook, Altbalaji, Netflix, Amazon Prime, Hoichoi, Addatimes and Spuul. By locating the language-specific content strategies of these platforms and portals, I foreground how these strategies can help the NSE to imagine local and global diasporas. Second, I extend the range of inquiry to the Marathi and Bengali languages, thus reiterating the importance of language-based content in the Indian NSE. Through a focus on original content and everyday labour practices of online creators that are specific to these languages, I investigate the industrial and cultural logics at play in building online persona and popularity and catering to 'spatial communities' (de Certeau 1984) that exist beyond the contours of India. I argue that the regional content strategies deployed by platforms/portals result from 'localization' strategies of creators, who invariably shape the 'algorithmic and representational logics'. Finally, the success and popularity of regional creators on YouTube and Facebook beyond India have acted as a motif for the platforms/portals to reimagine the economic potential of creating content in native Indian languages that have transnational and global appeal.

THE INDIAN REGIONAL LANDSCAPE

Sidharth Ravindran, Marketing Manager for Netflix, asserted that regional consumption was driven by the 'increased penetration of television, digital platforms and a large section of the audience taking pride in their roots' (Ravindran 2018). Ravindran's point corresponds with the fact that India is the fourth most

STATEMENT - 4 SCHEDULED LANGUAGES IN DESCENDING ORDER OF SPEAKERS' STRENGTH - 2011			
S. No.	Language	Persons who returned the language as their mother tongue	Percentage to total population
1	2	3	4
1	Hindi	52,83,47,193	43.63
2	Bengali	9,72,37,669	8.03
3	Marathi	8,30,26,680	6.86
4	Telugu	8,11,27,740	6.70
5	Tamil	6,90,26,881	5.70
6	Gujarati	5,54,92,554	4.58
7	Urdu	5,07,72,631	4.19
8	Kannada	4,37,06,512	3.61
9	Odia	3,75,21,324	3.10
10	Malayalam	3,48,38,819	2.88
11	Punjabi	3,31,24,726	2.74
12	Assamese	1,53,11,351	1.26
13	Maithili	1,35,83,464	1.12
14	Santali	73,68,192	0.61
15	Kashmiri	67,97,587	0.56
16	Nepali	29,26,168	0.24
17	Sindhi	27,72,264	0.23
18	Dogri	25,96,767	0.21
19	Konkani	22,56,502	0.19
20	Manipuri	17,61,079	0.15
21	Bodo	14,82,929	0.12
22	Sanskrit	24,821	N

N - Stands for negligible.

Figure 5.1 Scheduled Indian languages in descending order based on the speaker's strength (Ministry of Home Affairs 2018: 4).

linguistically diverse country in the world (Skutnabb-Kangas 2000). The Indian constitution recognizes 22 official languages as 'Scheduled Languages' based on the Census of India conducted in 2011 (Ministry of Home Affairs 2018: 4). However, there are also 99 unofficial or unscheduled languages, amounting to 121 languages in sum (ibid.). The cultural politics become even more complicated, as a total of 19,569 'mother tongues' are spoken in India (ibid.). The report (ibid., 3) defines 'mother tongue' as a 'language spoken in childhood by the child's mother to the child. If the mother died in infancy, the language mainly spoken in the person's home in childhood would be the mother tongue.' Figure 5.1 shows the scheduled Indian languages in descending order, based on the number of speakers.

As Figure 5.1 shows, Hindi, Bengali and Marathi are the three most spoken languages in India, followed by Telugu, Tamil and Gujarati.

India's prevalent cultural diversity and region-specific heterogeneity provide more compelling evidence that content in one language cannot be the basis for pan-Indian catering. Further evidence can also be traced from the populated language-specific film and television industries functioning within the Indian media and entertainment landscape.

The blurring of regionalization and localization boundaries

In his study of the television media landscape of India, Athique (2009: 163) notes that liberalization was instrumental in transforming television from 'Hindi-centric' government policies to regional players with the potential to cater to 'national, international and intensely local' interests. In evidencing the popularity and transnational ability of the Indian television industry, Athique (2009, 163–4) says:

> Kolkata-based Bengali broadcasters are seeking bigger audiences in neighbouring Bangladesh, where the majority of Bengali speakers are found. Tamil-language channels reach Tamil-speaking audiences in Sri Lanka and, despite a blanket ban on Indian-produced media in Pakistan, all of the Indian Hindi channels access substantial audiences there via satellite or cable operations.

Athique's commentary is critical, as it highlights the commercial potential of creating 'regional' content. However, as the 'local' content crosses 'regional' boundaries (also see Chapter 1, where I discuss Mohan, Kumar and Punathambekar's (2021) argument on the use of the Hindi language in India as well as Pakistan), Athique triggers the complexity that terms such as 'local' and 'regional' might entail while mapping the content-distribution practices that exist in India. Mohan and Punathambekar (2019: 14) also reflect on the blurring of frameworks that define 'regionalization' and 'localization' practices, given the community and culture that permeates both.

Consider, for example, the 'translocal' presence of the Bengali diaspora, not just within India but also in Bangladesh, Pakistan, the United States, Myanmar and the United Kingdom (Raghuram et al. 2008). While discussing the concept of translocal geography, Brickell and Datta (2011: 3) argue:

> Translocality is now widely seen to be a form of 'grounded transnationalism' – a space where deterritorialised networks of transnational social relations take shape

through migrant agencies. This means that translocality as a form of local–local relations exists primarily within the debates on transnationalism.

The linkage of geographical and cultural imaginations through the platformed economy results from the shared commonalities between locals who, in acting as viewers or creators, attempt to connect with their cultural identities. In highlighting one such case, Rahul Mukherjee (2012: 55) depicts how indigenous communities use the documentary medium to highlight the 'changing cultural politics of tribal identities'. These filmmakers 'redeploy historical experiences' to connect with the past and renew local ties to mobilize against the marginalization of their voices. Acknowledging these significant interventions, I contextualize 'regionalization' or 'region' as the geography from which the creator emanates and where they practise everyday content creation. In investigating the regional content and community formation of online creators, I subscribe to de Certeau's (1984: 117) idea of 'spatial stories', which define a space as 'the effect produced by the operations that orient it, situate it, temporalize it, and make it function in a polyvalent unity of conflictual programs or contractual proximities'.

Media studies scholars have also foregrounded the importance of regional and cultural dynamics within the spatial dimensions of platform localization practices (Tinic 2005; Venegas 2009). The transnational exchanges between media businesses and the migration of people across the world (Appadurai 1990) mean that geographical regions can no longer be imagined based on one language alone. These studies serve as an important intervention in iterating the importance of language and region in the diffusion of internet practices worldwide (Goggin and McLelland 2010). This is even more significant in India's case, as Indian regions and states were historically identified based on cultural and linguistic lines. Through their research on Indian Bhojpuri language content, academics such as Kumar (2013) and Hardy (2015) have already cautioned against India's narrow territorial imagination.

PLATFORM/PORTAL LOCALIZATION STRATEGIES

By 'localization' strategies, I allude to the cultural logics that the NSE employs in imagining language-specific communities. As shown in Chapter 3, the political economy of platforms/portals suggests that there has been a genuine attempt to expand their relevance across users, separated by boundaries, languages and culture. The NSE digital infrastructure has spent little time building interfaces in multiple Indian languages to expand its viewership. While discussing Amazon Prime Video's marketing strategy its Marketing Manager, Nabh Gupta, questions the concept of 'regional' content in relation to India's plurality:

In India, cultures and languages change every 10 kilometres. For example, if you are in Bengal, Hindi or English is the regional content. That is why, in India, there is no regional content. It is either Indian content or global content.

(Gupta 2018)

Gupta's exposition builds on the fact that people in Bengal use 'Bengali' as their common language (Chatterjee 1975). Like Athique's (2009: 163) findings about the translocal appeal of Indian regional television content, Indian platforms/portals are mimicking the television broadcasters by creating original content in regional languages to expand their viewer base beyond Hindi- and English-language speakers.

Altbalaji portal (see Chapter 3) offers 32 original web shows with a strong focus on Hindi-language content – although, one would find a solitary web series within the content library in other languages, such as Marathi, Tamil and Bengali. While discussing the local and contiguous appeal of the languages across borders, Sunil Nair (2018), Chief Operating Officer for Altbalaji, said:

> If you look at languages like Tamil, Telugu, Malayalam, Kannada, Gujarati, Punjabi, Awadhi or Bhojpuri, these put together are sizeable masses. We had one show in Bengali, which, when it went live, was viewed by the audience in Dhaka (Bangladesh). Before that, we had never seen Dhaka in the top 20 viewing cities of Altbalaji. Dhaka, actually, became number eight in terms of city-based viewership ranking.

The cultural politics and commercial potential of languages form an important part of the content strategy for streaming platforms. Bengali, or Bangla, is the seventh most spoken language globally and second most spoken after Hindi in India. It also serves as the official language for Bangladesh. Bengali language's national and global outreach makes it a significant value proposition for investment for the streaming platforms.

Priyam Ghose, who produces sketches and memes in the Bengali language on YouTube and Facebook, was invited to Facebook's creator camp in Kolkata as part of the platform's localization strategy. Detailing his experiences at the camp, Ghose (2018) noted:

> Facebook emphasised the importance of having a page for content creators as they have added many features, analytics – for example, the publishing tool where you can create, delete, expire, reupload your post with a new date. Analytics help you keep an eye on your top videos, overall page reach, and your fan base – be it the gender, age bracket, country and the city they are from. Besides that, they wanted us to make more regional content as the Bengali language-speaking audience is more than the Hindi language-speaking audience across the world.

The gender, time and location-specific insights provided by Facebook encourage creators like Ghose to 'tailor' their content according to the audience. Given that Ghose creates most of his content in the Bengali language, he finds that the majority of his audience is in West Bengal. The language-specific content appeal is evident because Ghose's content has more views from Dhaka (Bangladesh) than from some of the Indian territories.

The commercial, cultural and transnational prospect of catering to the Bengali-speaking audience has also resulted in the launch of two Bengali language-specific Indian SVoD portals, Hoichoi and Addatimes (discussed in Chapter 3). As a company specializing in catering to the 'Bengali' community, Vishnu Mohta, the co-founder of Hoichoi, emphasized the importance of language and culture in storytelling practices: 'It takes a lifetime to understand a particular community. Every community has a very distinct style of living and want to see stories in the languages that they understand' (Mohta 2018). By catering to a language-specific community, regional creators gain the knowledge of catering to their local taste and develop distinct industry norms as a part of their content strategy. Common content strategies include borrowing from celebrated authors such as Rabindranath Tagore and Sarat Chandra Chattopadhyay (Paul 2018) to assimilate the existing patronage for Bengali literature.

CREATOR LOCALIZATION STRATEGIES

Cunningham and Craig (2017) argue in their study of social media creators that maintaining authenticity constitutes a distinctive feature of social media creators as it helps them build trust and relevance with their audience. For Indian regional online creators, this authenticity is maintained by creating content in their native language and using themes and inferences relevant to their community.

The regional online creators I introduce in this chapter are located strategically at the intersection of films and television media industries and are separated by their content-production practices, styles and genres. Indrani Biswas, known to her YouTube and Facebook audience as 'Wonder Munna', argues that a part of her online identity is synonymous with the Bengali culture of having two names, 'one real and one nickname' (Biswas 2018). The word 'Munna' comes from her nickname, and her friends suggested 'Wonder'.

Biswas creates humorous sketches centred on the everyday lives of people from Kolkata. She writes, produces and edits all the videos herself. As a part of YouTube's corporate strategy, Biswas was also judged the winner of 'YouTube NextUp 2018', a concept conceived to recognize upcoming YouTubers with awards, production support and mentoring (Kundu 2018). She highlights the motivations behind creating content in Bengali, stating that it is her mother tongue. Moreover, she argues that the scant Bengali content on social media and the need to represent 'Kolkata' and the 'Bengali community' inspired her to create videos in the Bengali language. 'Wonder Munna' (Biswas 2018) outlines the relevance of her culture in her content-creation practices:

> Bengali sentiment is very important for my content because most of my subscribers are in Bengali. For example, there are a lot of videos on YouTube which are titled 'Durga Puja' (popular Bengali Festival) and not 'Pujo' despite the fact [that] 'Puja' is a word from the Sanskrit language, but 'Pujo' is from the Bengali language.

Biswas's emphasis on the word 'Pujo' as a term more relatable to the Bengali community is particularly interesting, as linguist scholar Anderson (1917: 1) notes in his study of phonetics in the Bengali language that the vowel 'a' is usually pronounced 'o'. Therefore, the usage of colloquial terminologies constitutes an important instrument for regional content creators to localize their content and build loyalty and trust with their audience.

Moreover, for many, it is a matter of pride to create content that is non-Hindi and non-English language. Saurav Kar, the Being Bong YouTube Channel creator, argues that online content creators do not need to leave their city of origin and move to Mumbai to make a name for themselves. This, he maintains, is a common perception among some creators. Kar (2018) also creates Bengali language content across diverse narratives from prank videos and vlogging to comedy sketches. He elaborates:

> Today, online creators making videos in the Bengali language are developing original ideas and not simply imitating other languages. The Bengali community will relate more to the video as they have a sense of belongingness with the language.

Kiran Dutta, who runs the YouTube channel The Bong Guy, is another example of an emerging regional creator from Kolkata. Dutta produces sketches offering satirical commentaries on previous Bengali-language films and television content. With a following of over half a million subscribers on YouTube (The Bong Guy n.d.), Dutta is one of the most popular vloggers from Kolkata. Incidentally, both Dutta's and Kar's YouTube channel names, 'The Bong Guy' and 'Being Bong' respectively, incorporate 'Bong'. The history of this word can be traced as far back as the seventh century BCE when the Bengal province was called 'Bong-long', and its inhabitants were known as 'Bong' (see Mazumdar 2000: 28). By reflecting on the roots of the Bengali community, the creators build a distinct relationship with the Bengali-speaking diaspora in India and Bangladesh (Dutta 2018). The cultural logic of using these naming conventions is also on display as they navigate the dispersed online communities. The content production and symbolic representation of these creators resemble the everyday practices of the 'Bengali' people, leading them to develop 'spatial stories'.

Sarang Sathaye, the co-founder of the digital media company (Bhartiya (Indian) Digital Party) which specializes in creating Marathi language content on YouTube's BhaDiPa (Bhartiya Digital Party n.d.), discussed the example of fellow Marathi YouTube channel, Khaas Re TV, to highlight the importance of localizing content practices:

> There is a huge difference in content creators who come from metropolitan cities as opposed to those who are coming from smaller cities. For example, the YouTube channel Khaas Re TV (Khaas Re TV n.d.) did a video (satire) called *Are you EUUUUU +ve?* (Khaas Re TV 2018) and none of us at BhaDiPa was aware of what that term actually meant. We found out later that 'EUUUUU' is a way of catcalling women in certain pockets of Maharashtra. The video went viral. This input cannot be picked up from someone who lives in a city like Mumbai or Pune. It is not possible for creators from metropolitan cities to identify a trend like this.

Founded by film industry professionals Paula McGlynn, Anusha Nandakumar and Sarang Sathaye in 2015, content on BhaDiPa is produced under the banner of Gulbadan Talkies. While both Anusha and Sarang come from India, Paula is from Canada, where she graduated from the film production programme at Simon Fraser University. Frustrated with the lack of creativity in the film and television medium, the team decided to form their enterprise. These narrative accounts exemplify the regional content creators' efforts to maintain 'authenticity' by conforming to what Hardy (2010: 239) describes in her study of Bhojpuri film professionals as a 'carefully constructed conglomeration of rural ethical markers embodied and authenticated by a literal pedigree'. These practices help them to build a loyal audience base of people who connect with their constructed political, social and cultural identities.

At the same time, being a native speaker or coming from a certain geographical region does not guarantee knowledge of 'ethical markers'. Regional online creators are often more precarious than Hindi- and English-language creators due to their exclusive dependency on the language and community. Staying relatable is as important as storytelling. The creators achieve this by observing the community's everyday practices through participation in community festivals, taking public transport and visiting public places, and even striking up conversations with strangers to understand everyday concerns that affect their lives. In observing their conversations and reactions to situations, the creators decide the upcoming topics for their sketches:

Whenever people visit a restaurant, the first thing they do is click a selfie and then post it on Facebook, and later when they are served with food, they will click the picture of the food and then post that too on Facebook.

While one might argue that there is a fair bit of generalization in this example, and the observations are not necessarily unique to the Bengali culture, reflecting on the city's youth trends emerges as an ethical marker of relatability. By assimilating the diaspora's linguistic, social and cultural traits into their localization practices, these creators build a distinct identity of everyday life of its viewers.

Regional creators also distinguish themselves from traditional mediums by establishing themselves as 'accurate' representors of their community. Biswas laments how Bengali films on Durga Puja rarely capture the 'craziness' of the festival, often using it as a backdrop for a 'love story', whereas Kar describes Bengali television as 'unrealistic'.

While discussing the state of Marathi films and television, Sathaye (2018), who has acted in both Hindi- and Marathi-language films, lamented that 'Television broadcasters, of late, had converted the medium into a factory' and the 'Marathi film industry was largely star-driven'. These self-theorized accounts suggest a lack of agency and even opportunity afforded to them as they reflect on frustrations with traditional media's industrial practices and content. As discussed in Chapter 2, the 'feudalistic creative' practices of the television industry and the closed network circuits of the film industry have driven emerging and existing creators to the internet as a preferred medium for creative expression. The popularity of these creators within their communities enables them to develop successful collaboration opportunities with streaming platforms and regional film industry talent with greater agency, as discussed below.

Exploiting the cultural politics of language

Even though 'Marathi' language is largely spoken in the Indian states of Maharashtra and Goa, Sathaye (2018) argues that catering to the language-based diaspora in India accounts for a greater number than the population of certain countries: 'The entire population of Canada is approximately 33 million, which is half of the Marathi speaking audience.' With over 83 million speakers, the 2011 Indian Census reported that 'Marathi' was the third most spoken language in India behind Hindi and Bengali. Overall, Marathi is the nineteenth most spoken dialect in the world.

Sathaye (2018) reflected on how shocked he was to find only 'three cinema halls within a stretch of 300 kilometres'. He also noticed the rampant circulation of pirated Marathi feature films among these audiences, who could now afford huge downloads over the internet. Sathaye acknowledged that Reliance

Jio's entry into the Indian telecom sector had triggered a motive for creating Marathi language content that could reach its regional audience. Media scholar Joy Mukherjee (2019) makes similar assertions about the 'Jio effect', illustrating how Jio's nationwide low-cost internet plans (discussed in Chapter 3) make data consumption accessible and effectively bring down fellow telecom competitors' rates, thereby ensuring an increase in internet penetration in the rural and semi-urban regions of India.

Despite being the highest producer of films globally, India suffers from a dire lack of screen infrastructure, with its current count of just 9,423 in 2021 (FICCI-EY 2022: 148). This means that there are only about eight screens for film exhibitions per million people – comparatively, about 20 per cent of the total screens in China and the United States. Such a shortage of cinema infrastructure leaves very little room for regional films that already face stiff competition from Hollywood and Bollywood. The situation is especially grim in the Marathi film industry, as it competes with Bollywood in sharing Mumbai as the common site of production, exhibition and even audiences (Ingle 2017). As Ingle points out, Marathi cinema also struggled for attention between 1960 and 1980, when Marathi audiences preferred other forms of entertainment, such as folk shows and theatre. Absorbed within the linguistically demarcated state of Maharashtra in 1960, Marathi cinema's proximity with Hindi or 'national' cinema in Mumbai led to an unending struggle between 'national concerns and regional representations' (Ingle 2017: 200).

BhaDiPa is one of India's emerging Marathi language-specific online content creators, with a subscriber base of over 700,000 (Bhartiya Digital Party n.d.) on YouTube. BhaDiPa's content focuses mostly on creating comedy sketches and music videos devoted to the social and cultural causes rooted within the Maharashtrian community's interests. However, given the limitations of funding within the regional online content on social media, Sathaye (2018) believes it is important for regional online creators to diversify their value propositions beyond the social media platforms:

> There are various other platforms that one should take benefit of to create a place for themselves. One has to be multi-dimensional in order to reach the audience. The other activities include on-ground activation, merchandising, meet and greet, etc. Our first successful on-ground activation was funded by 'Brewbot', Mumbai, where we conducted a Marathi Stand-Up comedy event at their brewery.

BhaDiPa has diversified its value proposition by signing emerging Marathi stand-up comedians. Based on the last fieldwork data, Sathaye's company was managing the business interests of fifteen Marathi-speaking stand-up comedians.

This strategy highlights how regional online creators seek to diversify their business practices by bringing together language-specific talent. The congruity of language and region-specific traits in content creation practices enables regional creators to connect with their online audience.

THE POTENTIAL OF REGIONAL ONLINE CREATORS

In Kolkata, I was genuinely surprised to witness Kiran Dutta's fan following. Until then, my imagination of on-site fandom practices within Indian regional media industries was rather 'elitist' and restricted to traditional media celebrities. This belief was quickly suspended when Dutta invited me to meet him for our interview in a Starbucks café located in a downtown mall, the Acropolis. The interview was interrupted every 10 minutes by eager young people wishing to take a selfie with him. Boys and girls, men and women, aged from 16 to 30, instantly recognized him and came up to him to touch him or share words of adulation for his work. In witnessing Dutta's popularity first-hand, I realized the influence of regional online creators within their local community.

Dutta's strategic use of social media for amassing popularity and gaining attention is similar to the assertions made by Senft (2013) in her study on 'camgirls', in which she identifies those engaging in self-branding exercises on social media networks as 'micro-celebrities'. In this case, the actualization of Dutta's online fan following in the mall blurred the lines of popularity between mainstream media celebrity and 'micro-celebrity'. The rising online and offline popularity of regional online creators gives them the agency to negotiate with mainstream traditional media talent and producers. For instance, Dutta confessed that he had rejected a collaboration opportunity with a popular Tollywood actor who sought changes in his content-creation practices (Chakraborty 2018), exemplifying a rare example of challenging the power appropriation between established talent from traditional media and new media.

In 2018, popular Tollywood actor Dev and portal Hoichoi collaborated with him, in a growing demonstration of the interdependence between films, portals and social media, to create 10-minute original scripted content on his channel to promote Hoichoi's upcoming web show *Hoichoi Unlimited* (Dutta 2018; see Chapter 3). Moreover, as discussed previously, social media platforms continue to engage with these emerging creators in lieu of tapping the Indian regional language audience. Dutta acknowledged that he was one of the invitees of the Facebook creator camp and divulged that the camp's primary objective was to notify regional online creators of the Facebook algorithms and monetization opportunities. Through Ghose's example, Dutta's exposition is compelling evidence of how the NSE shows interdependence in content and creator strategies.

As is clear from Dutta's exposition of his collaboration with the Bengali language film industry and streaming portal, Hoichoi, it is not uncommon for film celebrities to promote films on a regional online content creator's social media channel. Both Priyam Ghose and Karandeep Jassal, who create sketches and short videos on their YouTube channel Priyam and Karandeep (Priyam and Karandeep n.d.), asserted that one of their videos on YouTube helped Priyam to bag a small role in a Hoichoi web series, *Gariahater Ganglords* (Ghose and Jassal 2018). Ghose also noted that his popularity on social media had led to invitations for auditions and acting offers in advertisements and Tollywood feature films.

The popularity of regional online creators on social media is useful to the regional film industry as it helps them promote upcoming feature films on the creator's YouTube channel. For instance, in 2016 BhaDiPa developed a popular web series on its channel titled *Casting Couch with Amey and Nipun*. The show revolves around two protagonists, Amey and Nipun, disguised as rookie filmmakers and calling celebrities from the Hindi and Marathi film industry to convince them to collaborate in their upcoming film projects. Shows such as these serve two objectives: first, the actors get to promote their upcoming films with BhaDiPa's audience base; and second, they help BhaDiPa to showcase their ability to create engaging content with celebrities, attracting attention from brands and audiences alike. It is important to note Sathaye and his partner's well-entrenched network with these celebrities, owing to their previous work in theatre and films.

As discussed through extended examples in this chapter, collaboration with regional online creators helps the film industry reach out to regional audiences. Often, the creators' social media channels are used to spread awareness about a film. At the same time, these collaborations also can surpass national boundaries, as my respondents had received collaboration requests from Bangladeshi creators who were popular on YouTube. Thus, opportunities to translate social media credentials as a means for scoping future work across multiple mediums encourage regional creators to remain prominent on social media platforms and build a content portfolio and a large, loyal viewership.

CONCLUSION

By mapping the regional original content-creation space in the NSE, I have demonstrated how the NSE, through regional creators, comes to understand and negotiate India's linguistic and cultural logic in catering to the diverse online Indian audience. At the same time, the industrial regional content practices of the platform economy challenge the notion of 'mainstream' or 'regional' content. The selection of any language for content creation is eventually driven by its commercial, cultural and geographical politics. I concur that a platform/portal's strategy is determined as much by the creator's sense-making and content-creation practices as it is by its commissioning and facilitating practices. Building on the focus of English and Hindi language creators in the previous chapter, I have highlighted the emergence of new voices and broadcaster-led portals and TV renegades within the regional online space contributing to the distinctiveness of the Indian NSE.

The increase in creation, circulation and consumption of regional online content can be placed against a backdrop of pushback against the incumbent Indian Government's efforts to enforce Hindi language as a compulsory language within its National Draft Education policy under the garb of nationalism (Ranjan 2019) – bringing back memories of its historical push for the Hindi language as a part of the nation-building project. The thrusting of Hindi language, which in hindsight seems more of a strategy to invade the stronghold of regional parties in non-Hindi states, has led regional political parties – especially from Maharashtra, West Bengal and southern states of India – to protest jointly, eventually forcing the Government to backtrack on its proposition.

Within the Indian media landscape, the paucity of film screens, coupled with an over-concentration of Hollywood and Hindi films, has threatened the visibility of regional cinema. In these troubled times, the increased internet penetration beyond the Hindi-speaking belt and the demand for regional content from the local and global Indian diasporas has posed opportunities for regional content creators to exploit the cultural politics to their advantage. At the same time, marginalized by the 'closed door' and 'hegemonic' practices of Indian traditional regional media, the regional content creators amass loyal viewership by using the affordances of social media.

In the next chapter, we focus on the role of intermediaries, specifically examining the industrial and cultural practices of multi-channel networks and talent agents in enabling the creator labour movements across films, platforms and portals.

6
The Role of Intermediaries

Google conceptualization of MCNs as 'third-party service providers that affiliate with multiple YouTube channels to offer services that may include audience development, content programming, creator collaborations, digital rights management, monetization, and/or sales' (Google n.d.) highlights an out-dated and YouTube-centric definition of the term 'MCN' that fails to encapsulate the advances made by the MCNs across the screen industries as highlighted by Boyle. Boyle (2018: 132) acknowledges the problematization of MCNs due to their dynamic business model:

> The term 'multi-channel network', or MCN, has been around since the mid-2000s and was used to describe networks of online content clustered under a brand mostly curating short-form non-television content. Such is the pace of change that, while the phrase still exists, its meaning is shifting and moving from aggregators of online content and numerous online channels to a sense that generating and curating your own content and brand are becoming more important, not least as that age-old debate between content producers and platforms (and where the power lies) remains unresolved.

Similarly, Zelenski's (2002: 1) definition of talent agents as 'third parties' that help the talent in 'locating employment opportunities and assist them in making career decisions' is but a small part of the varied media and talent management activities that we are seeing in the Indian NSE today. This is also because, unlike talent agents in the United States, who are legally barred from becoming producers (Zelenski 2002), Indian talent agents can also actively produce, market and distribute their clients' content.

I argue that the Indian intermediaries such as talent agents and MCNs have successfully readjusted their image from marginalized, invisible mediators to become proactive media industry trendsetters by providing diverse services across the Indian screen industries. The MCNs and talent agents have been instrumental in developing revenue circuits through their distinct industrial and cultural practices of content production, distribution, marketing, syndication and talent management. In doing so, both these components of the NSE have diversified from their traditional business operations to create their niche by identifying the demands of the evolving Indian media landscape. The Indian NSE has developed a range of industrial practices that contribute to the flexibility and dynamism of the Indian media and entertainment industries under conditions of digital transformation.

CHARTING MCN AND TALENT AGENT DISTINCTIONS

Talent agents and MCNs have distinct motivations for diversifying their traditional business practices of talent management and YouTube-dependent creator services, respectively. As Lobato (2016) highlighted through the analysis of US MCNs, the rapid increase of MCNs led to a sudden excess, and their excessive YouTube dependency contributed to their collapse. However, in India's case, this collapse was averted by the transformation in MCN business practices – their more active role in content creation and circulation in India. Three reasons explain this transformation. First, MCNs' overarching dependence on YouTube had already made them a familiar entity among online content creators. Second, access to YouTube analytics also provided the MCNs with sufficient knowledge about the online users' content preferences. Third, prior experience in online talent management and production culture ensured a safe passage for MCNs to pivot towards less medium or platform dependency. In other words, by reinventing their value propositions, the MCNs diversified in content creation, production and talent management across media sectors (films/television/online).

Similarly, Cunningham and Craig (2019: 140) observe how the rise of social media platforms such as Vine, Instagram, Snapchat and Periscope transformed the MCNs into multiplatform networks (MPNs), seeking 'to craft management strategies for pursuing alternative revenue streams across numerous platforms and offer creators platform integration strategies and analytics superior to YouTube's'. However, in India's case, the MCNs did not just deal with platforms and portals but also, to some extent, with film and television. The MCNs capitalized on the success of social media talent, and their expertise in creating YouTube content with other mediums, by pitching talent or content.

On the other hand, talent agents who were often reduced to piecemeal collaborations with traditional media (film and television), owing to factors like less 'talent and more star-driven' industries (Dutta 2018) and a lack of trust (Kohli-Khandekar 2018), capitalized on socio-technological transformations in the creator culture and took an active role in brokering the deals between talent and portals. By guiding the content strategies of platforms, portals and creators, the talent agents gradually gained prominence in the Indian screen industries from 2014, when Indian portals slowly started commissioning original content.

The market intelligence gathered from industry sources also led the Indian talent agents to assist the NSE with talent and content strategies. By trading these insights for economic and social benefits, the intermediaries bridge links between traditional media and the NSE and create multimedia opportunities. In this chapter, I argue that by identifying gaps within the circuits of creation, production and commissioning practices, the intermediaries diversified their value propositions to operate as negotiators, producers, distributors and marketers of content and talent. I demonstrate how and why the intermediaries operate differently, and to what extent, in the NSE compared with the traditional media industries (film and television).

The entry of the global portals Netflix and Amazon Prime Video in 2016 played a key role in facilitating the growing importance of intermediaries. These portals were already playing catch-up against the transformative content practices led by individuals and native digital media companies on social media as well as incumbent portals such as SonyLIV (2013), Hotstar (2015) and TVFPlay (2015). In order to gain a foothold among Indian digital users, both Netflix and Amazon Prime actively began to seek collaboration with local producers and storytellers, as we saw earlier when discussing the commissioning practices of portals in Chapter 3. Having anticipated this entry due to industry sources, the talent agents established trust and partnership through knowledge and resource sharing with these portals, helping them commission content by pitching scripts and their internet-popular clientele. Their earlier experience of dealing with media practitioners helped talent agents streamline the launch of portals by facilitating partnerships with credible and successful media professionals. As Indian MCNs and talent agents converge through media creation, management and distribution activities, retracing their histories helps us illuminate the key distinctions in their value propositions.

Thus, while MCNs originated first on YouTube, talent agents have had a longstanding relationship with the film and television industries. MCN clientele typically are creators with a dominant social media presence but, more importantly, those who are camera-friendly. On the other hand, because talent agents are broadly situated across the media industries, they have come to represent writers and directors who might not be 'influencers' or 'celebrities' but nevertheless play a key role in the media-making process. This is not to suggest that MCNs are any less capable than talent agents – indeed, I would argue that MCNs have played a significant role in shaping career trajectories on digital media. However, as I discussed in this section, the specific histories of talent agents and MCNs provide them with certain distinctions conducive to the development of Indian NSE.

In outlining these intermediary field practices, this chapter contributes to the small but growing literature on those who operate at the 'high building' meso level of CMIS's multiscalar topography, while also answering Research Objective 3, related to the roles played by intermediaries in facilitating the distinctiveness of the NSE.

BACKGROUNDING INTERMEDIARIES

Maguire and Matthews' (2014) edited collection serves as a useful link when conceptualizing and mapping the dynamism of cultural intermediaries. The book forms a critical point of investigation and articulates the role of intermediaries as cultural tastemakers and constructors of legitimacy through the affirmation of content and talent. Maguire and Matthews' scholarship also highlights the perils of intermediaries, who are often under-studied due to their 'inconspicuous' working style. Kuiper's work (2014: 52) discusses the invisibility of the labour of intermediaries, as they work 'behind the scenes of cultural production':

> The actual work of intermediaries often is hard to observe, let alone 'measure'. It typically consists of long hours spent behind computers, emailing, browsing, twittering, and writing, interspersed with meetings that are often off-limits to researchers. Moreover, much of the work done by cultural intermediaries does not look like work. Their professional encounters and activities look deceivingly casual: sipping lattes at Starbucks, having lunch in hip venues, flipping through magazines, browsing stands at festivals and fairs, and most of all: talking to people.

However, Boyle's (2018: 6) study of UK intermediaries reminds us that such a misperception only occurs 'because their power and influence exist away from the screen itself'. The industrial practices of the intermediaries have often been obscured or trivialized due to their often-perceived non-conforming standards of business practices, which Kuiper (2014) highlights in his work. It is thus increasingly important to articulate the practices of the intermediaries to assess their influence in determining a creative decision-making process.

Boyle (2018: 103) argues that the creative industries is part of the wider gig economy owing to the 'uncertainty of employment and career development'. As observed in the previous chapter, the social media activities and medium-agnostic approaches of Indian creators are driven because of job insecurities and symbolizes Fuch's (2015) theorization of digital labour as a practice that exploits the creator's value-generation by underpaying them. From this perspective, platforms, too, become intermediaries of cultural production by mediating the social, cultural and economic transactions of the creators.

While analysing the practices of Hollywood talent management companies and the specialized educational courses offered in talent management, Stephen

Zafirau (2008) argues that talent agents perform similar roles to producers. He emphasizes how talent agencies build media projects by consulting with their diverse clientele, consisting of actors, writers and directors, and eventually selling the project to studios for profit. Roussel (2016) asserts that as the convergence of content keeps blurring the media, the roles of intermediaries such as talent agents keep being reinvented. He emphasizes that as the boundaries between television and films become blurred, the agents need to promote, negotiate and market their talent to promising areas for growth. Roussel suggests that these measures require increasing specialization and departmentalization among the agents, ultimately contributing to new departments of talent management based on genres, sub-genres and talent.

However, in this chapter, the significance of intermediaries will be limited to talent agents and MCNs and their contributions will be analysed by identifying their India-specific cultural and commercial practices, and discussing their relevance within the contemporary Indian screen industries. Parthasarathi and Athique (2020: 11) highlight the 'synergistic combinations of formal and non-formal practices' to demonstrate the interdependences within the Indian media economy. Building on Parthasarathi and Athique, I show how the industrial and cultural dynamics of the intermediaries shape the formal and non-formal practices between platforms, portals and films.

INDIAN TALENT AGENTS

This chapter offers a critical analysis of the role of talent agents in negotiating the demands of creators across the Indian screen industries with specific attention to the NSE. At the same time, contemporary media management issues related to managing multiple talents, multiple aspirations of talents, assisting global media businesses in localization and venturing into production as a means of diversification are discussed in detail. In the following section I discuss the contemporary industrial practices of the Indian talent agents in the Indian NSE to articulate their influence in shaping the content strategies of platforms and portals.

Perhaps the strongest intervention that the talent agents have made is in the field of stand-up comedy. An outstanding case is that of Only Much Louder (OML), which launched its operations in 2002 as India's first artist management company for independent music bands. Over the past two decades, OML has diversified its business portfolio to event management, content production and talent agenting, representing popular comedians such as the All India Bakchod (AIB) team, Kenny Sebastien, Anuvab Pal, Naveen Richards and Sumuki Suresh (Samtani 2017). By uploading the stand-up comedy content of their clientele on social media, the talent agents have expanded their talent's fan base and created an additional revenue stream on YouTube. As discussed in Chapter 5, social media content also acts as a 'calling card' to obtain more work from the producers. By 2019, OML's worth was estimated at around US$10 million (Alves 2019).

Using the prior experience of event management skills, OML has successfully led its stand-up comedians – who are already popular on social media – to perform shows across India, in locations ranging from metropolitan cities such as Mumbai, Delhi and Kolkata to smaller towns and cities such as Kottayam, Vijaywada, Pudducherry and Vellore (Choudhary 2018). This has expanded the scope of stand-up comedy to include a wider audience while also mainstreaming the idea that being a full-time stand-up comedian is a lucrative profession. Performing across diverse states has augmented the demand for regional creators, who are now practising stand-up comedy in diverse languages and collaborating with established stand-up comedians.

At the same time, helping its creators launch YouTube channels has enabled OML to draw audiences and commercial deals. Raica Mathews (2018), a Senior Producer at OML, said:

> Any artist can just perform and directly connect with their audience. These social media platforms have helped us, as it is easier to explain what we see in talent. We do not need to set up a meeting or chase producers (broadcasters, brand executives) for months.

As Mathews notes, it can be difficult to sell a talent's reach to the producers where an agency lacks metrics to prove its popularity and skills. Furthermore, the Indian media industry is relatively new to the talent-management business, as producers are wary of relying on a talent agent's expertise. They would rather deal directly with an established talent than pay to acquire a talent managed by the agency (Dave 2018). Unlike earlier times, where getting access to producers and convincing them about the talent's potential proved to be a challenging task, the sociotechnical affordances of social media have helped the talent agency convince producers of a talent's potential and negotiate better deals.

Reflecting on his association with OML, AIB co-founder Rohan Joshi argued that the terminology of a talent agent undermines the services it provides. Joshi (2018) identifies them more like 'business partners', as he explains:

> It is important to find the correct talent agents as, often, creative people are not good at handling business. We [AIB] need people who can understand our business well and help us get the right brands onboard and, at the same time, will not go around spoiling our company's reputation by pitching everyone.

Joshi's views were echoed by Kopal Khanna, co-founder of a Tape A Tale, a business venture that provides opportunities to selected individuals to narrate their stories and poetries and then commercializes them through live events, YouTube channel, brand integration and content aggregation on other services such as Saavn, a music portal. Khanna (2018) reasoned that OML's relationship with brands improved her venture's business prospects:

> Sometimes, while pitching, one does not know how much one should quote to a brand. At other times, it is also important to manage the brand once they are onboard. This is where OML chips in with its experience.

She explained that the association with OML could help her diversify her content, beyond recording or videotaping 'one person talking'. Talent agents have also performed their traditional role of connecting talent with suitable opportunities and, in some cases, even creating one where a handful of OML stand-up comedians wrote several web series for Amazon Prime to help it localize in India.

In 2017, Amazon Prime signed fourteen comedians from OML's talent roster to mark its launch in India (Pathak 2017). Buoyed by the reception of these shows, Amazon Prime teamed up with six other stand-up comedians from OML's roster to create web series. It also collaborated with OML talent to launch India's first-ever digital talent hunt for stand-up comedians, *Comicstaan* (DNA 2018). The strategic collaboration with Amazon Prime for a talent show helped OML to keep an eye out for emerging talent while also popularizing the idea of stand-up comedy as a full-time career.

Between 2017 and 2018, OML stand-up comedians Biswa Kalyan Rath, Zakir Khan and Sumukhi Suresh debuted in web series by conceptualizing and writing shows such as *Laakhon Mein Ek* (One in 100,000), *Chacha Vidhayak Hain Humare* (My Uncle is a Legislator) and *Pushpavalli*, respectively. In doing so, OML made a crucial intervention for stand-up comedians with no formal storytelling background to experiment with fictional long-form storytelling such as web series. In helping the comedians transition from performing stand-up comedy to writing and acting (Zakir Khan and Sumukhi Suresh) for Amazon Prime, OML has created new opportunities for comedians keen to work as actors/writers in high production-based content. Involving stand-up comedians in conceptualizing, writing, and role-playing for fiction stories has helped the comedians develop new skills and imagine the various possibilities of engagement with narratives and storytelling that are not limited to performing on stage.

OML has thus helped stand-up comedians transition from stand-up comedy to writing web series for a global portal. It is crucial to examine how talent agents can translate an artist's aspirations into a viable business proposition while helping a global portal localize its production. Although these efforts were realized through Amazon Prime's investment in stand-up comedians, analysing these developments alongside OML's industrial practices helps us understand the talent agency's critical interventions. As for Amazon Prime, this partnership allows them to achieve three objectives. First, it helps them create localized content by identifying talent that has already been cherry-picked by the talent agent and assures the platform of the talent's quality. Second, it helps Amazon Prime launch with faces already popular on social media platforms, thereby reducing the risks associated with the project. Finally, it creates a distinct value proposition for Amazon Prime to compete with existing local and global portals that have already entered the marketplace.

The association between Amazon Prime and OML highlights the talent agent's increasing influence in the NSE and its ability to contribute both culturally and commercially. It does so by developing projects that the portals perceive as commercially lucrative, pushing stand-up comedy as a genre, creating revenue opportunities for the talent and offering innovative and localized programming to the audience.

Diversification and localization practices of talent agents

By investing resources in local, regional, national and international media-management operations across films, television and new media, Indian talent agencies have taken a more active, strategic role in the NSE than previously. Consider the case of India's marquee celebrity management firm Kwan, which represents some of the biggest celebrities across categories like Bollywood, regional cinema, sports and music. Kwan opened a new division, Kwanabler, to facilitate global investments in Indian sports as well as the entertainment industry while simultaneously creating opportunities for local brands seeking to enter the global marketplace (Tewari 2018). Other investments include a stake in music streaming platform Saavn, actress Deepika Padukone's apparel brand All About You and Gigstart, a marketplace platform to discover artists ('Silly Monks Entertainment History' 2018). Kwan also holds a majority stake in Mojostar, a joint venture with marketing and licensing firm Dream Theatre, which focuses on developing retail brands through partnerships with celebrity talent (Choudhary 2017a).

To strengthen the talent database in the South Indian film industry, Kwan entered into a partnership with actor Rana Daggubati's production house, Suresh Productions. Having set up a team of twenty personnel for its Chennai office, Kwan offers diverse services such as talent and event management, content packaging, brand partnerships, endorsements and production assistance ('KWAN South Aims' 2018). The investment in regional media businesses highlights Kwan's further attempts to diversify and commercialize celebrity culture beyond Bollywood. In 2018, Kwan also signed up India's online creator Bhuvan Bam, the first Indian to reach 10 million views on YouTube, to strengthen its repertoire of talent in online comedy, featuring talents like Mallika Dua, Vir Das, Bollywood Gandu aka Karan Talwar, Amit Tandon and Suresh Menon.

Having signed diverse and successful celebrities across different genres and fields allows Kwan to influence negotiations with media businesses while also building a portfolio as a preferred company for representing talent. The global operational approach of its subsidiary, Kwanabler, highlights the transnational ambitions of talent agents by creating opportunities for collaboration with global brands. These strategies help to create space for emerging talent for circulation within the media industry landscape and gradually become a 'one-stop-shop' for talent and content-led solutions. Kwan and OML's micro-movements challenge the closed-network circuit of traditional media that prefers kinship over talent (Punathambekar 2013). The diversity and strength of its roster also enable Indian talent agencies to have a greater say in negotiations while attracting newer talent looking for representation.

Localizing the Indian operations of Netflix

My fieldwork coincided with Netflix's premiere of its first Indian original web series, *Sacred Games*. Around the same time, I read a post on my Facebook feed from Datta Dave, co-founder of the Tulsea talent agency, sharing the *Sacred Games* trailer with a congratulatory note to the writers, all of whom were represented by Tulsea. Interviewing Tulsea also made sense, purely because thirty of its clientele were collaborating with portals other than Amazon Prime Video and Netflix (Bengali 2018). Tulsea's talents have contributed in different capacities for Netflix-released Indian originals such as *Ajji* (director Devashish Makhija), *Ghoul* (director Patrick Graham), *Brij Mohan Amar Rahe* (director Nikhil Bhat) and *Sacred Games* (writers Varun Grover, Vasant Nath, Smita Singh; co-director Vikramaditya Motwane).

Tulsea identifies itself as a strategic talent and content management company, representing around 200 media practitioners, the majority of whom are writers, directors and actors. Content management in this context refers to the content strategies (conducting writers' rooms and offering content ideas) to the producers and portals. Since its inception in 2010, Datta Dave and Chaitanya Hegde have employed sixteen executives to cater to the professional needs of their talent. Tulsea also has a creative team, which cumulatively read around 100 scripts in a month. Radhika Gopal, Business Development Associate with Tulsea, recounted that Dave already knew about Netflix's launch in India and had regular contact with Netflix's executives from the LA office. This helped

Tulsea to ascertain the kind of content Netflix was seeking and position its talent accordingly.

Elaborating on Tulsea's collaboration with Netflix's first web series in India, *Sacred Games*, Gopal (2018) shared the details of a series of events that contributed to their writers working on it:

> When Netflix came to India, it had already bagged the rights of the book *Sacred Games* and offered the same for adaptation to Phantom Productions, whose co-founder, Vikramaditya Motwane, was exclusively represented by Tulsea. Further discussions around the content led to the need for a writers' room. Accordingly, it was decided that three writers represented by Tulsea would adapt Sarat Chandra's novel, *Sacred Games*, with Motwane as the showrunner and co-director.

Besides offering its talent to producers, the agency also mediates by conducting writers' rooms for web series. For *Sacred Games*, Tulsea put together a writers' room consisting of their three writers to facilitate a joint writing expedition of the 947-page novel to be released over two seasons (Kohli-Khandekar 2018).

By facilitating a collaborative scriptwriting process among writers, the talent agents achieve a three-pronged objective of 'localizing' Netflix, improving their talent's storytelling skills and acquiring new expertise in organizing a writers' room for portals. The success of such projects also enables a recurring source of income for the talent and agents. Moreover, as conducting meetings with producers is a part of the talent agent's everyday routine, they are well-versed with most media producers' content strategies and budget details. This information is often used as a source for pitching the right talent, influencing business outcomes and circulating market gossip for strategic interests.

Datta Dave (2018) articulated that the motivation to launch Tulsea was to represent writers who had often been marginalized in India's audio-visual entertainment industry:

> In India, there is an over-emphasis on the actors and an under-emphasis on the writers. Ideally, 20 per cent of the budget should be spent on the star cast, but here, 60 to 70 per cent of the budget is spent on stars.

Here, Dave addresses wider concerns regarding the unpaid and underpaid labour practices involving writers that plague the Indian media industry. Such practices also help to distinguish Tulsea from other talent agencies, which Dave suggests are 'mostly focused on stars and celebrities'. In raising the lack of respect for a writer's talent in the Indian media industry, Dutta positions Tulsea as the writers' champion as he questions Indian media industry practices (Mehta 2018):

> Do we truly respect our writers? Are we okay with the writer (lead writer/showrunner) being the creative producer on the show? Can we fathom the showrunner earning more than the star of the show? Are we comfortable with the production company reporting to the showrunner?

In the same article, Dutta offers ways in which industry personnel could support writers through fair compensation, legal policies that protect the interests of the writers and a writer-friendly culture that would allow them to work freely. By voicing the needs of writers, Dutta addresses wider concerns that plague the Indian media industry and outlines the steps needed to give creators a platform that will enable them to focus their energies on one project at a time, leading to a better quality of content production for the media industry in general.

By fixing the price of its writers and negotiating assertively for them, the talent agents ensure that the writers are compensated fairly at market rates. This positions them as problem-solvers offering distinct solutions to both talent and producers. By addressing the marginalized and often neglected voices of writers, talent agents perform an important intervention by addressing the systemic pay inequities that persist within the Indian screen industries – much to the producers' chagrin, whose budgets are impacted by fairer compensation.

Managing multiple talents

One of the crucial challenges for talent agents in the NSE is to manage the aspirations of multiple talents at any given time. The agency is tasked with the challenge of scheduling events, shooting dates, timely communication and due diligence of every talent's contract. Any negligence on the agency's part can destabilize its relationship with the talent and collaborators while also directly impacting its potential revenues.

Pankaj Mandal (2018), Digital Marketing and Analytics lead at OML, summarized these challenges:

> I think ten years ago it was more traditional that singers and bands do live shows only. However, now it is so much convergent because the same artist is doing live shows and television shows. Biswa Kalyan Rath [comedian] is making his web series on Amazon Prime, also doing stand-up comedy and consulting. This is also the reason why the [talent] managers must know every trick of the trade.

So how did OML work this out? Mandal (2018) explained:

> We have multiple managers – one who looks after his live events and another who looks after his content. There is also one brand team, which only manages the

branded content. Since it is difficult for one person to be good at everything, we have different teams managing different functions.

As talent agencies manage multiple clients and their multimedia aspirations, this often leads to insecurities and competition between talent in the same profession. In 2018, creator Mallika Dua accused OML of sexism and alleged that she was paid half the sum offered to her fellow creator Zakir Khan for appearing on the *Great Indian Laughter Challenge* television show. Such instances offer perspectives on the quotidian challenges of talent agents as they look to expand their roster. Determining a market price for multiple clients operating in the same genre with a similar fan following can be a difficult exercise, especially when a talent agency is also negotiating for the same show. The challenge of managing the profiles of multiple online content creators and establishing a uniform level of trust is a tedious task, which calls for effective communication between the talent and the agency.

A mutually agreeable price for negotiation can help alleviate the tensions between talent and agents. Ultimately, the perceived value proposition that the talent agency can offer should override any inhibitions that the talent feels it can negotiate or any threats from the talent agency's competitors. On the other hand, the blurring of boundaries between their personal and professional lives in building the talent's trust is an unavoidable social transaction that has to be undertaken. A distinct aspect of these times is the opportunities that arise from new platforms and portals, increasing brand investments in the online space, managing multimedia aspirations and the ability to negotiate fair market rates in a nascent and emerging NSE.

In sum, Indian talent agents have undergone a metamorphic change to cope with the contemporary demands of the growing platform economy. By assisting creators to transition from social media, they circulate the flow of talent to other platforms and mediums (films/television). Tulsea's testimony also highlights the initiatives taken by talent agents in safeguarding and advocating for the interests of writers. Moreover, they have also played a crucial role in expanding the popularity of stand-up comedy as a cultural product for creation and consumption. There seems to be an invisible protocol in the industry whereby talent represented by intermediaries is invariably paid well and recognized for their contribution through fair contractual agreements. In helping the stand-up comedians navigate from writing stand-up comedy acts to episodic narrative writing for Amazon Prime, the talent agents have inadvertently challenged the conventional US industry practices of hiring established film and television writers. These emerging practices blur the boundaries between 'amateurs', 'professionalizing amateurs' and 'professionals', thereby questioning Western scholarship such as that of Cunningham and Craig (2019), which principally situates social media creators as 'amateurs' and distinguishes them from the 'professional' film and television creators that create content for portals.

MCNs AS INTERMEDIARIES

Lobato (2016) argues that MCNs play an active role in the career of YouTube celebrities as talent agents or managers. He reasons that the current YouTube creators sign a direct agreement with the platform for commercial benefits and link up with MCNs to expand their audience base and advertising revenue. Based on his study of intermediaries in the United Kingdom, Boyle (2018) credits MCNs with discovering new talent and promotion in newer forms of storytelling.

In tracing the history of SME intermediaries from the pre-MCN to the post-MCN era, Cunningham and Craig (2019: 90) define social media entertainment (SME) intermediaries as the 'bridge between SME creators and SME platforms, traditional media and advertising'. However, much of the available scholarship identifies the business models of MCNs as YouTube dependent.

I build on Boyle's (2018) analysis, discussed earlier in the chapter, by highlighting a transformation within the MCN approach: embracing a more talent- and content-driven strategy as they try to distance themselves from YouTube. MCNs in India only began to emerge in 2012–13 compared to their presence in the United States since 2008–9 (Cunningham and Craig 2019). Through an analysis of Indian MCNs such as Culture Machine, One Digital, Silly Monks and Qyuki Media, I show how Indian MCNs have reworked their business operations to focus more on a creator-centric approach instead of a YouTube or social media-centric model. An important part of transformation means functioning as a producer, organizing a creator network and localizing its services. MCNs are becoming producers like talent agents, in contrast to the screen industries in the West that restrict this transition due to conflicts of interest. I highlight the platform-agnostic approach of MCNs in distancing themselves from being called a 'multi-channel network' to be more of a 'creator network' or 'producers'.

MCNs as 'creator network'

MCNs in India, such as One Digital Entertainment, Culture Machine, PING network, Silly Monks and Qyuki, actively produce and partner with content aggregators and scout digital talent to offer diverse content across genres of food, music and drama within the new media ecosystem. As mentioned earlier, previous scholarship (Cunningham and Craig 2019; Lobato 2016) has articulated MCNs' over-dependence on YouTube. However, the growth of digital platforms in India, coupled with the precarity of income on YouTube, has led Indian MCNs to quickly move from YouTube dependency.

Gurpreet Singh, the founder of One Digital Entertainment (ODE), voices strong reservations about using MCN terminology. He reasons that ODE's business is about developing a 'creator network', invariably hinting towards a less medium-specific and more talent-driven model. According to Singh, operating as an MCN is just one part of many business activities performed by ODE, which sums up the MCN strategy to shed YouTube dependency:

> When we are collaborating with a creator, our purpose is not just to increase the viewership of the videos to earn money through it. It is more about converting a creator into a brand by using YouTube's reach and affinity.
>
> (Singh 2018)

This strategy is not unique to ODE. For most Indian MCNs and their Western counterparts (Cunningham and Craig 2019), the burden of responsibility is not so much about monetizing YouTube but highlighting the client's creativity to maximize their reach and seek prospective collaborations with brands and producers. Singh's approach reflects MCN's dependency on the creator rather than platforms. Singh discusses the cultural differences between a process led by multinational companies and the 'Indian' way of collaborating with creators:

> There is a code of conduct decided by YouTube as the way to carry on business as MCN. There have been several examples where the MCNs have not let off creators even when their contract expires, as the contract is between the creator and the MCN. So, a policy came in stating that the artist can discontinue from the MCN whenever they want to, and the MCN will have 30 days to convince them. From one side, it benefits the creators, but if we look at it from the perspective of the MCN, it can prove to be a major setback for them as they invest many resources in the creator. But all these scenarios are uncommon in India, as India is a 'relationship'-driven market.
>
> (Singh 2018).

Singh's emphasis on the relationship also articulates his sensemaking of the term 'creator network' as a more 'human-led' approach that looks beyond platform-specific advantages. Thus, even though YouTube is the defining point of the relationship between the MCNs and the creators, the creator's dependency on the MCN goes beyond YouTube.

The term 'creator network' involves multiple concepts. First, because the creator is in direct correspondence with the MCN to receive guidance on quotidian content creation practices, MCNs gain the status of being dependable and trustworthy. Second, the role of MCNs is not limited to content creation. It often begins with identifying talent, convincing them to consider switching to online content creation as a full-time profession and offering a team of content, marketing and public relations personnel to enable and support an encompassing, long-term career trajectory.

Prajakta Koli, a popular vlogger with over four million YouTube subscribers, is a case in point. Koli was previously employed as a radio DJ before switching to vlogging as a full-time career. Singh spotted her communication skills while his enterprise was creating a promotional video for the radio channel. After several meetings, Koli finally agreed to pursue content creation on YouTube with ODE as her talent agent. As a third concept, MCN leverages the 'network' of its existing clientele of talents, brands and producers in pushing the new creators for collaborations, multimedia exposure and an expanding audience base. In Koli's case, ODE leveraged clients such as popular rapper Badshah to promote Koli's channel.

In continuing with their creator-driven strategy, MCNs have also focused on offering content creation and production services, thus diversifying from talent to production, as is evident in Qyuki Digital Media's and Culture Machine's cases. Founded by BAFTA award-winning director Shekhar Kapur and Oscar-winning singer-musician, A. R. Rahman in 2012 and joined by Samir Bangara in 2014 (Bhadani 2015), Qyuki Media operates as a production house and talent management agency with specific attention to the music, animation, lifestyle, religion and comedy genres (Qyuki 2013). With a set-up of 45 to 50 employees, Qyuki runs operations from its Bandra office in Mumbai. Speaking about the company's business operations, senior producer Arunesh Kripal, who also worked on YouTube original show *Arrived* as the writer, stated:

> Qyuki mostly works with many social media stars/creators who mushroomed in the last decade owing to the grand success of YouTube. Qyuki Media provides these YouTube stars/creators with contracts and represents them, which in turn help them in getting better exposure and more sources of revenue. Qyuki Media constantly tries to bridge the gap between mainstream media (film, TV) and YouTube artists by producing and conceptualising television and web shows.
>
> (Kripal 2018)

Qyuki has diversified from a talent agency to a production company. It has achieved this transition through conceptualization and production of shows like *Arrived*, *Jammin* – a singing-based reality show on television channel Sony Entertainment Television (SET) – and *Boss Dialogues*, a talk show that began on YouTube but later migrated to broadcaster NDTV Prime.

MCN Culture Machine operates 715 YouTube channels and owns five YouTube channels, namely 'Being Indian (youth entertainment), Blush (a lifestyle channel for the modern Indian woman), Put Chutney (entertainment and comedy, Tamil), Viva (entertainment and comedy, Telugu) and Awesome Sauce (food)' (Mulki 2017). In 2018, Culture Machine partnered with Amazon Prime Video to launch Put Chutney's original stand-up comedy show, marking its entry into the subscription-based global streaming space (Panjari 2018). It also struck a deal with Star Vijay's regional television channel to create original content under Put Chutney ('Culture Machine's "Put Chutney"' 2017).

As discussed in Chapter 6, Mohan and Punathambekar (2019) map the localization practices of Indian MCNs by studying Put Chutney's everyday content practices and ascertain how linguistic and cultural diversities in South India are utilized to amass a native online audience. Such instances reflect the ability of the MCNs to go beyond the management of YouTube channels and venture into content creation. Culture Machine's versatility in dealing across multimedia and diverse platforms and portals reflects the skilful ways MCNs strategize their business operations. Pitalwalla (2018) also affirmed that the company's business model had diversified from 'YouTube and inventory-based business to creating content for brands and streaming businesses'. By expanding the value propositions to portals and brands, MCNs reduce their YouTube dependency and transition from talent management to content-creation practices.

Diversification and localization practices of MCNs

In an interview with MCN Qyuki's co-founder, Prasanto Das, Cunningham and Craig (2019) highlighted Qyuki's strategy of focusing on language-specific markets to exploit India's multicultural diversity. Like Qyuki, Silly Monks Entertainment Pvt. Ltd., a Hyderabad-based digital media entertainment company launched by entrepreneurs Sanjay Reddy and Anil Pallala in 2013, offers creative services in south Indian languages Tamil, Telugu, Kannada and Malayalam. Pallala initially planned to launch a television channel but instead went ahead with an 'all-digital' entertainment company as the investors were hesitant to make the larger investment required for a television channel (Ranipeta 2018), thereby reflecting the advantage of the NSE over traditional television in securing investment, as well as the flexibility of the digital infrastructure over television.

As an MCN, Silly Monks Entertainment works with 651 YouTube channels in varying roles of content aggregator, producer and acquisition, clocking an estimate of a billion views a month. As the company's tagline 'ride on digital' (Ranipeta 2018) suggests, its operations are not limited to YouTube alone. Silly Monks also syndicates content to Netflix, Amazon Prime, YuppTV, Vuclip, mobile careers, and streaming music platforms Ganna and Saavn. Additional revenue sources include operating as a creative consultant to promote brands, celebrities and producers. Over the last few years, Silly Monks has diversified its business operations to encompass events, merchandise and the music business as a strategy to cater to its fragmented audience base across distinct categories.

Silly Monks also manages its content operations under its three subsidiaries: Dream Boat Entertainment Pvt. Ltd., Monkstar Music LLP and Event Monks ('Silly Monks Entertainment History' 2017). Silly Monks' financial structure makes it India's first digital entertainment company to be listed on the country's National Stock Exchange, raising INR 15.12 crores (approximately US$2 million) through an initial public offering (IPO) in 2018 ('Silly Monks Plans to Buy' 2018). Silly Monks also launched a portal to provide multilingual content focusing on Tamil, Telugu and Malayalam (Ranipeta 2018). With offices in Hyderabad, Bangalore, Chennai and Kochi, Silly Monks has strategically located itself within the spatial dynamics of the South Indian media industry and created a strong network between film and online media.

The industrial, cultural and spatial dynamics of Silly Monks offers insights as to how the localization of regional digital media businesses helps the company to play within its strengths and compete with other MCNs that are more focused on capturing the Hindi and English-speaking audience. Prior knowledge of the cultural tastes of their audiences, based on the success of their YouTube channels and the creators they manage, enable MCNs to become a reliable source for media ventures looking to tap into regional markets. By finding their niche within a fragmented audience base, MCNs attract partnerships and collaboration from platforms, brands, portals and producers looking to accommodate region-centric cities within their ambit.

In 2018, Silly Monks produced Amazon Prime's first web series in the Telugu language titled *Gangstars*, a 12-episode series, with Silly Monks as co-producer with Early Monsoon Tales ('Amazon Prime Video Launches' 2018). It also ventured into Telugu language content production with its maiden film, *24 Kisses*, in November 2018 (Kumar 2018). Its strong digital presence in Telugu language content has helped the company secure Telugu films such as *Brand Babu*, *Mallesham*, *Keshava* and *KGF*.[1] Additionally, Mumbai-based production company Aurous Avatar partnered with Silly Monks to produce and distribute Telugu films ('Sillymonks Ties Up with Aurous Avatar' 2019), reflecting Silly Monks' growing dominance in offering multidimensional services. The diversification of content spanning films, platforms in varying creation roles, distribution, marketing and syndication, and investment in the regional sports category is indicative of the growing portfolio of a company that began as a regional language-focused MCN. Unlike Western countries, most Indian MCNs have outgrown YouTube-centricity by diversifying into production, talent and media-management activities, thereby signalling a shift towards a medium-agnostic, creator-focused approach. The lack of dependency on YouTube has assisted India's MCNs to remain afloat while numerous MCNs worldwide have failed.

RISE OF 'NEW INTERMEDIARIES'

New forms of intermediary business are emerging. The Story Ink venture earned its fee by selling novel adaptation rights to studios, independent producers, and portals. The founder of The Story Ink, Sidharth Jain, is an international producer, having worked with 65 writers across Los Angeles, New York, London and India. The Story Ink's business operations revolve around scouting for novels that can be adapted into screenplays for films and portals; however, instead of a straightforward deal with authors, The Story Ink acts more like an intermediary, pitching these novels to producers. However, any commercial deal between The Story Ink and the authors is dependent on a deal with the producers. Thus, Jain manages to broker author–producer relationships and manage them by utilizing his social networking skills and creating a risk-free economic model.

Jain elaborated as to how he curates several books before shortlisting them for adaptation. The shortlisted novels are subsequently developed into commercial pitches by identifying potential producers and offering them creative solutions on ways to adapt them. The Story Ink thereby aims to provide consultancy on pre-production and production activities for its content without doing the production activities itself. Jain also assists producers to identify writers for adaptation from his earlier experience as Hotstar's content head.

Jain sees The Story Ink as a development producer rather than a talent agent:

> It is a business-to-business solution. We are the enablers of stories where our role is curating, consulting, and connecting. It is like an 'Uber' of stories where all kinds of stories can aggregate.
>
> (Jain 2018)

By 'aggregator', Jain alludes to the access to novel titles that he can barter with the producers and portals. There seems to be scope in this model, considering the initial investments made by Netflix, to adapt novels like *Sacred Games* and *Bard of Blood*. As of August 2018, The Story Ink has managed to secure the adaptation rights of novels such as *More Bodies will Fall*, *Remember Death* and *Dead Meat* as a part of a three-film deal with a leading production house. Furthermore, it has also secured screen adaptation rights with leading production houses for Indian novels such as the comic book *Caravan* and the ancient mythology novel *Avishi*. Given the sheer demand for localized fiction content in films and portals, such a value proposition corresponds directly with the needs of the NSE and the film industries and enables The Story Ink to retain its distinction from the rest.

CONCLUSION

To conclude, the intermediaries contribute to the NSE (Research Objective 3) by developing talent and pushing newer forms of storytelling by facilitating writers' rooms, active production and consultation with prospective funders (portals, film producers). In return, the intermediary practices offer creators the freedom to pursue their art without worrying about the producers' predatory contract policies. There seems to be an informal understanding within the Indian media industry that the talent represented by intermediaries is remunerated, irrespective of the project's outcome, and that writers are duly recognized for their contribution through fair contractual agreements (Khandekar- Kohli 2019). Intermediary services are also invariably sought by producers and portals to facilitate writers' rooms and scout for novels suitable for adaptation on screen.

Together, through their diverse industrial practices, these intermediaries are becoming indispensable to the new media and are therefore better positioned to negotiate contracts for themselves and their talent. Their ability to mediate the quotidian content-creation practices on new media demonstrates their power to influence the content that shapes the algorithmic culture of portals. My findings on the significance of the intermediaries within the Indian new media offer a meso-level perspective of how social relations mediate the industrial and cultural logics between the creators, intermediaries and portals, and articulate the various ways in which intermediaries influence on-screen media texts.

7

Conclusion

In exploring the Indian New Screen Ecology's (NSE) social relations and economic exchanges, my findings highlight how creators adapt to the NSE to situate themselves within the Indian screen industries. The book has demonstrated the continuities and disjunctures between the NSE and traditional screens (film, television) and examined how informal–formal media dynamics shape the contemporary production culture of Indian NSE.

OVERVIEW

The fluidity and complexity of the digital environment arising out of the convergence of broadcast, internet-based distribution and telecommunications companies have impacted film and television industries, regulators and content creators. The fundamental question that I answer in this book is how the digital transformation of the Indian screen industries has impacted on production cultures, through investigation of its industrial practices and exploration of social contexts within which its key players (platforms, portals, intermediaries, creators) operate. Through a multiscalar CMIS framework (helicopter view for mapping platform–portals, top of the building view for mapping intermediaries and on-the-ground view for mapping creators) (Herbert, Lotz and Punathambekar 2020: 184), my research has examined the three different layers of operations of creators, intermediaries, platform and portals that exist within the Indian NSE. This approach aligns with the three research objectives that sought to investigate the interdependencies between platforms, portals, creators and intermediaries within NSE.

The convergence between diverse media and technology sectors has led to a wide array of formal–informal interdependencies in the Indian screen industries, as characterized in the NSE, and is demonstrated at three levels, as discussed below.

'Helicopter' view

At a macro-level, the ownership structures of television-led broadcasters signal the interdependencies between traditional television and the NSE. Reliance Jio's entry as a portal and into the original content-creation space and syndication deals between telecom players and portals highlights the interdependencies between telecommunications and portals. The macro-level interdependencies between film and portals can be observed through sole ownership of studios and portals (Sony Pictures and SonyLIV, Hotstar and Fox Star Studios, ZEE5 and Zee Studios, Viacom18 and Viacom18 Studios). Finally, the entry of a native portal like TVFPlay, previously a social media creator, signals the platform–portal interdependency. As discussed in Chapter 3, these macro-level interdependencies also highlight a distinct concatenation of global, local and multinational platforms and portals offering diverse value propositions to target the growing Indian local, regional and global internet-savvy Indian diaspora.

A critical point that has emerged from the study of the competitive Indian NSE is that a vast content library does not naturally offer a leadership position to any broadcaster-led portal. While a healthy television content library does promise an existing audience base, the rise of internet native portals and the increase in original content creation by broadcaster-led portals shows that consumers are looking for newer forms of content. The creation of original web series like *Asura*, *Sone bhi do Yaaron* and *Scam 1992*, amongst others, by broadcaster-led portals like Voot, ZEE5 and SonyLIV, respectively, signal this intent.

One of the significant findings of my book relates to how platforms and portals facilitate creator and content movement through talent and content interdependencies. As discussed in the introduction of the book, the interaction between the informal and formal economy plays an integral role in developing Indian screen industries. Specifically, in Chapter 1, we saw how the Indian film industry was driven by a range of informal practices in film financing (black money) and distribution (piracy). However, these informal practices were also vital in helping the Government and the investors of the Indian film industries' economic potential. Similarly, another layer of informality in the form of nepotism governed Indian film industries' business transactions.

My research into the industrial culture of Indian NSE shows how the Indian NSE emerged as a site of continuity that formalizes the 'informality' of the Indian film industries by offering aspiring filmmakers that lie outside the social circles an opportunity. While offering new means for monetization and distribution, portals have also challenged the exclusive theatrical distribution of the cinemas. Chapters 2, 4, and 5 show how in offering an alternative medium for distribution, the NSE challenges the social relations in the film industry between financers, producers, actors, and star directors.

NSE's global distribution network challenges Bollywood's informal economic and social reciprocity nexus with exhibitors that frequently marginalized the theatrical exhibition of small and medium-budget non-mainstream and regional films. The NSE also serves as another medium alongside television for films to sell its distribution rights. In that vein, many films such as *Lootcase, Dil Bechara, Gunjan Saxena, Gulabo Sitabo, Penguin, Ghoomketu, V, C U Soon* have bypassed the traditional step-by-step film distribution model of theatrical exhibition, television broadcast and digital release to premiere directly on portals. More than 100 films were streamed exclusively on portals (FICCI-EY 2022: 148).

Chapter 3, in particular, is important to highlight how YouTube became the unconscious carrier for facilitating global creator ambitions due to its early mover advantage as an internet-based UGC platform from 2008 onward. The launch of Facebook also offered Indian creators an alternative platform to help develop an emerging audience on the internet although the viewership-based monetization of videos on social media was largely restricted to YouTube. The strategic use of YouTube's monetization policies and Facebook's reach in India enabled Indian YouTube channels TVF, Pocket Aces, and several individual creators like Zakir Khan, Aditi Mittal, Indrani Biswas and Dhruv Sehgal to create a space within Indian popular culture and emerge as an alternative to film and television viewing. The contrasting industrial dynamics between the television and NSE in India, as shown in Chapter 4, have resulted in distinctions based on young, entrepreneurial and newcomer talent and content that is experimental, innovative, realistic and cosmopolitan.

As observed in Chapter 2, the Indian television industry could not cope with the sudden proliferation of local and global television channels and the growing television consumption in Indian urban and rural households. Its heavy reliance on melodramatic soap operas driven by perceptions of the audience based on gender and class (rural–urban) divides and hegemonic practices of broadcasters stifled the creativity of emerging and existing creators. Thus, despite leading in advertising revenues, and viewership, Chapter 2 unfolds how television broadcasting is plagued by the lack of a 'comprehensive system of regulation, the increasing political control of regional television channels and distribution networks and a structural problem with its business model and delivery platforms' (Mehta 2012: 614), and how the NSE benefits from this perception. The creator and content-based linkages between the UGC and PGC landscape signal the continuity in formal–informal practices within the NSE and show how the Indian screen industries continue to be shaped by formal and informal social, cultural and economic contexts.

Thus, the mapping of incumbent platforms and portals operating in India offers a distinct understanding of their interdependencies, based on the similarities of content and talent. Despite clear differences in the business models, architectures, and objectives between platforms and portals, this book shows how the Indian screen industries' complex structure creates reasons for interdependencies between platforms, portals and films. This underpins one of my key arguments: that, at the 'helicopter' level of the CMIS framework, the Indian NSE is underpinned by interdependencies between platforms and portals, which is in clear contrast to dominant Western models and answers the research objective concerning the distinctiveness of India's NSE and the role of platforms/portals in facilitating creator careers.

Top of the building view

The meso-level is dominated by the work of intermediaries that, as seen in Chapter 7, serve as bridges between the UGC–PGC, amateur–professional, platform–portal–film landscapes. Their work is personified by their duality of industrial practices in creating suitable market conditions by exploiting producers' economic potential on the one hand and widening the network of creators on the other. The work of talent agents and MCNs in shepherding the local strategies of Amazon Prime Video and Netflix, as highlighted in Chapter 6, is an important addition from the perspective of intermediary intervention. By diversifying their business practices into media management and other media-related businesses, the intermediaries have successfully developed dynamic solutions for talent and producers.

In demonstrating the NSE's dynamism, my book highlights the critical interventions by talent agents and multi-channel networks in establishing the platform–portal–film links through the facilitation of content and creators. As we witnessed in Chapter 6, Indian intermediary transformation is characterized by distinct industrial practices such as assuming a medium-agnostic approach, diversifying from talent management to content creation and media management practices, and mediating content strategies within the Indian screen industries by facilitating communications between talent and producers. The intermediaries not only help to enable these movements but also take an active part in the NSE's industrial cultures through production, marketing and media management.

To conclude this section, the research findings evidence the transformation of intermediaries in India as they have assumed a more hands-on approach to media production, marketing and management activities, apart from talent management. Intermediary contribution to the shape of the NSE is visible in the form of spearheading talent migration from platforms to portals as they transition from writing short-form content to long-form web-shows, actively producing content from their clients, helping the likes of Netflix and Amazon Prime with localization in India, and providing an impetus for stand-up comedy in online and offline circuits.

'On-the-ground' view

My analysis of NSE creators in Chapters 4–6 highlights how they utilize the concomitant relationship between the Indian formal–informal media economy to create opportunities across the Indian media landscape. The early popular culture on the internet was mediated by newcomers who neither belonged to the elite social class of film or television fraternity nor possessed any credentials to be a part of their insiders' circle.

My cohort of NSE creators offered a mix of urban and rural narratives with a strong claim of offering a 'realistic' portrayal of Indian society – that is, more realistic than the melodramatic templates of television. Comedy and drama genres gained prominence and are key to my cohort of creators who resorted to low-cost sketches and limited episodic web series to build a strong relationship between story characters and the audience. The early success of these genres and creators was exploited by subsequent portals like Hotstar, SonyLIV, Amazon Prime and Netflix as a part of their launch strategy to entice the growing NSE audience. Chapters 4–6 also showed how my creator cohort successfully leveraged the success and popularity of their content on social media to satisfy their desires for working in films and portals. In this way, the platform–portal links show a remarkable continuity in carrying forward the formal–informal practices that continue to pervade the Indian media economy. My book findings have shown that portals such as Amazon Prime, Netflix and Hotstar provide a larger canvas for my cohort of creators, reaching a regional and international diaspora with their creative capabilities.

Chapter 6 details NSE exploited India's transnational cultural appeal by facilitating content and creators from multiple Indian languages. In that vein, the focus on Marathi and Bengali language creators suggests yet another synergy in creator mobilization between platforms, portals and films. The NSE provides an alternative and cheaper distribution option for those existing and emerging regional creators who may not possess the financial capacity to indulge in traditional film marketing and exhibition expenses. One of the significant findings of this book is that localization strategies of the platforms and portals are as much a result of creator innovation. The 'rural and ethical markers' employed by regional creators on social media on their content brought fame and popularity to both creators and platforms. Creators' fan-following eventually led YouTube and Facebook to consider non-Hindi and non-English creators as a part of their creator development, monetization and localization strategies.

The increasing internet penetration into rural Indian households presents a significant opportunity for regional creators to withstand the hegemony of Hindi and English language content on mass media. The prospect of catering to Indian language internet users, who were expected to rise from 234 million in 2016 to 536 million in 2021, has led to a growth in demand for regional content on the internet (KPMG 2019: 48). NSE regional creators can bypass the informal producer–exhibitor–distributor relations by creating a direct relationship with the Indian audience. Ultimately, the creators' success on social media becomes a synecdoche for regional content creators to create demand for online regional content and form partnerships with regional film industries.

The inroads that creators have made from UGC platforms such as YouTube and Facebook to PGC landscapes of portals and films signify a form of media agnosticism, which is supported by the fact that many do not wish to be labelled based on just one platform, such as being known as 'YouTubers' or 'Instagrammers' (see Chapter 4). There is undoubtedly a significant difference in production cost between the content created on platforms and portals. This difference is obviously due to the heavy reliance of the YouTube creators on brand sponsorships, advertising and viewership, as opposed to the upfront payment that is offered by the portals. However, the similarity between the Indian platform and portal content is the creators' ability to create content for the younger demographics. Those creators who can transition from platforms to portals have been able to do so by introducing political, social or culturally relevant issues of a modern India that is witnessing dynamic changes in terms of access to resources (affordability of the internet and the resulting access to global content) and consumption (transition from a single-screen to a multiscreen viewing culture).

A distinctive feature of the NSE is its entrepreneurial set-up, whereby intermediaries adopt the roles of producers, stand-up comedians transition into web series writers, and individuals with limited media management and production exposure have floated successful digital media companies that include Pocket Aces, TVF and AIB (see, for example, Chapters 4 and 5). Through the examples of ScoopWhoop, Arré, Bhuvan Bam, Pocket Aces, Shitty Ideas Trending (SIT) and Dhruv Sehgal, I have shown how new as well as existing Indian media practitioners have exploited platform and portal affordances to build career trajectories that previously seemed impossible to achieve within the film and television industries.

Central to their everyday NSE practices are the tensions between precarity caused by platform–portal algorithmic culture, elitism within film industries, the hegemony of television broadcasters and their desire to achieve a medium-agnostic sustainable career by establishing a direct relationship with the audience. The uncertainty surrounding the kinds of content the portals seek leads creators to adopt a multiplatform strategy to reduce their dependency on a single platform and portal. While this has produced advantageous results for select creators and digital media companies, as shown in Chapter 4, it has also resulted in unpaid labour from multiplatform content creation.

Moreover, precarity is not only financial or algorithmic; it is also highly gendered. The safe haven provided to #MeToo accused creative professionals, and the lopsided focus on heteronormative programming is a gentle reminder for academic scholars who distinguish portals for their ability to cater to individualized tastes through 'informed' readings. Especially since much of the processing of this information is biased and rooted in privileging the privileged. Global portals must also play an (im)balancing act of chasing established career professionals and offering chances to newcomers. The findings of this research are a growing reminder that the ability to draw talent with higher social capital determines your worth in the industries rather than the subscriber numbers. The findings on the impact of the #MeToo movement in the Indian NSE (see Chapter 4) highlight how on-screen liberal expressions on the internet do not correspond with off-screen working conditions. The various #MeToo cases in India's NSE indicate the dire need for institutional and policy-level changes, which the Indian screen industries need to promote as a safe working culture for women media practitioners.

While Indian television remains the dominant medium in broader popular culture, the NSE is more dynamic in addressing the diverse viewership and convenience-based needs of Indian audiences. While different business models continue to populate the Indian NSE, the popularity of creators and content amongst the audience play a critical role in driving platform–portal content strategies. In this book, I have shown how outsiders have their task cut out in establishing this bond in a country where films still occupy a central place in popular audio-visual culture. Finally, in analysing the creators' industrial and cultural practices, I provided evidence of their multimedia aspirations and the precarious efforts to situate themselves within the Indian screen industries.

THE FUTURE OF THE INDIAN NSE

There has been an increase in the number of online audio-visual content productions, owing to the emergence of new players who previously were invested in different business practices. This section charts the evolving NSE trajectories that continue to build on this book's findings through industrial practices that evidence diversification among creator profiles, the impact of an intermediary intervention and the launch of new platforms/portals that could further blur the creator-based platform–portal divide.

Platforms/portals

This section primarily focuses on launching new platforms and portals to articulate how their diverse value propositions could create new possibilities for monetization and career sustainability for creators. The Indian NSE landscape has witnessed new trends outside the timeframe of this book in the form of consolidation, shutdown, and entry of niche portals. The frenetic movements within the Indian NSE are evidence of its emerging potential, and yet, the departures and arrivals of portals highlight the unpredictability of the market. As an example, consider Netflix's change in the revenue model from subscription to a hybrid (advertising and subscription) system (see Chapter 3). It is even more difficult for me to offer clear implications for the NSE future in such a case. While the entry of companies from other sectors into the NSE serves as a means for capital injection, the launch of Chinese and native social media platforms challenges the monopoly of the US-led Indian SME platform landscape. This section offers an overview of these developments to highlight the rapid growth of the Indian NSE.

Since the beginning of this project, several new global and local platforms–portals have been launched in India. Reports estimate that portals developed 2,512 hours of original content in 2021 in comparison to 1,187 in 2020 and 2,033 in 2019 (FICCI-EY 2022: 234). However, the biggest development has been Netflix's decision to launch the AVoD service (Fitzgerald 2022). With a monthly plan of US$6.99, four to five minutes of advertisements per hour will be shown. Portals such as ZEE5 and MXPlayer have forayed into the UGC landscape by introducing short-form video platforms such as HiPi and MxTakaTak, respectively (Sarkar 2020). Similarly, Netflix India introduced a Take Ten talent-hunt competition in 2022 in which the portal would award a $10,000 grant to select filmmakers to develop short films ('Take Ten' 2022). These short films would eventually premiere on its YouTube channel. These developments bear well with the book's findings showing an intricate relationship between UGC and PGC landscapes.

As an example of market instability, HOOQ, a Singaporean portal borne out of a joint venture between Singapore telecom Singtel, Sony Pictures and Warner Bros, shut down on 30 April 2020 (KPMG 2020). Their failure to localize their programming is understood to be one of the main reasons behind their closure (Frater 2020). Alongside HOOQ, Malaysian freemium service Iflix met a similar fate owing to its focus on Western-centric content, as noted by its co-owner Mark Britt (Frater 2020). These developments highlight the criticality of comprehending region-specific contexts while catering to multiple countries at the same time. Simultaneously, niche portals such as 'Mubi' and 'Cinemapreneur' have been launched to capture non-mainstream independent cinephiles (KPMG 2020). Similarly, an industry report estimated that 177 non-Hindi titles were produced in 2021 with an increase in regional content from 27 per cent in 2020 to 46 per cent in 2021, highlighting the overall significance of regional content in the NSE (FICCI-EY 2021).

As an example of convergence between media and other sectors within India, Flipkart, a Walmart owned e-commerce platform, has launched a 'Video' and an

'Ideas' toolbar to support its e-commerce business and engage in multiple ways with its consumers. Flipkart 'Ideas' is a curated feed that merges brands' and influencers' content in multimedia formats (videos, polls, stories, GIFs, quizzes) to influence consumer shopping decisions (Khatri 2019a). On the other hand, for its 'Video' section, Flipkart features syndicated content from multiple online creators such as Arré and Pocket Aces, as well as portals such as Voot and TVFPlay.

Similarly, Paytm, an e-commerce platform and digital wallet company owned by a slew of investors, such as Softbank, SAIF Partners, Alibaba Group and Ant Financial (Sorrells 2019), is planning to venture into short-form video content, news and live television (Khatri 2019b). Such diversification is akin to Amazon's 'eco-sphere' business model (see Tiwary 2020) and signals the convergence between diverse industrial sectors, and serves as a means of capital injection into the growing NSE. The increased attention to the media business also offers positive news for NSE media start-ups to exchange their content library for a fixed cost while also offering an alternative to consider for content creation.

The diversity of their value propositions, evident from their business ventures, genres and formats, presents some distinct opportunities for creators of every format to expand their footprints beyond Facebook and YouTube. To further challenge the domination of Facebook, a trio of Indian engineers – Bhanu Singh, Ankush Sachdeva and Farid Ahsan – have launched Sharechat, a social media application that facilitates 14 Indian languages and has amassed over 120 million users in 2021 (see FICCI-EY 2022: 65). The Indian user-centric start-up operates from Bengaluru and has embraced Indian multilingual diversity, with close to 100 employees from 21 states (Biswas 2018). Sharechat boasts high-profile investors such as Twitter, Trustbridge Partners, Lightspeed Venture Partners, Shunwei Capital, Hill House, Morningside Venture Capital, India Quotient and SAIF Capital (*India Business Law Journal* 2019). In 2020, Sharechat facilitated 28 million creators, 750 million UGC with a daily average user time of 24 minutes ('Eight Women amongst Top 10 Creators' 2020). Sharechat's entry offers a critical dimension to the Indian NSE.

By focusing strictly on Indian languages, Sharechat promotes and fosters a creator culture. To that effect, it has already started offering monetary incentives to regional language creators who are currently using YouTube and Facebook. Such a local intervention is crucial as, unlike the Indian portal scene, Indian social media entertainment is still dominated by US players like Google and Facebook. Sharechat presents Indian NSE with a distinct opportunity to boost Indian regional and local creators' profiles whose popularity is highly subjected to their success on YouTube and Facebook.

India's free marketplace and its rising online viewership have attracted interest from Chinese companies that are not content with just being investors in Indian media ventures (Russell 2019). Competing alongside Sharechat and Facebook in India is China's social media platform Helo, launched by Chinese technology company Bytedance in 2018 and available in 14 Indian languages; it offers a mix of videos, memes, GIFs, jokes, *shayaris* and film gossip, among other content genres (Ahuja and Dalal 2018). Bytedance takes pride in its success of two million daily active Indian users. Bytedance's backend machine learning and deep learning algorithms allow the platform to track user time and interaction on content and actions such as 'taps swipes, pauses and comments' (Shaikh 2018).

In 2019, Helo launched its third season of Helo Superstar. This campaign encourages Indian creators to speak in any of the nine Indian languages such as 'Hindi, Tamil, Telugu, Malayalam, Kannada, Punjabi, Marathi, Bengali and Gujarati' to create content across ten different categories, such as entertainment, education, sports and food among others ('Helo Launches 3rd Season' 2019). The commercial prospects of catering to large numbers of native Indian language internet users, which were estimated to increase from 234 million in 2017 to 536 million in 2021 as compared to 175 million English users, is not lost on Chinese investors, who developed 44 out of the top 100 downloaded apps in India on Google Playstore (Russell 2019).

TikTok was first launched in China in 2012 and has rapidly grown to emerge as a globally successful short-form content destination in 150 countries and about 75 languages (Fannin 2019). Its low-barrier entry and 15-second limited duration have made it an eclectic medium of expression for Indian users, who may not have the wherewithal to shoot high-quality videos. TikTok's popularity in India can be traced from its numbers. However, the Indian Government's ban of TikTok and 58 Chinese applications in 2020 citing national integrity and sovereignty issues as a response to India's skirmish with China in the Galwan Valley in Ladakh signals an era where wars are fought on digital borders (Poddar 2020).

The listing of emerging local and global platforms and portals is meant to indicate the growing economic appeal of the Indian NSE in the minds of private investors. However, NSE's potential as a lucrative international market depends on how the Indian Government deals with national security and censorship issues. Moreover, as we saw in Chapter 4, the Indian Government's perception of NSE as another vehicle for enforcing pro-Hindu policies, monitoring 'cultural expressions', and implementing digital surveillance in the name of welfare (see Thomas 2019) will do little to assuage its claims of being a neo-liberal market-friendly country.

Another critical aspect to consider while comprehending the sudden burst of UGC platforms is the ability to monetize short-form videos. Short-video applications such as MxTakaTak, Snapchat, Sharechat and Josh accumulated 290 monthly active users, with the advertisements on these platforms contributing to

5 per cent of the overall advertising spending in 2021 (FICC-EY 2022: 72). As observed in Chapter 5, sketches and short-form content were vital to several cash-strapped Indian SME creators' early successes. The ability to commercialize short-form videos was critical to some of my creator cohort's survival, who successfully practised their video-making skills in the shorter format before transitioning to web series. The existence of multiple short-form friendly video sites, while offering more alternatives for commercialization, also signals a more significant opportunity for commercializing amateurs to work their way towards the PGC landscape.

Central to NSE growth is the role of the Indian Government in resolving the lingering issues of the digital divide. As Thomas (2019: 60) argues, 'closing the digital divide will also result in the resolving of other divides in society'. Taken together, these developments contribute to the arguments I have made in this book regarding the distinctiveness of the Indian NSE and the ability of these emerging content-delivery systems to offer new socio-technological affordances in cultivating an influencer culture that can be sustained across the Indian screen industries.

Shifting power dynamics of intermediaries?

As witnessed earlier, the advent of the NSE has also enabled talent agents to diversify themselves besides dealing with Amazon Prime and Netflix. The NSE has therefore helped talent agents and multi-channel networks to establish their role and significance in mediating the decisions that shape the cultural modes of negotiating creative practices. However, as the demand for content and content creators continues to increase, the businesses of those who can identify the talent and produce content will emerge as the driving force for running the marketplace. As highlighted in Chapter 7, the talent agents and multi-channel networks have assumed a stronger position than ever in negotiating the value propositions regarding the demand and supply of content and talent. However, the rise of intermediaries posits new concerns, as such a power imbalance marginalizes creators' ability to choose their projects. I hope future researchers will investigate the implications of intermediaries' growing influence on the media industries.

While my cohort agreed to the influence of talent agents in gaining work for creators, helping them navigate through contracts and negotiations with producers, they acknowledged that the growing power of talent agents and multi-channel networks also meant there was pressure to affirm deals that were brought by them. Some established creators (acclaimed writers and directors who did not wish to be named) alluded to the fact that often the deals brought by agents had to be responded to, despite their reluctance due to the perceived control of the producer over the content creating disharmony between the agency and the talent. At other times, creators lamented that talent agencies pressured writers to develop new content to stay 'in the minds' of producers. Thus, the constant pressure to 'remain in the game' affected the creative space of the creator, leading to tensions between the agency and its talent.

Creators elaborated that the capitalistic tendencies of talent agencies would often harm the interests of the talent. The talent agency would pursue five deals instead of the one deal that might interest the talent the most. However, the five deals would enable talent agents to maximize their earnings. The aspiration to make the most money out of the talent could therefore lead to subversive exploitation methods, which slipped under the veil of providing more opportunities to their talent.

My creator cohort asserted how the Indian screen industry is fraught with relationships often cultivated through periods of a long collaboration. Writers and directors develop these relationships and, over a period, maintain informal networks with producers. Often these networks are later utilized to discuss business opportunities without any direct assistance from the talent agents. There is thus a tone of informality in the way Indian media practitioners operate, resulting in an added challenge on behalf of talent agents to rationalize their services. Furthermore, Chapter 6 underlines how there is a huge risk of the talent moving on as it reflects a loss of business (economic) and goodwill (social capital) for intermediaries. On the other hand, if the talent feels cheated or does not see growth, the partnership is not mutually beneficial, and it is only fair that they part ways with their agents. Thus, there is a constant struggle on the intermediaries to be relevant in an already precarious screen industry.

Creators

If there is one thing that various case studies and testimonies of creators in this book attest to, it is the privilege of opportunity. Indian film industries, for years, have romanticized the notion of turning a 'nobody' into a 'star'. However, this notion is just too good to be true. Whereas the careers of creative professionals from privileged backgrounds are rarely ever affected by their performance at the box office, the newcomers are left playing the catch-up game in struggling to get a single opportunity. They are either too raw or, put differently, unprofitable. As Chapters 4 and 5 demonstrated, the platforms and portals, with their precarity, still offer opportunities for creators to imagine a media career. The continuous development of diverse online creators from practising short-form videos and uploading stand-up comedy acts and sketches on social media to featuring in web series on portals and securing prominent roles in feature films will only challenge the elitist distinctions such as UGC and PGC that have been made based on platforms' and portals' affordances respectively.

As we witness an increase in the movement of creators across the media ecologies, creators are increasingly leveraging their popularity to exercise their agency in prioritizing opportunities within the NSE.

What began as a reliant and over-dependent relationship on one platform has evolved into a much more nuanced and complex political economy between platforms, portals, broadcasters, studios and producers and creators. For example, Abhishek Banerjee, the founder of Casting Bay (see Chapter 3), who appeared in short films and sketches on YouTube, appeared as a protagonist in the Amazon Prime web series *Paatal Lok* (Hell) in 2020 and VootSelect web series *The Great Indian Wedding of the Munnes* in 2021. *Paatal Lok* was put together by the talent agency Tulsea (see Chapter 6) as growing evidence of intermediary intervention and creator mobilization (from casting to acting on YouTube to appearing as a protagonist). Kiran Dutta (The Bong Guy), whose fandom was elaborated in Chapter 5, will be acting in Tollywood feature film *Kolkata Chalontika*. Also, Arré, a digital media company (see Chapter 4) with popular social media verticals for sketches and web shows across multiple genres, developed a web series for the newly launched portal MXPlayer in further evidence of platform–portal creator interdependency.

In building on the evidence of creator porosity between Bollywood and global portals discussed in Chapter 3, the book's findings signal the desire of Hindi media practitioners to be seen as global talent. Amazon Prime's and Netflix's global outreach makes them lucrative destinations for Bollywood personnel. In concluding her formative study on Bollywood's production culture, Ganti (2012: 366) recalls how the allure of receiving global fame and circulation of Bollywood content continues to trouble several emerging and existing Bollywood directors and producers. The desire to be seen as global media practitioners and be known 'not as the Indian Scorsese – but the Scorsese' (film director Abhishek Chaubey, cited in Ganti 2012: 366) by demonstrating high levels of production and engaging storytelling practices has stepped up with the presence of portals such as Amazon Prime Video and Netflix.

I recount Ganti's (2012) epilogue on Bollywood's attempts to situate its production culture on par with the international film culture by highlighting how my cohort of creators use the NSE for satisfying their global ambitions. As an example, while discussing his career aspirations, the head of TVF's YouTube vertical Screenpatti (see Chapters 4 and 5), Amrit Gupta (2018), remarked:

> A person like me dreams of making a show of the level of Netflix. I want to achieve something as big as Narcos in India, I need the required amount of investment, and if the brand does not support me in giving me the required investment, I will pitch to OTT portals like Amazon and Netflix.

The opportunity to unpack complex political, social and cultural themes and experiment with freedom on uncensored portals has also attracted Bollywood producers such as Dharmatic Entertainment (the digital arm of popular film production company Dharma Productions), Loneranger Productions (owned by Director Vikram Bhatt), Excel Entertainment Pvt. Ltd. (owned by actor/writer/producer/director Farhan Akhtar and producer Ritesh Sidhwani), JAR Pictures (owned by producers Ajay Rai and Alan McAlex), D2R films (owned by director/writer/producers DK and Raj Nidimoru) and Red Chillies (owned by popular actor Shah Rukh Khan), as discussed in Chapter 3.

While discussing the benefits of distributing the film on Netflix, filmmaker Makhija pointed out that his feature film *Ajji* (Grandmother) was censored in film theatres but was uncut when streamed by Netflix. My cohort of creators also alluded to these portals' ability to take risks in commissioning original content driven by the script rather than stars. Actress Radhika Dugal, whose profile was elaborated in Chapter 4, remarked that 'at the end of the day, [both] Netflix and Amazon Prime have the reach and the capital to support new creators and actors'.

In examining the proximity between the portals and Bollywood, I argue that Bollywood assumes a different characteristic on these portals, whereby its industry status is no longer defined by being 'aggressively oriented toward box-office success and broad audience appeal' (Ganti 2013: 3). In placing Indian content alongside international content, global portals have also exposed and challenged the star-driven narratives of Bollywood. In times to come, it will be interesting to see whether the NSE portals will continue to challenge Bollywood's informal networks by offering opportunities to 'outsiders' or, like film studios, conform to elitist practices by preferring kinship in the recruitment of its employees or buying 'star-driven' films over merit.

CLOSING NOTE

This study contributes to a growing body of research that is mapping the political, social and cultural dynamics of Indian media. It addresses gaps in the media industry studies literature on the dynamics of digital transformation in the screen industries in a region-specific context and contributes to a body of literature on Indian digital production cultures. As a critical media scholar, my book has explored who gets these opportunities and the extent to which they not only shape one's media career but ultimately also affect the existing structures within which the screen industries operate.

As for the creators aspiring to build media careers, social media platforms' concentration offers new ways to express creativity, gain fame, and reach and improve commercial possibilities within the screen industries. My findings show that the distinctiveness of the Indian NSE arises from the platform–portal–film interdependencies that are actualized through the industrial practices of creators, platform/portal executives and intermediaries, and the NSE's contrasting production culture with the television industry.

Because a clear divide between platforms and portals does not exist in India, and it's contemporary enmeshing of industrial practices results from the past and present film and television industrial cultures, future studies must consider platforms and portals' practices when studying the production and consumption of digital audio-visual cultures. A distinctive feature of the inherently informal screen industries like India is to enable players from diverse sectors to expand the financial, cultural and social potential of industrial transactions that erstwhile hegemonical structures do not allow. In this light, I urge future scholars to not be deterred by the scale of informality (within and beyond UGC) and investigate the various linkages that contribute to the development of the media industries.

Notes

CHAPTER 2
1. Available online: http://www.bigsynergy.tv (accessed 2 October 2020).
2. Available online: http://mumbainewsnetwork.blogspot.com/2018/03/abhishek-banerjee-anmol-ahuja-co.html (accessed 18 November 2019).
3. Available online: https://scroll.in/reel/869836/cult-tv-series-powder-is-finally-getting-the-platform-and-attention-it-deserves?fbclid=IwAR2eqS-VY_Q6lZGG-PCPAD1ZktwJvpfZLDsO2MwczC6eafaCRQk5f4ngVgU (accessed 17 July 2021).
4. Available online: https://www.imdb.com/title/tt6522580/?ref_=nv_sr_2?ref_=nv_sr_2s (accessed 9 September 2019).
5. Available online: https://www.imdb.com/name/nm3832707/ (accessed 9 September 2019).

CHAPTER 3
1. Available online: https://www.facebook.com/PriyamGhoseComedy (accessed 9 September 2019).
2. Available online: https://www.hotstar.com/sports (accessed 9 September 2019).
3. Available online: https://www.zeeentertainment.com (accessed 9 September 2019).
4. Available online: https://spuul.com/about (accessed 9 September 2019).
5. Available online: https://www.addatimes.com/sports (accessed 9 September 2019).

CHAPTER 4
1. Samar, Zoom interview with author, 22 December 2021.
2. Neetha, Zoom interview with author, 14 November 2021.

CHAPTER 6
1. Available online: https://sillymonks.com/movie-promotions (accessed 9 September 2019).

References

Abidin, C. (2015), 'Communicative Intimacies: Influencers and Perceived Interconnectedness', *Ada*, 8: 1–16. Available online: http://adanewmedia.org/2015/11/issue8-abidin/ (accessed 18 August 2020).

Ahluwalia, H. (2018), 'Zee Entertainment Launches New Video Streaming Platform Zee5', *Livemint*, 14 February. Availabe online: https://www.livemint.com/Consumer/c7MymlBR4d5jIrLUeFWRkO/Zee-Entertainment-launches-new-video-streaming-platform-Zee5.html (accessed 24 March 2020).

Ahooja, R. and T. Sarkar (2021), 'How (Not) to Regulate the Internet: Lessons from the Indian Subcontinent', Lawfare. Available online: https://www.lawfareblog.com/how-not-regulate-internet-lessons-indian-subcontinent (accessed 24 January 2022).

Ahuja, A. and M. Dalal (2018), 'Chinese Start-Up Says Helo to India, Set to Take on ShareChat', clip, *Livemint*. Available online: https://www.livemint.com/Technology/oanSCMhXkOTx6xINpvGPTL/Chinese-startup-says-Helo-to-India-set-to-take-on-ShareCha.html (accessed 9 October 2019).

Alambayan, S. (2017), In-person interview, 5 January, Mumbai.

Alves, G. (2019), 'Vijay Nair: This College Dropout Now Heads a Biz Worth 10 million!', *Economic Times*. Available online: https://economictimes.indiatimes.com/magazines/panache/vijay-nair-this-college-dropout-now-heads-a-biz-worth-10-million/articleshow/44905195.cms (accessed 11 April 2020).

'Amazon Prime Video Launches Its 1st Telugu Series "GangStars"' (2018), *United News of India*. Available online: http://www.uniindia.com/amazon-prime-video-launches-its-1st-telugu-series-gangstars/entertainment/news/1246331.html (accessed 28 July 2019).

Anderson, J. D. (1917), 'The Phonetics of the Bengali Language', *Bulletin of the School of Oriental and African Studies*, 1 (1): 79–84.

Appadurai, A. (1990), 'Disjuncture and Difference in the Global Cultural Economy', *Theory, Culture & Society*, 7 (2–3): 295–310.

Arora, A. (2021), 'Disney+ Hotstar Unveils 18 New Indian Movies and Series', Gadgets 360, 27 July. Available online: https://gadgets360.com/entertainment/news/hotstar-specials-multiplex-movies-series-18-new-ajay-devgn-jacqueline-fernandez-disney-plus-2495893 (accessed 8 August 2022).

Arora, N. (2016), 'Bollywood is the Final Stop for YouTube Star Bhuvan Bam', *Hindustan Times*, 4 July. Available online: https://www.hindustantimes.com/delhi-news/bollywood-is-the-final-stop-for-youtube-star-bhuvan-bam/story-tfitRMWWxYlusMqlUDFsWK.htmls (accessed 18 March 2022).

Athique, A. (2006), 'Bollywood and "Grocery Store" Video Piracy in Australia', *Media International Australia*, 121: 41–51.

Athique, A. (2005), 'Watching Indian Movies in Australia: Media, Community and Consumption', *South Asian Popular Culture*, 3 (2): 117–33.

Athique, A. (2008), 'The Global Dynamics of Indian Media Piracy: Export Markets, Playback Media and the Informal Economy', *Media, Culture and Society*, 30 (5): 699–717.

Athique, A. (2009), 'From Monopoly to Polyphony: India in the Era of Television', in G. Turner and J. Tay (eds), *Television Studies after TV*, 169–77, London: Routledge.

Athique, A. (2012), *Indian Media*, London: Polity.

Athique, A. (2014), 'Transnational Audiences: Geocultural Approaches', *Continuum*, 28 (1): 4–17.

Athique, A. (2019), 'Digital Emporiums: Platform Capitalism in India', *Media Industries Journal*, 6 (2). Available online: https://quod.lib.umich.edu/m/mij/15031809.0006.205?view=text;rgn=main (21 March 2022).

Athique, A. (2020), 'Integrated Commodities in the Digital Economy', *Media, Culture and Society*, 42 (4): 554–70.

Athique, A. and V. Parthasarathi (2020), 'Platform Economy and Platformization', in A. Athique and V. Parthasarathi (eds), *Platform Capitalism in India*, 1–19, Cham: Palgrave Macmillan.

Athique, A., V. Parthasarathi and S. V. Srinivas, eds (2017), *The Indian Media Economy, Vol. I: Industrial Dynamics and Cultural Adaptation* and *Vol. II: Market Dynamics and Social Transactions*, New Delhi: Oxford University Press.

Baddhan, R. (2018), 'ZEE5 Announces Launch of Eight Tamil Originals', *BizAsia*. Available online: https://www.bizasialive.com/zee5-announces-launch-of-eight-tamil-originals (accessed 2 April 2020).

Ball, M. (2022), 'What the Metaverse Will Mean', *The Wall Street Journal*, 11 August. Available online: https://www.wsj.com/articles/what-the-metaverse-will-mean-11660233462 (accessed 13 August 2022).

Baltruschat, D. (2010), *Global Media Ecologies: Networked Production in Film and Television*, vol. 6, New York and London: Routledge.

Bam, B. (2016), 'BB Ki Vines YouTube channel'. Available online: https://www.youtube.com/channel/UCqwUrj10mAEsqezcItqvwEw (accessed 19 October 2019).

Banerjee, Abhishek (2018), Co-founder, Casting Bay, in interview, 22 June, India.

Baym, N. (2015), *Personal Connections in the Digital Age*, 2nd edn, Cambridge: Polity.

BB ki Vines (2018), *Plus Minus / Divya Dutta and Bhuvan Bam / Short Film*, video. Available online: https://www.youtube.com/watch?v=jKyXUJceZ6k (accessed 2 April 2020).

Being Bong (n.d.), Home page, YouTube channel. Available online: https://www.youtube.com/channel/UCeBOZ6kDRQ2yQSB9WP52VLw/about (accessed 27 February 2019).

Bengali, S. (2018), 'Big-Budget TV Meets Bollywood as Amazon and Netflix do Battle in India', *LA Times*, 3 March. Available online: http://www.latimes.com/world/asia/la-fg-india-netflix-amazon-2018-story.html (accessed 3 March 2022).

Bhadani, P. (2015), 'Redefining Online Content', *Indian Express Screen*. Available online: http://epaper.screenindia.com/408116/Screen-/Jan-2-Jan-8#dual/46/1 (accessed 2 April 2020).

Bhartiya Digital Party (n.d.), Home page, YouTube channel. Available online: https://www.youtube.com/channel/UCUw8vQF-X7CJqdVpxBYcavQ (accessed 2 April 2020).

Bhartiya Digital Party (2018), 'Kajol Speaks Marathi on *Casting Couch with Amey and Nipun* – Helicopter Eela'. Available online: https://www.youtube.com/watch?v=gYf9GSGaZe0 (accessed 2 April 2020).

Bhatt, S. (2019a), Homecoming: What's motivating boomerangs to take a chance. Available online: https://economictimes.indiatimes.com/small-biz/startups/features/giving-up-starting-up-whats-motivating-boomerangs-to-take-chance/articleshow/71457298.cms?fbclid=IwAR0G6ZFUxQpsgB-1u7u8QgEotHtqDJF4ObK9rjfQMPcKZuM2RcEjwE_yUsandfrom=mdr (accessed 9 October 2019).

Bhatt, S. (2019b), 'How Aram Nagar in Mumbai became the Silicon Valley of Indian Media and Entertainment Industry', *India Times*, 3 March. Available online: https://economictimes.indiatimes.com/industry/media/entertainment/the-mumbai-neighbourhood-that-has-become-a-creators-paradise/articleshow/68335634.cms?fbclid=IwAR0Mp8Y2-0u_qzpSc2J1w8-XXK5Bz8RGPBY4fSRJPoVue8cvnwhNPq-udV8 (accessed 9 October 2019).

Bhatt, V. (2017), VB on the web, YouTube channel. Available online: https://www.youtube.com/channel/UC9RQ7KVTqWiv9XAy8O5cUIA/videos?view=0andsort=daandflow=grid (accessed 25 March 2019).

Bhatt, V. (2018), Video. Available online: https://www.youtube.com/channel/UC9RQ7KVTqWiv9XAy8O5cUIA (accessed 25 March 2019).

Bhattacharjee, M. (2019), 'Is Digital-Only Release the Way Forward for Small or Medium Budget Films'. Available online: https://www.financialexpress.com/brandwagon/is-digital-only-release-the-way-forward-for-small-or-medium-budget-films/1794727/ (accessed 20 December 2020).

Bhattacharyya, A. (2016), 'Amazon Launches Premium Service Prime in India', *Financial Express*, 27 July. Available online: https://www.financialexpress.com/industry/amazon-launches-premium-service-prime-in-india/330027 (accessed 25 March 2019).

Bhattacharya, A. (2018), 'How a Viral Indian Web Series went from YouTube to Netflix'. Available online: https://qz.com/india/1404182/youtubes-little-things-goes-big-with-netflix/ (accessed 3 March 2019).

Bhushan, N. (2017), 'Amazon Inks Groundbreaking Deal for 14 Indian Stand-Up Comedy Specials', *Hollywood Reporter*, 27 January. Available online: https://www.hollywoodreporter.com/news/amazon-inks-ground-breaking-deal-14-indian-stand-up-comedy-specials-966401 (accessed 25 March 2019).

Bhushan, N. (2019), 'Netflix to Invest $400M in Indian Content over Two Years, CEO Reed Hastings Says', *Hollywood Reporter*, 6 December. Available online: https://www.hollywoodreporter.com/news/netflix-invest-400m-indian-content-says-ceo-reed-hastings-1260159 (accessed 1 April 2020).

Bhushan, N. and G. Szalai (2020), Netflix Expected to Bring Mobile-Only Plan to More Markets, *Hollywood Reporter*, 8 January. Available online: https://www.hollywoodreporter.com/business/business-news/netflix-expected-bring-mobile-plan-more-markets-1259093/ (accessed 5 August 2022).

Bishop, S. (2018), 'Anxiety, Panic and Self-Optimization: Inequalities and the YouTube Algorithm', *Convergence*, 24 (1): 69–84.

Bisht, N. (2018), Associate Director, *The Viral Fever*, in interview, 14 March, India.

Biswas, I. (2018), Creator, in interview, 9 April, India.

'Bollywood Streaming Service Spuul Launches Initial Coin Offering' (2018), Mumbrella Asia. https://www.mumbrella.asia/2018/06/bollywood-streaming-service-spuul-to-raise-funds-through-cryptocurrency (accessed 9 October 2019).

Booth, G. D. (2008), *Behind the Curtain: Making Music in Mumbai's Film Studios*, New York: Oxford University Press.

Boston Consulting Group (BCG) (2021), *Blockbuster Script for the New Decade*, Mumbai, December. Available online: https://web-assets.bcg.com/7b/a8/1eff85904e408c18fb8284a299f9/blockbuster-script-for-the-new-decade.pdf (accessed 2 February 2021).

Bouquillion, P. (2020), 'Industrial and Financial Structures of Over-the-Tops (OTTs) in India', in A. Athique and V. Parthasarathi (eds), *Platform Capitalism in India*, 129–49, Cham: Palgrave Macmillan.

Bourdieu, P. (1985), 'The Forms of Capital', in J. G. Richardson (ed.), *Handbook of Theory and Research for the Sociology of Education*, 241–58, New York: Greenwood.

Boyle, R. (2018), *The Talent Industry: Television, Cultural Intermediaries and New Digital Pathways*, London: Palgrave Macmillan.

Boyle, R. (2019), 'The Television Industry in the Multiplatform Environment', *Media, Culture and Society*, 41 (7): 919–22.

Brickell, K. and A. Datta (2011), 'Translocal Geographies: Spaces, Places, Connections', *Australian Planner*, 50 (2): 178–9.

Burgess, J. (2006), 'Hearing Ordinary Voices: Cultural Studies, Vernacular Creativity and Digital Storytelling', *Continuum*, 20 (2): 201–14.

Burgess, J. and J. Green (2018), *YouTube: Online Video and Participatory Culture*, 3rd edn, Cambridge: Polity Press.

Burgess, J. and J. Green (2013), *YouTube: Online Video and Participatory Culture*, 2nd edn, Cambridge: Polity.

Carey-Simos, G. (2018), 'Facebook Launches Watch, a Platform to Watch Your Favourite Shows'. Available online: https://wersm.com/facebook-watch-tv (accessed 24 March 2020).

Castells, M. and A. Portes (1989), 'World Underneath: The Origins, Dynamics, and Effects of the Informal Economy', in A. Portes, M. Castells and L. A. Benton (eds), *The Informal Economy: Studies in Advanced and Less Developed Countries*, 11–38, at 12, Baltimore, MD, and London: Johns Hopkins University Press.

Chacko, B. (2022), 'Voot Exploring Entry into Short-Form Video Content Space', afaqs!, 8 August. Available online: https://www.afaqs.com/news/media/voot-forays-into-short-form-videos-with-shots (accessed 8 August 2022).

Chakraborty, I. (2018), Chief executive officer, Big Synergy Productions, in interview, 22 March, India.

Chakraborty, S. (2018), 'My Parents Don't Really Understand What I Do, Says Web Sensation Kiran Dutta', *Times of India*, 31 January. Available online: https://timesofindia.indiatimes.com/city/kolkata/my-parents-dont-really-understand-what-i-do-says-web-sensation-kiran-dutta-/articleshow/62721848.cms (accessed March 2019).

Chatterjee, P. (1975), 'Bengal: Rise and Growth of a Nationality', *Social Scientist*, 4 (1): 67–82.

Chatterjee, S. (2019), Self-Regulatory Online Content Code May Not Serve Interests of Indian Consumers, Creators', *Technology News*. Available online: https://www.firstpost.com/tech/news-analysis/self-regulatory-online-content-code-may-not-serve-interests-of-indian-consumers-creators-5991191.html (accessed 9 October 2019).

Chaturvedi, A. (2018), 'YouTube Will Speak in Your Language More'. https://economictimes.indiatimes.com/industry/media/entertainment/youtube-will-speak-in-your-language-more/articleshow/66079094.cms (accessed 9 October 2019).

Chauhan, K. (2017), 'Regional OTT Content more than Just Catch-Up TV'. http://www.indiantelevision.com/iworld/over-the-top-services/regional-ott-content-more-than-just-catch-up-tv-171122 (accessed 9 October 2019).

Chauhan, K. (2018), '2017: The Year OTTs went Regional in India'. https://www.indiantelevision.com/specials/year-enders/2017-the-year-otts-went-regional-in-india-180104 (accessed 9 October 2019).

Chitrapu, S. (2017), 'Associations and Networks: Inequalities in Film and TV Production', in A. Athique, V. Parthasarathi and S. V. Srinivas (eds), *The Indian Media Economy, Vol. 2: Market Dynamics and Social Transactions*, 152–70. New Delhi: Oxford University Press.

Chopra, V. (2018), Writer/actor, in interview, 12 March, India.

Choudhary, V. (2017a), 'Kwan Entertainment, Dream Theatre form JV Mojostar to Create New Brands', Livemint, 25 August. Available online: https://www.livemint.com/Industry/DugEJ9HQ2iZAePzPpdeRxH/Kwan-Entertainment-Dream-Theatre-form-joint-venture-Mojosta.html (accessed 9 October 2019).

Choudhary, V. (2017b), 'RIL Buys 25% Stake in Balaji Telefilms for Rs413 Crore'. Available online: https://www.livemint.com/Companies/bKu1z9YYSqfVqo8HT4N1xM/RIL-buys-25-stake-in-Balaji-Telefilms-for-Rs413-crore.html (9 October 2019).

Choudhary, V. (2018), 'Jokes Apart, Stand-Up Comedy is Serious Business in Small Towns'. Available online: https://www.livemint.com/Consumer/ngeEKRoLkCXMg1SGjsfGjN/Jokes-apart-standup-comedy-is-serious-business-in-small-to.html (accessed 1 April 2020).

Chowdhury, D. (2018), Co-founder, Friday Night Originals, in interview, 10 April, India.

Cohen, D. (2018), 'Facebook is Making Some Changes to Its Branded Content Tag', *Adweek*. Available online: https://www.adweek.com/programmatic/facebook-is-making-some-changes-to-its-branded-content-tag (accessed 1 April 2020).

'Comicstaan Emerges as the Most Watched Show on Amazon Prime Video in Its First Week' (2018), Available online: https://www.dnaindia.com/entertainment/report-comicstaan-emerges-as-the-most-watched-show-on-amazon-prime-video-in-its-first-week-2639724 (accessed 1 April 2020).

'Complaint Against Netflix for "Defaming" India, Hurting Hindu Sentiments' (2019), Available online: https://thewire.in/politics/shiv-sena-netflix-complaint (accessed 9 October 2019).

Corbin, J. M. and A. Strauss (2008), 'Elaborating the Analysis', *Basics of Qualitative Research: Techniques and Procedures for Developing Grounded Theory*, 195–228, Thousand Oaks, CA, and London: Sage.

Corrigan, T. (2015), 'Media and Cultural Industries Internships: A Thematic Review and Digital Labor Parallels', *tripleC: Communication, Capitalism and Critique. Open Access Journal for a Global Sustainable Information Society*, 13 (2): 336–50.

'Creativity: It's Kolkata's Business Buzz' (2019), *Kolkata News – Times of India*. Available online: https://timesofindia.indiatimes.com/city/kolkata/creativity-its-kolkatas-business-buzz/articleshow/70969190.cms (accessed 9 October 2019).

'Culture Machine's "Put Chutney" to Air on Star Vijay Every Sun' (2017). Available online: http://www.indiantelevision.com/iworld/video-on-demand/culture-machines-put-chutney-to-air-on-star-vijay-every-sun-170609 (accessed 1 April 2020).

Cunningham, S. (2015), 'The New Screen Ecology: A New Wave of Media Globalisation?', *Communication Research and Practice*, 1 (3): 275–82.

Cunningham, S. and D. Craig (2017), 'Being "Really Real" on YouTube: Authenticity, Community and Brand Culture in Social Media Entertainment', *Media International Australia*, 164 (1): 71–81.

Cunningham, S. and D. Craig (2019), *Social Media Entertainment: The New Intersection of Hollywood and Silicon Valley*, New York: New York University Press.

Cunningham, S., D. Craig and J. Silver (2016), 'YouTube, Multichannel Networks and the Accelerated Evolution of the New Screen Ecology', *Convergence*, 22 (4): 376–91.

'Curated by Arré, Tathaastu Claims to Make Your Wishes Come True' (2019), *Exchange4media*. Available online: https://www.exchange4media.com/marketing-news/curated-by-Arré-tathaastu-claims-to-make-your-wishes-come-true-94775.html (accessed 1 April 2020).

Curtin, M. and K. Sanson (2016), *Precarious Creativity: Global Media, Local Labor*, Oakland, CA: University of California Press.

Curtin, M. and K. Sanson (2017), *Voices of Labor: Creativity, Craft, and Conflict in Global Hollywood*, Oakland, CA: University of California Press.

D'Souza, T. (2018), Head, TVF Girliyapa, in interview, 3 April, India.

Das, J. (2018), Director/scriptwriter/creative head, Big Synergy Productions, in interview, 15 March, India.

Dasgupta, A. (2017), Stand-up comedian/writer, in interview, 28 October, India.

Dasgupta, P. (2017), 'How Indian TV Universe Expanded', *Economic Times*. Available online: https://economictimes.indiatimes.com/blogs/et-commentary/how-indian-tv-universe-expanded (accessed 1 April 2020).

Dave, D. (2018), Co-founder, Tulsea, in interview, 26 March, India.

de Certeau, M. (1984), *The Practice of Everyday Life*, Berkeley, CA: University of California Press.

Deb, A. (2018), Creative director, in interview, 13 March, India.

Deep, A. (2020), 'A Complete Guide to Streaming Services Content Regulation in India', *MediaNama*, 29 July. Available online: https://www.medianama.com/2020/07/223-ott-content-regulation-reading-list/ (accessed 3 July 2021).

Delmestri, G., F. Montanari and A. Usai (2005), 'Reputation and Strength of Ties in Predicting Commercial Success and Artistic Merit of Independents in the Italian Feature Film Industry', *Journal of Management Studies*, 42 (5): 975–1002.

Deloitte (2020), 'Economic Impact of the Film, Television, and Online Video Services Industry in India'. Available online: https://www2.deloitte.com/content/dam/Deloitte/in/Documents/about-deloitte/in-about-deloitte-economic-impact-of-the-film-television-and-osv-industry-noexp.pdf (accessed 1 April 2020).

Devasundaram, A. I. (2016), 'Bollywood's Soft Power: Branding the Nation, Sustaining a Meta-Hegemony', *New Cinemas: Journal of Contemporary Film*, 14 (1): 51–70.

Dijck, J. van (2013), *The Culture of Connectivity: A Critical History of Social Media*, New York: Oxford University Press.

DNA (2018), 'Comicstaan Emerges as the Most Watched Show on Amazon Prime Video in Its First Week'. Available online: https://www.dnaindia.com/entertainment/report-comicstaan-emerges-as-the-most-watched-show-on-amazon-prime-video-in-its-first-week-2639724 (accessed 28 July 2019).

Doyle, G. (2016), 'Digitization and Changing Windowing Strategies in the Television Industry: Negotiating New Windows on the World', *Television and New Media*, 17 (7): 629–45.

Dua, A. (2018), 'Reliance Jio Could Soon Implement Freemium Model for JioTV, JioCinema and JioMusic Apps', *MySmartPrice*. Available online: https://www.mysmartprice.com/gear/reliance-jio-soon-implement-freemium-model-jiotv-jiocinema-jiomusic-apps (accessed 1 April 2020).

Duffy, B. and E. Hund (2015), '"Having It All" on Social Media: Entrepreneurial Femininity and Self-Branding among Fashion Bloggers', *Social Media + Society*, 1 (2). Doi: 10.1177/2056305115604337.

Dugal, R. (2018), Actress, in interview, 26 June, India.

Dutta, K. (2018), Creator, in interview, 12 April, India.

Dwibhashyam, G. (2018), Content head, Spuul portal, in interview, 31 May, India.

Dwivedi, A. B. (2013), 'Arunabh Kumar – The Man Behind Qtiyapa', YourStory. Available online: https://yourstory.com/2013/10/arunabh-kumar-qtiyapa (accessed 1 April 2020).

Dyondi, R. and S. K. Jha (2015), 'Strategic Risk Issues for FilmDdistributors of Hindi Film Industry in Mumbai: A Grounded Theory Approach', *International Journal of Social, Behavioral, Educational, Economic, Business and Industrial Engineering*, 9 (6): 2076–82.

EA (2012), 'Zee launches Ditto TV'. Available online: http://magnetfish.com/zee-launches-ditto-tv-1 (accessed 24 March 2020).

'Eight Women amongst Top 10 Creators on ShareChat: UGC Trends Report – ET BrandEquity (2020), *Economic Times*. https://brandequity.economictimes.indiatimes.com/news/marketing/eight-women-amongst-top-10-creators-on-sharechat-ugc-trends-report/79854091 (accessed 20 January 2021).

'Ekta Kapoor on ALTBalaji: "Our Target Group is the Big World between Narcos and Naagin"' (2017), 'Entertainment', *Firstpost*. Available online: https://www.firstpost.com/entertainment/ekta-kapoor-on-altbalaji-our-target-group-is-the-big-world-between-narcos-and-naagin-3383816.html (accessed 24 March 2020).

'Entertainment Education Report: The Best Film Schools In 2018' (2018), *Variety*, 25 April. Available online: http.variety.com/2018/film/spotlight/entertainment-education-film-school-stars-1202785789/ (accessed 7 October 2019).

'Entertainment Industry Will Promote Economy, Create Jobs: Suresh Prabhu' (2018), *Economic Times*. Available online: https://economictimes.indiatimes.com/industry/media/entertainment/entertainment-ind-will-promote-economy-create-jobs-suresh-prabhu/articleshow/63203472.cms

'Facebook Launches Creator App for Video Developers, to Rival YouTube's Channel Services' (2017), *Indian Express*. Available online: https://indianexpress.com/article/technology/social/facebook-launches-creator-app-for-video-developers-to-rival-youtubes-channel-services-4941617 (accessed 1 April 2020).

'Facebook Makes Ad Breaks Available for Video Creators in India' (2018), *Hindustan Times*. https://www.hindustantimes.com/tech/facebook-makes-ad-breaks-available-for-video-creators-in-india/story-rIAArazWzzKiK9kikl72QJ.html (accessed 1 April 2020).

'Facebook Watch Now Available on Desktop, Four Originals Renewed for 2nd Season' (2018), *Indian Express*. Available online: https://indianexpress.com/article/technology/social/facebook-watch-now-available-on-desktop-four-originals-renewed-for-2nd-season-5493635 (accessed 24 March 2020).

Fannin, R. (2019), 'The Strategy Behind TikTok's Global Rise'. Available online: https://hbr.org/2019/09/the-strategy-behind-tiktoks-global-rise (accessed 9 October 2019).

Farooqui, M. (2018), 'Why Regional Content is Gaining Steam on Online Video Platforms'. Available online: https://www.moneycontrol.com/news/entertainment-2/why-regional-content-is-gaining-steam-on-online-video-platforms-3071461.html (accessed 9 October 2019).

Farooqui, M. (2022), 'IPL Rights Auction: Disney Settles for Legacy Media; Hotstar May Lose out', *Moneycontrol*, 14 June. Available online: https://www.moneycontrol.com/news/trends/sports-trends/ipl-rights-auction-disney-settles-for-legacy-media-hotstar-may-lose-out-8686691.html (accessed 5 August 2022).

Fazal, S. (2009), 'Emancipation or Anchored Individualism? Women and TV Soaps in India', in K. Moti Gokulsing and W. Dissanayake (eds), *Popular Culture in a Globalised India*, 61–72, London: Routledge.

FICCI-EY (2018), *Re-imagining India's M&E Sector*, New Delhi: FICCI – Federation of Indian Chambers of Commerce & Industry.

FICCI-EY (2019), 'A Billion Screens of Opportunity', *India's Media and Entertainment Sector*, 31 March. Available online: https://assets.ey.com/content/dam/ey-sites/ey-com/en_gl/topics/tmt/ey-how-a-billion-screens-can-turn-india-into-a-m-and-e-powerhouse.pdf?download (accessed 27 February 2020).

FICCI-EY (2022), *Tuning into Customer*, India, March. Available online: https://assets.ey.com/content/dam/ey-sites/ey-com/en_in/topics/media-and-entertainment/2022/ey-ficci-m-and-e-report-tuning-into-consumer_v3.pdf (accessed August 2022).

'First Ever YouTube Pop-Up Space Delhi Opens Its Doors at Kingdom of Dreams and We're also Bringing the YouTube NextUp Camp to Delhi!' (2018), Blog. Available online: https://india.googleblog.com/2018/10/first-ever-youtube-pop-up-space-delhi.html (2 July 2020).

Fitzgerald, S. (2019), 'Over-the-Top Video Services in India: Media Imperialism after Globalization', *Media Industries Journal*, 6 (1): 89–115.

Fitzgerald, T. (2022), 'Will People Flock to Netflix's New Ad-Supported Service? Experts Weigh In', *Forbes*, 14 October. Available online: https://www.forbes.com/sites/tonifitzgerald/2022/10/14/will-people-flock-to-netflixs-new-ad-supported-service-experts-weigh-in/?sh=3c8aff367aa3 (accessed 28 October 2022).

Fleming, D. (2016), 'How Arunabh Kumar Made TVF a Bigger Cult than MTV and Even Beat Netflix to the Online Television Race'. http://www.mensxp.com/culture/people/31886-how-arunabh-kumar-made-tvf-a-bigger-cult-than-mtv-and-even-beat-netflix-to-the-online-television-race.html (accessed 1 October 2019).

Frater, P. (2020), 'Hooq May Have Fallen but a Business Case for Southeast Asian Streamers Endures', *Variety*, 1 April. Available online: https://variety.com/2020/biz/asia/hooq-collapse-singtel-southeast-asia-streaming-1203550122/ (accessed 1 August 2021).

Frater, P. and N. Ramachandran (2021), 'Sony Pictures Networks and Zee Sign Definitive Agreement towards Creating Indian Broadcast Giant', *Variety*, 22 December. https://variety.com/2021/global/news/sony-pictures-networks-zee-merger-complete-1235140626/ (accessed 8 August 2022).

Fuchs, C. (2015), 'The Digital Labour Theory of Value and Karl Marx in the Age of Facebook, YouTube, Twitter, and Weibo', in E. Fisher and C. Fuchs (eds), *Reconsidering Value and Labour in the Digital Age*, 26–41, London: Palgrave Macmillan.

Gadgets Now Bureau (2015), 'AIB, TVF First Indian YouTube Channels to Hit 1 Million Followers', *Gadget Now*. Available online: https://www.gadgetsnow.com/social/AIB-TVF-first-Indian-YouTube-channels-to-hit-1-million-followers/articleshow/46632767.cms (accessed 23 April 2019).

Gandhi, G. (2018), Chief operating officer, Voot portal, in interview, 16 March, India.

Gandini, A. (2016), 'Digital Work: Self-Branding and Social Capital in the Freelance Knowledge Economy', *Marketing Theory*, 16 (1): 123–41.

Ganguly, S. (2018a), 'Facebook Announces Video Monetisation for Indian Users'. https://inc42.com/buzz/facebook-announces-video-monetisation-for-indian-users (accessed 23 April 2019).

Ganguly, S. (2018b), 'YouTube Bullish on Growing Business via Vernacular Content in India'. https://inc42.com/buzz/youtube-bullish-on-growing-business-via-vernacular-content-in-india/ (accessed 23 April 2019).

Ganti, T. (2012), *Producing Bollywood: Inside the Contemporary Hindi Film Industry*, Durham, NC: Duke University Press.

Ganti, T. (2013), *Bollywood: A Guidebook to Popular Hindi Cinema*, London: Routledge.

Ghose, A. (2018), 'Bhuvan Bam: The New Face of Indian Comedy', *Man's World India*. Available online: https://www.mansworldindia.com/currentedition/covers/bhuvan-bam-new-face-indian-comedy (accessed 19 October 2019).

Ghose, P. (2018), Creator, in interview, 11 April, India.

Ghose, P. (2019), *When Bengalis Speak Hindi*, video. https://www.facebook.com/watch/?v=373619410189832 (accessed 1 April 2020).

Gill, R. (2002), 'Cool, Creative and Egalitarian? Exploring Gender in Project-Based New Media Work in Euro', *Information, Communication and Society*, 5 (1): 70–89.

Goggin, G. and M. McLelland, eds (2010), *Internationalizing Internet Studies: Beyond Anglophone Paradigms*, London: Routledge.

Google (n.d.), 'Multi-Channel Network (MCN) Overview for YouTube Creators – YouTube Help'. Available online: https://support.google.com/youtube/answer/2737059?hl¼en (accessed 28 July 2019).

Gopal, R. (2018), Business development associate, Tulsea, in interview, 10 September, India.

Govil, N. (2007), 'Bollywood and the Frictions of Global Mobility', in D. K. Thussu (ed.), *Media on the Move: Global Flow and Contra-Flow*, 84–98.

Govil, N. (2013), 'Recognizing "Industry"', *Cinema Journal*, 52 (3): 172–6.

Govil, N. (2016), 'Envisioning the Future: Financialization and the Indian Entertainment Industry Reports', *South Asian Popular Culture*, 14 (3): 219–34.

Guha, P. (2021), *Hear #MeToo in India: News, Social Media, and Anti-Rape and Sexual Harassment Activism*, New Brunswick, NJ: Rutgers University Press.

Gulati, S. (2016), 'How to Write a *Saas-Bahu* Saga'. Available online: https://caravanmagazine.in/reportage/lather-rinse-repeat-saas-bahu-saga?fbclid=IwAR2iscw7XTD2sctcpKAZR6hGKayHkfuJR-mPXM2F4jMYuce40kOr7CyAi9g (accessed 31 March 2020).

Gupta, A. (2018), Director/writer/creative head, TVF Screenpatti, in interview, 2 April, India.

Gupta, N. (2018), In-person interview, 27 March.

Hallinan, B. and T. Striphas (2016), 'Recommended for You: The Netflix Prize and the Production of Algorithmic Culture', *New Media and Society*, 18 (1): 117–37.

Hardy, K. C. (2010), 'Mediating Bhojpuriya: Migration, Circulation, and Bhojpuri Cinema', *South Asian Popular Culture*, 8 (3): 231–44.

Hardy, K. C. (2015), 'Constituting a Diffuse Region: Cartographies of Mass-Mediated Bhojpuri Belonging', *BioScope: South Asian Screen Studies*, 6 (2): 145–64.

Havens, T. (2008), *The Evolution of Industry Lore in African American Television Trade*, Montreal: International Communication Association.

Havens, T. and A. Lotz (2017), *Understanding Media Industries*, Oxford: Oxford University Press.

Havens, T., A. D. Lotz and S. Tinic (2009), 'Critical Media Industry Studies: A Research Approach', *Communication, Culture and Critique*, 2 (2): 234–53.

'Helo Launches 3rd Season of *Helo Superstar* Campaign' (2019). Available online: http://www.businessworld.in/article/Helo-Launches-3rd-Season-Of-Helo-Superstar-Campaign/16-09-2019-176183 (accessed 9 October 2019).

Herbert, D., A. D. Lotz and A. Punathambekar (2020), *Media Industry Studies: A Short Introduction*, Cambridge: Polity Press.

Herman, E. and R. McChesney (2003), 'The Rise of the Global Media', in L. Parks and S. Kumar (eds), *Planet TV: A Global Television Reader*, 21–39, New York: New York University Press.

Hobson, D. (2003), 'Housewives and the Mass Media', in S. Hall, D. Hobson, A. Lowe and P. Willis (eds), *Culture, Media, Language*, 103–12, London: Routledge.

'Hoichoi Announces 100 Hours of Original Content' (2018), *Exchange4media*. Available online: https://www.exchange4media.com/digital-news/hoichoi-announces-100-hours-of-original-content--92149.html (accessed 1 May 2020).

'Hoichoi: In Expansion Mode' (2018), *Financial Express*. Available online: https://www.financialexpress.com/industry/technology/hoichoi-in-expansion-mode/1349086 (accessed 24 March 2020).

Holt, J. and K. Sanson, eds (2013), *Connected Viewing: Selling, Streaming, and Sharing Media in the Digital Age*, New York and London: Routledge.

'I Have Never Evaluated Myself as a Female Comedian: Mallika Dua' (2018), *Times Now News*. Available online: https://www.timesnownews.com/entertainment/news/

bollywood-news/article/i-have-never-evaluated-myself-as-a-female-comedian-mallika-dua/291845 (accessed 7 October 2019).
'India a Bigger Market for Paywalled Content than China: Netflix CEO Reed Hastings' (2018), *Economic Times*. Available online: https://economictimes.indiatimes.com/small-biz/startups/newsbuzz/india-a-bigger-market-for-paid-content-than-china-netflix-ceo-reed-hastings/articleshow/63044139.cms (accessed 1 April 2020).
'India Has Been on Radar for Everyone at YouTube for Past Two Years: Marc Lefkowitz' (2018), *New Indian Express*. Available online: http://www.newindianexpress.com/nation/2018/oct/23/india-has-been-on-radar-for-everyone-at-youtube-for-past-two-years-marc-lefkowitz-1889042.html (accessed 1 April 2020).
'India has Over 120 Women YouTubers with more than 1 Million Subscribers' (2020). Available online: https://yourstory.com/herstory/2019/09/india-women-youtube-million-subscribers (accessed 31 March 2020).
Ingle, H. (2017), 'Marathi Cinema: Notes towards a Liminal History', *Asian Cinema*, 28 (2): 199–218.
'Introducing the Class of 2018 for YouTube NextUp Delhi!' (2018), Blog. Available online: https://india.googleblog.com/2018/09/introducing-class-of-2018-for-youtube.html (accessed 1 April 2020).
Iyengar, R. (2018), 'Disney's Next 700 Million Viewers Might be in India'. Available online: https://money.cnn.com/2018/07/09/media/disney-fox-deal-star-india/index.html (accessed 1 April 2020).
Jadhav, R. (2017), Creator, in interview, 29 November, India.
Jaggi, R. (2011), 'The Great Indian Television Soap Opera: Issues of Identity and Socio-Cultural Dynamics', *Media Asia*, 38 (3): 140–5.
Jain, S. (2018), Founder/producer, The Story Ink, in interview, 31 March, India.
Jain, R. and S. Pareek (2018), 'Gendered Portrayals of Domestic Work in Indian Television', *Journal of International Women's Studies*, 19 (6): 106–17.
Jalan, T. (2018), 'YouTube to Take Originals Out of Paywall in 2019'. Available online: https://www.medianama.com/2018/11/223-youtube-originals-no-pawall-2019 (accessed 24 March 2020).
Jassal, K. (2018), Creator, in interview, 11 April, India.
Jayachandran, S. (2015), 'The Roots of Gender Inequality in Developing Countries', *Economics*, 7 (1): 63–88.
Jeffrey, R. and A. Doron (2013), *Great Indian Phone Book*, New York: C. Hurst and Co.
Jenkins, H. (2008), *Convergence Culture: Where Old and New Media Collide*, New York: New York University Press.
Jensen, R. (2012), 'Do Labor Market Opportunities Affect Young Women's Work and Family Decisions? Experimental Evidence from India', *Quarterly Journal of Economics*, 127 (2): 753–92.
Jesrani, B. (2018), 'Abhishek Banerjee and Anmol Ahuja, Co-founders, Casting Bay', http://mumbainewsnetwork.blogspot.com/2018/03/abhishek-banerjee-anmol-ahuja-co.html (accessed 24 March 2020).
Jha, L. (2018), 'Indian Families Sill Watch TV Together: BARC'. Available online: https://www.livemint.com/Consumer/2x8i6gMoNbrHU1uZcx10VO/Indian-families-still-watch-TV-together-BARC.html (accessed 4 February 2021).
Jha, L. (2019a), 'Content Investment across TV, Film, Online Video in India at $3.6 Bn in 2018'. Available online: https://www.livemint.com/technology/tech-news/online-video-content-investment-in-india-now-at-3-6-billion-report-1563969692466.html (accessed 12 August 2019).

Jha, L. (2019b), 'ZEE5 Goes Global, Launches in 190 Countries'. https://www.livemint.com/Companies/WgtidIx9OztvNt0tMUgLwL/ZEE5-goes-global-launches-in-190-countries.html (accessed 24 March 2020).

Jha, L. (2022a), '41% Consumers in India Okay to Share Ott Account Details: YouGov', *mint*, 12 May. https://www.livemint.com/industry/media/41-consumers-in-india-okay-to-share-ott-account-details-yougov-11652340891337.html (accessed 5 August 2022).

Jha, L. (2022b), 'Disney+ Hotstar to Stream New Original "Ghar Waapsi" on 22 July'. *mint*. https://www.livemint.com/industry/media/disney-hotstar-to-stream-new-original-ghar-waapsi-on-22-july-11658380469291.html (accessed 8 August 2022).

Jha, L. and S. Gupta (2017), 'Balaji Launches Online Streaming' Platform ALTBalaji'. Available online: https://www.livemint.com/Consumer/TZKZSgraxfEBbjY7TyNqeN/Balaji-launches-online-streaming-platform-ALTBalaji.html (accessed 24 March 2020).

Joshi, R. (2018), Writer/All India Bakchod co-founder, in interview, 30 March, India.

K, Balakumar (2021a), 'India has 353 Million OTT Users and 96 Million Active Paid Subscriptions'. Available online: https://www.techradar.com/in/news/india-has-353-million-ott-users-and-96-million-active-paid-subscriptions (accessed 6 September 2021).

K, Balakumar (2021b), 'What's Netflix's Strategy in India? Even its CEO is not Sure'. Available online: https://www.techradar.com/in/news/whats-netflixs-strategy-in-india-even-its-ceo-is-not-sure (accessed 2 September 2021).

Kadam, A. (2018), Senior supervising producer, Voot, in interview, 30 January, India.

Kanchwala, M. (2018), 'AIB and Feminism: Sumedh Natu and Aayushi Jagad Make One of the Best Articulated Videos Ever'. Available online: https://www.social-samosa.com/socialketchup/sumedh-natu-aayushi-jagad-criticize-aib-response (accessed 24 March 2020).

Kanga, S., B. Kappal and A. Das Sharma (2018), 'How Only Much Louder Failed the Women in its Ranks', *The Caravan*. Available online: https://caravanmagazine.in/gender/how-oml-failed-women-ranks?fbclid=IwAR1Eszj4M-TGyB5Mr-tk_lil9G9NTZTm9NFQHWiceyAysVyJA015l8Vm_MI (accessed 9 October 2019).

Kar, A. (2022), 'Indian Women Shunning Facebook Due to Safety, Privacy Concerns: Study', *The Hindu BusinessLine*. Available online: https://www.thehindubusinessline.com/info-tech/indian-women-ditching-facebook-due-to-safety-privacy-concerns-study/article65666502.ece (accessed 13 August 2022).

Kar, S. (2018), Creator, in interview, 9 April, India.

Kar, S. (2019), 'Brands Follow Their New-Age Audience to TikTok Videos', *Economic Times*. Available online: https://economictimes.indiatimes.com/industry/services/advertising/brands-follow-their-new-age-audience-to-tiktok-videos/articleshow/71269148.cms (accessed 9 October 2019).

Kashyaap, S. (2019), 'Who Owns the Video You Upload on TikTok or ShareChat?' Available online: https://yourstory.com/2019/09/tiktok-sharechat-content-ownership-conflict?fbclid=IwAR1ZpA1BwaV7Y5WcS5uEz6_epi-xdyWmWHyAP-ULzLDKZl85eqXBqyCw8xg (accessed 9 October 2019).

Kasturia, N. (2018), Writer/actor, in interview, 24 March, India.

Kathuria, R., M. Kedia and R. Sekhani (2019), *An Analysis of Competition and Regulatory Intervention in India's Television Distribution and Broadcasting Services*, New Delhi: Indian Council for Research on International Economic Relations. Available online: https://think-asia.org/bitstream/handle/11540/9810/An_Analysis_of_Competition_and_Regulatory_Interventions.pdf?sequence=1ss (accessed 24 March 2020).

Kawoosa, V. (2018), 'How Languages Intersect in India', *Hindustan Times*. Available online: https://www.hindustantimes.com/india-news/how-languagesintersect-in-india/story-g3nzNwFppYV7XvCumRzlYL.html (accessed 24 March 2020).

Kay, K. (2018), *New Indian Nuttahs*, Cham: Springer.

Keen, A. (2007), *The Cult of the Amateur: How Blogs, MySpace, YouTube and the Rest of Today's User-Generated Media are Destroying Our Economy, Our Culture, and Our Values*, New York: Doubleday.

Khaas Re TV (n.d.), Home page, YouTube channel. Available online: https://www.youtube.com/channel/UCKgr6HfwNolb_8t6t8aEuog (accessed 24 March 2020).

Khaas Re TV (2018), Euuuuuu +ve | Awareness Video | Khaas Re TV. https://www.youtube.com/watch?v=GHzaoYf8eXA (accessed 24 March 2020).

Khan (2011), Home page, YouTube channel. Available online: https://www.youtube.com/user/zakirkhan208/about (accessed 24 March 2020).

Khanna, K. (n.d.), Tape A Tale, Facebook page. Available online: https://www.facebook.com/TapeAtale (24 March 2020).

Khanna, K. (2017), Home page, YouTube channel. Available online: https://www.youtube.com/channel/UCWMGibmCqz-J7U_08ziHzdg/videos (accessed 24 March 2020).

Khanna, K. (2018), Co-founder, Tape A Tale, in interview, 19 March, India.

Khatri, A. (2017), Stand-up comedian, in interview, 23 May, India.

Khatri, B. (2018), 'YouTube Ready to Wage War against Netflix, Amazon, Hotstar with Originals, Premium Service'. Available online: https://inc42.com/buzz/youtube-ready-to-wage-war-against-netflix-amazon-hotstar-with-originals-premium-service (accessed 24 March 2020).

Khatri, B. (2019a), ''Flipkart Launches Videos and Instagram-Like Ideas Feed for Influencers'. Available online: https://inc42.com/buzz/flipkart-videos-launched-along-with-instagram-like-ideas-feed-for-influencers (accessed 24 March 2020).

Khatri, B. (2019b), 'Paytm is Now Betting on Content and Short Videos to Reach 250 Mn Users'. Available online: https://inc42.com/buzz/paytm-is-betting-on-content-and-short-videos-to-reach-250-mn-users (accessed 9 October 2019).

Khdair, D. (2013), 'Piecing Together the Puzzle: Kahaani, Talaash and the Complex Narrative in Popular Hindi Cinema', *Studies in South Asian Film and Media*, 5 (2): 179–94.

Kim, D. (2018), 'Is Facebook Watch a Serious Streaming Platform? These 6 Shows Say Yes', *New York Times*, 6 September. https://www.nytimes.com/2018/09/06/watching/is-facebook-watch-a-serious-streaming-platform-these-6-shows-say-yes.html (accessed 24 March 2020).

Kim, J. (2012), 'The Institutionalization of YouTube: From User-Generated Content to Professionally Generated Content', *Media, Culture & Society*, 34 (1): 53–67.

Klasen, S. and J. Pieters (2015), 'What Explains the Stagnation of Female Labor Force Participation in Urban India', *World Bank Economic Review*, 29 (3): 449–78.

Kohli-Khandekar, V. (2010), *The Indian Media Business*, New Delhi: Sage Publications India.

Kohli-Khandekar, V. (2018), 'How Talent Management Firms Make Stars', *Rediff News*, 17 October. Available online: https://www.rediff.com/movies/special/how-talent-management-firms-make-stars/20181017.htm (accessed 4 June 2020).

Kohli-Khandekar, V. (2022), 'The Future of Television', *Business Standard*, 14 July. Available online: https://www.business-standard.com/article/opinion/the-future-of-television-122071401490_1.html (accessed 4 August 2022).

KPMG (2018), 'Media Eco-Systems: The Walls Fall Down', Mumbai. Available online: https://assets.kpmg.com/content/dam/kpmg/in/pdf/2018/09/

StandaloneExecSummary.pdf-KPMG INDIA (accessed November 2019 and 7 December 2020).

KPMG (2019), 'India's Digital Future, Mass of Niches', KPMG in India's Media and Entertainment Report 2019. Available online: https://assets.kpmg/content/dam/kpmg/in/pdf/2019/08/india-media-entertainment-report-2019.pdf (accessed 21 September 2020).

KPMG (2020), *A Year Off-Script*, Mumbai: KPMG. Available online: https://home.kpmg/in/en/home/insights/2020/09/media-and-entertainment-report-kpmg-india-2020-year-off-script.html (accessed 21 December 2020).

Kripal, A. (2018), Creative producer, Qyuki, in interview, 10 January, India.

Krishna, N. (2018), 'YouTube Channels in Regional Languages are Growing and How', *The Hindu*. Available online:: https://www.thehindu.com/society/youtube-channels-in-regional-languages-are-growing-and-how/article25335529.ece (accessed 8 April 2019).

Kuipers, G. (2013), 'Ethnographic Research and Cultural Intermediaries', in J. Smith Maguire and J. Mathews (eds), *The Cultural Intermediaries Reader*, 52–63, Los Angeles, CA, and London: Sage.

Kumar, A. (2013), 'Provincialising Bollywood? Cultural Economy of North-Indian Small-Town Nostalgia in the Indian Multiplex', *South Asian Popular Culture*, 11 (1): 61–74.

Kumar, A. (2014), 'The Aesthetics of Pirate Modernities: Bhojpuri Cinema and the Underclasses', in R. Kaur and P. Dave-Mukherji (eds), *Arts and Aesthetics in a Globalizing World*, 185–203, London and New York: Routledge.

Kumar, A. (2019a), 'Informality in the Time of Platformization', *Media Industries Journal*, 6 (2). Doi: 10.3998/mij.15031809.0006.207.

Kumar, A. (2019b), 'Insurrectionary Tendencies', in A. Athique and E. Baulch (eds), *Digital Transactions in Asia: Economic, Informational, and Social Exchanges*, 242–59, New York and London: Routledge.

Kumar, M. and A. Punathambekar (2019), 'Beyond the Nation: Cultural Regions in South Asia's Online Video Communities', in S. Cunningham and D. Craig (eds), *Creator Culture*, 236–62, New York: New York University Press.

Kumar, S. (2010), *Gandhi Meets Primetime: Globalization and Nationalism in Indian Television*, Urbana, IL: University of Illinois Press.

Kumar, S. (2014), 'Media Industries in India: An Emerging Regional Framework', *Media Industries Journal*, 1 (2). Available online: https://quod.lib.umich.edu/m/mij/15031809.0001.205?view=text;rgn=main (accessed 1 June 2020).

Kumar, S. (2015), 'Contagious Memes, Viral Videos and Subversive Parody: The Grammar of Contention on the Indian Web', *International Communication Gazette*, 77 (3): 232–47.

Kumar, S. (2016), 'Online Entertainment. YouTube Nation: Precarity and Agency in India's Online Video Scene', *International Journal of Communication*, 10: 5608–25.

Kumar, S. (2021), *The Digital Frontier: Infrastructures of Control on the Global Web*, Bloomington, IN: Indiana University Press.

Kumar, S., S. Mohan and A. Punathambekar (2021), 'Beyond the Nation Cultural Regions in South Asia's Online Video Communities', in S. Cunningham and D. Craig (eds), *Creator Culture: An Introduction to Global Social Media Entertainment*, 170–88, New York: New York University Press. Doi: 10.18574/nyu/9781479890118.003.0013.

Kundu, K. (2018), 'YouTube NextUp Delhi 2018 Winners Include Magicians, Comediennes and More'. Available online: https://beebom.com/youtube-nextup-delhi-2018-winners (accessed 1 June 2020).

Kutty, P. (2018), Founder/producer/actor, Vaishnave Media Works Pvt. Ltd., in interview, 31 May, India.

'KWAN Entertainment and Ravi Krishnan Team Up to Launch KWANAbler' (2018). Available online: https://brandequity.economictimes.indiatimes.com/news/business-of-brands/kwan-entertainment-and-ravi-krishnan-team-up-to-launch-kwanabler/63908473 (accessed 1 June 2020).

'KWAN South Aims to Herald a New Era for the Entertainment Ecosystem of South India' (2018). Available online: http://everythingexperiential.businessworld.in/article/KWAN-South-aims-to-herald-a-new-era-for-the-entertainment-ecosystem-of-South-India/23-07-2018-155508 (accessed 1 June 2020).

Laghate, G. (2018), 'Indian MandE Industry to Reach Rs 2 Trillion by 2020: FICCI-EY Report'. Available online: https://economictimes.indiatimes.com/industry/media/entertainment/media/indian-me-industry-to-reach-rs-2-trillion-by-2020-ficci-ey-report/articleshow/63159594.cms (accessed 1 June 2020).

Largeshort Films (2016), *Chutney | Tisca Chopra | Royal Stag Barrel Select Large Short Film*, video. Available online: https://www.youtube.com/watch?v=0krwKbsQscw (accessed 1 June 2020).

Lazzarato, M. (1996), 'Immaterial Labor', in M. Hardt and P. Virno (eds), *Radical Thought in Italy: A Potential Politics*, 133–47, Minneapolis, MN: University of Minnesota Press.

Little Things (2016), YouTube channel Dice Media. Produced by Pocket Aces Pvt. Ltd., Mumbai. Available online: https://www.youtube.com/watch?v=YoFoKZ9HgfQandlist=PL4x7Of-X4XhgNBVfFpd1N4cSU_X1x96gU (accessed 1 June 2020).

Little Things (2018), Netflix. Produced by Pocket Aces Pvt. Ltd., Mumbai.

Livingstone, S. (2008), 'Taking Risky Opportunities in Youthful Content Creation: Teenagers' Use of Social Networking Sites for Intimacy, Privacy and Self-Expression', *New Media and Society*, 10 (3): 393–411.

Lobato, R. (2016), 'The Cultural Logic of Digital Intermediaries: YouTube Multichannel Networks', *Convergence*, 22 (4): 348–60.

Lobato, R. (2019), *Netflix Nations: The Geography of Digital Distribution*, New York: New York University Press.

Lobato, R. and J. Thomas (2018), *The Informal Media Economy*, London: John Wiley & Sons.

Locklear, M. (2018), 'Europe Moves Forward Fith Content Quotas for Netflix and Amazon'. Available online: https://www.engadget.com/2018/10/04/europe-approves-content-quotas-netflix-amazon (accessed 1 June 2020).

Lorenzen, M. and F. A. Täube (2008), 'Breakout from Bollywood? The Roles of Social Networks and Regulation in the Revolution of Indian Film Industry', *Journal of International Management*, 14 (3): 286–99.

Lorenzen, M. and F. A. Taeube (2010) 'The Banyan and the Birch Tree: Family Ties and Embeddedness in the Indian Film Industry in Bollywood,' *Creative Encounters Working Paper*, No. 40, Copenhagen: Copenhagen Business School.

Lotia, N. (2014), 'Be You Nick YouTube Channel'. https://www.youtube.com/user/beyounick (accessed 19 October 2019).

Lotz, A. D. (2014), *The Television Will Be Revolutionized*, New York: New York University Press.

Lotz, A. D. (2017), *Portals: A Treatise on Internet-Distributed Television*, Ann Arbor, MI: Maize Books.

Lotz, A. D. (2018), *We Now Disrupt this Broadcast: How Cable Transformed Television and the Internet Revolutionized it All*, Cambridge, MA: MIT Press.

Lotz, A. D. (2019), 'Teasing Apart Television Industry Disruption: Consequences of Meso-Level Financing Practices before and after the US Multiplatform Era', *Media, Culture and Society*, 41 (7): 923–38.

Lotz, A. D. (2022), *Netflix and Streaming Video: The Business of Subscriber-Funded Video on Demand*, Cambridge: Polity.

Madhavan (2018), Actor/producer, in interview, 23 March, India.

Maguire, J. S. and J. Matthews, eds (2014), *The Cultural Intermediaries Reader*, Thousand Oaks, CA: Sage.

Mahadevan, S. (2019), 'TikTok Wants to Grow its Content Creator Base in India'. https://www.thenewsminute.com/article/tiktok-wants-grow-its-content-creator-base-india-103371 (accessed 9 October 201).

Mahendra, V. (2022), 'How Voot Clocked a 58% Growth in Revenue; Is it Volume Versus Value', *The Financial Express Stories*. Available online:: https://www.financialexpress.com/brandwagon/how-voot-clocked-a-58-growth-in-revenue-is-it-volume-versus-value/2624197/ (accessed 10 August 2022).

Maheshwari, S. (2018), 'Facebook's Version of YouTube Takes Shape with Pranksters, Magicians and Cartoons'. Available online: https://www.nytimes.com/2018/12/16/business/media/facebook-watch-advertising.html?fbclid=IwAR3dCc7ZtBkP2IS05a0Ls3RNx60MkM9Dvp9sMcbKLE5d0uOjpY9G9PpysXk (accessed 24 March 2020).

Maiti, D., F. Castellacci and A. Melchior (2020), 'Digitalisation and Development: Issues for India and Beyond', in D. Maiti, F. Castellacci and A. Melchior (eds), *Digitalisation and Development*, 3–29, Singapore: Springer.

Makhija, D. (2018), Director/writer, in interview, 2 June, India.

Malhotra, V. (2019), 'Indian Govt Could Soon "Censor" Netflix and Other Streaming Services, But is it Needed?' https://fossbytes.com/indian-govt-could-soon-censor-netflix-other-streaming-services (accessed 9 October 2019).

Malhotra, S. and E. M. Rogers (2000), 'Satellite Television and the New Indian Woman', *International Communication Gazette*, 62 (5), 407–29. Doi: 10.1177/0016549200062005004.

Malik, A. (2022), 'Meta to Roll Out New Monetization Tools on Instagram and Facebook, Including a Creator Marketplace', *TechCrunch*. Available online: https://techcrunch.com/2022/06/21/meta-new-monetization-tools-on-instagram-facebook-creator-marketplace/ (accessed 13 August 2022).

Mallapragada, M. (2006), 'Home, Homeland, Homepage: Belonging and the Indian American Web', *New Media and Society*, 8 (2): 207–27.

'Mallika Dua Says Zakir Khan was Paid Twice as Much as Her for Great Indian Laughter Challenge' (2019), *Entertainment News*. Available online: https://www.firstpost.com/entertainment/mallika-dua-says-zakir-khan-was-paid-twice-as-much-as-her-for-great-indian-laughter-challenge-5329961.html (accessed 7 October 2019).

Mandal, P. (2018), Digital marketing and analytics head, Only Much Louder, in interview, 15 March.

Mandavia, M. (2020), 'Facebook Says Watch Emerges as Preferred Platform for Fans to Connect with Creators'. Available online: https://economictimes.indiatimes.com/industry/media/entertainment/facebook-says-watch-emerges-as-preferred-platform-for-fans-to-connect-with-creators/articleshow/73068544.cms (accessed 23 March 2020).

Mangure, C. (2018), 'Bombay HC Issues Notice to IandB Ministry after PIL Demands Censorship of Online Shows', *News18*. Available online: https://www.news18.com/news/india/bombay-hc-issues-notice-to-ib-ministry-after-pil-demands-censorship-of-online-shows-1901313.html (accessed 23 March 2020).

Mankekar, P. (1993), 'National Texts and Gendered Lives: An Ethnography of Televiion Viewers in a North Indian City', *American Ethnologist*, 20 (3): 543–63.

Mankekar, P. (1998), 'Entangled Spaces of Modernity: The Viewing Family, the Consuming Nation, and Television in India', *Visual Anthropology Review*, 14 (2): 32–45.

Manral, A. (2017), 'Sexism in Stand-Up Comedy? No Laughing Matter, as this Anupama Chopra-Led Panel Proves', *Entertainment News*. Available online: https://www.firstpost.com/entertainment/sexism-in-stand-up-comedy-no-laughing-matter-as-this-anupama-chopra-led-panel-proves-3496531.html (accessed 7 October 2019).

Mathews, R. (2018), Vice president, creator management, Only Much Louder, in interview, 15 March.

Mayer, V. (2008), 'Studying Up and F**cking Up: Ethnographic Interviewing in Production Studies', *Cinema Journal*, 47 (2): 141–8.

Mazumdar, R. (2015), '"Invisible Work" in the Indian Media Industries', *Media Industries Journal*, 1 (3): 26–31.

Mazumdar, B. C. (2000), *The History of the Bengali Language*, New Delhi: Asian Educational Services.

McCarthy, N. (2018), 'How Languages Used Online Compare to Real Life [Infographic]', *Forbes*. Available online: https://www.forbes.com/sites/niallmccarthy/2018/07/27/how-languages-used-online-compare-to-real-life-infographic/#66337f4c2c7c (accessed 25 June 2020).

McGlynn, P. (2012), *About Me*, blog. Available online: https://paulamcglynn.wordpress.com/about-me (accessed 23 March 2020).

McKelway, M. (2019), 'Vicious and Virtuous Cycles: Self-Efficacy and Employment of Women in India', unpublished manuscript, Massachusetts Institute of Technology (MIT), Cambridge, MA.

McMillin, D. C. (2001), 'Localizing the Global: Television and Hybrid Programming in India', *International Journal of Cultural Studies*, 4 (1): 45–68.

McRobbie, A. (2002), 'Clubs to Companies: Notes on the Decline of Political Culture in Speeded Up Creative Worlds', *Cultural Studies*, 16 (4): 516–31.

'Meet the 2018 Creators for Change Global Ambassadors' (2018), Blog. https://youtube.googleblog.com/2018/05/meet-2018-creators-for-change-global.html (accessed 23 March 2020).

Mehra, R. (2018), Founder, Addatimes portal, in interview, 8 April, India.

Mehta, B. (2018), 'Getting it Write'. Available online: https://boxofficeindia.co.in/getting-it-write (accessed 11 April 2020).

Mehta, N. (2012), 'Ravana's Airforce: A Report on the State of Indian Television', *South Asian History and Culture*, 3 (4): 614–25.

Mehta, N., ed. (2008), *Television in India: Satellites, Politics and Cultural Change*, London: Routledge.

Merchant, N. (2018), Vice president, Arré, product and business development, in interview, 19 April, India.

'Meta's Facebook Growth Sees Woes in India 2022' (2022), *New York Post*, 21 July. Available online: https://nypost.com/2022/07/21/metas-facebook-growth-sees-woes-in-india-its-biggest-market/ (accessed 8 November 2022).

MICA (2022), *Indian OTT Platforms Report*, Ahmedabad: MICA. Available online: https://communicationcrafts.in/wp-content/uploads/2022/04/Indian-OTT-Platforms-Report-2021.pdf (accessed 11 February 2022).

Ministry of Electronics and Information Technology (2021), 'Notification Dated the 25th February 2021 GSR 139(E): The Information Technology (Intermediary Guidelines and Digital Media Ethics Code) Rules, 2021: Ministry of Electronics and Information Technology, Government of India'. Available online: https://www.

meity.gov.in/content/notification-dated-25th-february-2021-gsr-139e-information-technology-intermediary (accessed 19 March 2021).

Ministry of Home Affairs (2018), 'Language – India, States and Union Territories', *Census India*. Available online: http://censusindia.gov.in/2011Census/Language_MTs.html (accessed 11 April 2020).

Mishra, S. (2019), 'The Stand-Up Comedy Scene in India'. Available online: https://www.outlookindia.com/magazine/story/entertainment-news-a-strained-laugh-lingers/301477 (accessed 11 April 2020).

Mistry, J. (2018), YouTube Spaces head, in interview, 29 March, India.

Mistry, P. (2018), Creative director, TVF, in interview, 12 March, India.

Mitra, A. (2006), 'Towards Finding a Cybernetic Safe Place: Illustrations from People of Indian Origin', *New Media and Society*, 8 (2): 251–68.

Mittal, A. (2017), Stand-up comedian, in interview, 22 May, India.

Mittal, C. (2018), Founder, Shitty Ideas Trending, in interview, 23 March, India.

Mitter, S. (2018a), 'Meet Hoichoi, a Regional Language OTT Platform that is Redefining Innovation'. Available online: https://yourstory.com/2018/09/meet-hoichoi-regional-language-ott-platform-redefining-innovation (accessed 11 April 2020).

Mitter, S. (2018b), 'Netflix Announces 9 New Originals from India, Brings Focus on Regional Content', *YourStory.com*. Available online: https://yourstory.com/2018/11/netflix-announces-9-new-originals-india-brings-focus-regional-content (accessed 11 April 2020).

Mitter, S. (2018c), 'YouTube has 225 Million Monthly Users in India, Reaching 80 pc of the Internet Population'. Available online: https://yourstory.com/2018/03/youtube-monthly-user-base-touches-225-million-india-reaches-80-pc-Internet-population (accessed 16 September 2019).

Mohan, S. and A. Punathambekar (2019), 'Localizing YouTube: Language, Cultural Regions, and Digital Platforms', *International Journal of Cultural Studies*, 22 (3): 317–33.

Mohanty, A. K. (2010), 'Languages, Inequality and Marginalization: Implications of the Double Divide in Indian Multilingualism', *International Journal of the Sociology of Language*, 205: 131–54.

Mohanty, P. C. (2020), 'Is India Digitally Divided? Identifying the Determinants of ICT Diffusion at the Household Level', in D. Maiti, F. Castellacci and A. Melchior (eds), *Digitalisation and Development: Issues for India and Beyond*, 265–86, Singapore: Springer.

Mohta, V. (2018), Co-founder, Hoichoi, in interview, 8 April, India.

Moorti, S. (2007), 'Imaginary Homes, Transplanted Traditions: The Transnational Optic and the Production of Tradition in Indian Television', *Journal of Creative Communications*, 2 (1–2): 1–21.

Mosco, V. (1996), *The Political Economy of Communication: Rethinking and Renewal*, vol. 13, London: Sage.

Mukherjee, D. (2020), *Bombay Hustle: Making Movies in a Colonial City*, New York: Columbia University Press.

Mukherjee, R. (2012), 'Travels, Songs and Displacements: Movement in Translocal Documentaries Interrogating Development', *BioScope: South Asian Screen Studies*, 3 (1): 53–68.

Mukherjee, R. (2019), 'Jio Sparks Disruption 2.0: Infrastructural Imaginaries and Platform Ecosystems in "Digital India"', *Media, Culture and Society*, 41 (2): 175–95.

Mukherjee, R. (2020), *Radiant Infrastructures: Media, Environment, and Cultures of Uncertainty*, Durham, NC: Duke University Press.

Mukherjee, S. (2018), Vice president, revenue and strategy, Hoichoi, in interview, 7 April, India.

Mulchandani, L. (2017), 'Sex, Drugs, Rebellion: New Tales are Being Told as Web Series Go Regional', *Hindustan Times*, 31 July. https://www.hindustantimes.com/tv/sex-drugs-rebellion-new-tales-are-being-told-as-web series-go-regional/story-cR9JsooG1x5m0MGAwu19VI.html (accessed 11 April 2020).

Mulki, S. (2017), '"We Have a Warship": Culture Machine's Sameer and Venkat'. Available online: http://www.afaqs.com/interviews/index.html?id=549_We-have-a-warship-Culture-Machines-Sameer-and-Venkat (accessed 11 April 2020).

Munshi, S. (2012), *Prime Time Soap Operas on Indian Television*, New Delhi: Routledge.

Murdeshwar, T. (2022), 'Disney+ Hotstar Revamps Its Subscription Plans w.e.f 1st September – Smartprix', *Smartprix Bytes*, 10 June. https://www.smartprix.com/bytes/new-disney-plus-hotstar-plans-2021/ (accessed 8 August 2022).

Mustaquim, M. (2022), 'Rural Markets Drive India's Internet Usage Growth: Survey', *Rural Marketing*, 29 July. Available online: https://ruralmarketing.in/stories/rural-markets-drive-indias-internet-usage-growth-survey/ (accessed 5 August 2022).

Nagy, P. and G. Neff (2015), 'Imagined Affordance: Reconstructing a Keyword for Communication Theory', *Social Media + Society*, 1 (2): 1–9.

Nair, S. (2017), 'Black Magic and Child Brides in TV Soaps'. Available online: https://www.theweek.in/webworld/features/lifestyle/Of-black-magic-and-child-brides-in-tv-soaps.html (accessed 11 April 2020).

Nair, S. (2018), Chief operating officer, Altbalaji portal, in interview, 19 March, India.

Narayan, S. S. and S. Narayanan, eds (2016), *India Connected: Mapping the Impact of New Media*, New Delhi: Sage.

Naregal, V. (2000), 'Cable Communications in Mumbai: Integrating Corporate Interests with Local and Media Networks', *Contemporary South Asia*, 9 (3): 289–314.

Natu, S. and A. Jagad (2017), *How AIB Uses Feminism*, video. Available online: https://www.youtube.com/watch?v=wLIT9buq-FQandfeature=youtu.be (accessed 11 April 2020).

'Naveen Richard, Sumukshi Suresh on Better Life Foundation Cancellation: One Should Recognise Other Artistes' Efforts' (2018), 'Entertainment', *Firstpost*, 23 October. Available online: https://www.firstpost.com/entertainment/aveen-richard-sumukshi-suresh-on-better-life-foundation-cancellation-one-should-recognise-other-artistes-efforts-5431561.html (accessed 11 April 2020).

Neff, G. (2012), *Venture Labor: Work and the Burden of Risk in Innovative Industries*, Cambridge, MA: MIT Press.

'Netflix and Amazon Prime to Face Local Quotas' (2016). Available online: https://www.rte.ie/entertainment/2016/0526/791072-netflix (accessed 11 April 2020).

Ok tested (2017), Home page, YouTube channel. Available online: https://www.youtube.com/channel/UC7lmZqhJeTzeQQkqNvfmjqw/about (accessed 12 May 2020).

'Online Video Market to Reach $5 Billion in India by 2023: Report' (2018), *Tech News*. Available online: https://www.timesnownews.com/technology-science/article/online-video-market-to-reach-5-billion-in-india-by-2023-report/317518 (accessed 12 May 2020).

'Only Much Louder Responds to #MeToo Allegations against the Company, Founder Vijay Nair' (2019), *Firstpost*. Available online: https://www.firstpost.com/india/only-much-louder-responds-to-metoo-allegations-against-the-company-founder-vijay-nair-5542961.html (accessed 9 October 2019).

Oxford Economics (2021), 'A Platform for India Opportunity'. Available online: https://www.oxfordeconomics.com/wp-content/uploads/2022/12/YouTube-India.

pdf?utm_source=website_resource_hub&utm_medium=organic&utm_campaign=economic_impact (accessed 18 December 2022).

Pagnamenta, R. (2018), 'Amazon Prime Eyes India and Its 1.3bn Audience', *The Telegraph*, 18 November. Available online: https://www.telegraph.co.uk/technology/2018/11/18/amazon-prime-eyes-india-13bn-audience (accessed 12 May 2020).

Pai, V. (2016), 'Zee Digital Launches Online Streaming Platform OZEE', *MediaNama*. Available online: https://www.medianama.com/2016/02/223-zee-launches-ozee (accessed 24 March 2020).

Pal, A. (2018), Writer/actor, in interview, 18 March, India.

Pandita, A. (2018), In-person interview, 14 March, Mumbai.

Panjari, S. (2018), 'Culture Machine Inks Content Deal with Amazon Prime Video', *TelevisionPost*, 17 April. Available online: https://www.televisionpost.com/culture-machine-inks-content-deal-with-amazon-prime-video (accessed 9 October 2019).

Pant, R. (2014), 'I'm a Drama Queen . . . But I'm the Star You Love to See!', *Subversions*, 3 (1): 1–28.

Pant, S. (2017), Stand-up comedian, in interview, 5 June, India.

Parthasarathi, V. (2017), 'Market Dynamics of the Media Economy', in A. Athique, V. Parthasarathi and S. V. Srinivas (eds), *The Indian Media Economy, Vol. 2: Market Dynamics and Social Transactions*, 152–70, New Delhi: Oxford University Press.

Parthasarathi, V. and A. Srinivas (2016), 'Networks of Influence', *The Caravan*, 9 (2): 24–7.

Parthasarathi, V. and A. Srinivas (2019), 'Problematic Ownership Patterns: The Evolution of the Television Distribution Networks in India', *Economic and Political Weekly*, 54 (12), 23 March.

Parthasarathi, V. and A. Srinivas (2022), 'Labyrinths behind the Screen: Ownership and Control in TV Cable Distribution', *South Asian Popular Culture*, 20 (1): 133–47.

Parthasarathi, V., S. Chitrapu and S. P. Elavarthi (2020), 'Media Economics in India: Traversing the Rubicon?', *Management and Economics of Communication*, 30: 441.

Pasquale, F. (2015), *The Black Box Society*, Cambridge, MA: Harvard University Press.

Pathak, A. (2017), 'Amazon Video has Signed 14 Top Indian Stand-Up Comics, Promises Zero Censorship', *Huffington Post*. Available online: https://www.huffingtonpost.in/2017/01/19/amazon-video-has-signed-these-14-top-indian-stand-up-comics-pro_a_21658257 (accessed 9 October 2019).

Pathak, A. (2019a), 'Bollywood is Strategically Rehabilitating All the Men Accused of Sexual Misconduct', *Huffington Post*. Available online: https://www.huffingtonpost.in/entry/alok-nath-me-too-de-de-pyaar-de_in_5cdec7bbe4b09e057802d0c6?utm_hp_ref=in-metoo (accessed 9 October 2019).

Pathak, A. (2019b), 'Woke to Broke: The Stunning Rise and Fall of AIB', *Huffington Post*. Available online: https://www.huffingtonpost.in/entry/aib-tanmay-bhat-rohan-joshi-collapse_in_5cf38febe4b0e8085e3b5060 (accessed 9 October 2019).

Paul, S. (2018), 'Bengali Content Finds Pan-India Audience with Growth of Hoichoi, a Regional Language OTT Player', 'Entertainment', *Firstpost*. Available online: https://www.firstpost.com/entertainment/bengali-content-finds-pan-india-audience-with-growth-of-hoichoi-a-regional-language-ott-player-5231051.html (accessed 9 October 2019).

Pendakur, M. (2003), *Indian Popular Cinema: Industry, Ideology, and Consciousness*, New York: Hampton Press.

Pendakur, M. (2013), 'Twisting and Turning: India's Telecommunications and Media Industries under the Neo-Liberal Regime', *International Journal of Media and Cultural Politics*, 9 (2): 107–31.

Permanent Roommates (2014), TVFPlay. Produced by Contagious Online Media, Mumbai.

Permanent Roommates (2016), TVFPlay (Season 2). Produced by Contagious Online Media, Mumbai.

Pitalwalla, S. (2018), Co-founder, Culture Machine, in interview, 2 August, India.

Pitchers (2015), TVFPlay. Produced by Contagious Online Media, Mumbai.

'Plus Minus: YouTuber Bhuvan Bam and Divya Dutta to Star in Short Film' (2018), *News18*. Available online: https://www.news18.com/news/movies/plus-minus-youtuber-bhuvan-bam-and-divya-dutta-to-star-in-short-film-1871477.html (accessed 9 October 2019).

Poddar, P. (2020), 'Digital Borders – The Banning of Chinese TikTok in India', Copenhagen University, 8 July. Available online: https://www.thinkchina.ku.dk/insights/blog/digital-borders/ (accessed 7 November 2020).

Powder (2010), Sony TV. Produced by Yash Raj Productions, Mumbai.

Pratap, R. (2018), 'From Theatres, Movies Hit OTTs, not Satellite TV'. Available online: https://www.thehindubusinessline.com/news/variety/from-theatres-movies-hit-otts-not-satellite-tv/article25727342.ece (accessed 9 October 2019).

Priyam, G. and J. Karandeep (2018), In-person interview, 11 April, Kolkata.

Priyam and Karandeep (n.d.), Home page, YouTube channel. Available online: https://www.youtube.com/channel/UCx1RX4LRg_uLYkPWumohvMw (accessed 22 April 2019).

Punathambekar, A. (2008), 'We're Online, Not on the Streets: Indian Cinema, New Media, and Participatory Culture', *Global Bollywood*, 282–99.

Punathambekar, A. (2013), *From Bombay to Bollywood: The Making of a Global Media Industry*, vol. 5, New York: New York University Press.

Punathambekar, A. and S. Mohan (2019), *Global Digital Cultures: Perspectives from South Asia*, Ann Arbor, MI: University of Michigan Press.

PwC (2019), 'Video on Demand: Entertainment Reimagined'. Available online: https://www.pwc.in/assets/pdfs/publications/2018/video-on-demand.pdf (accessed 9 October 2019).

Qyuki (2013), 'About Qyuki Music', YouTube video. Available online: https://www.youtube.com/user/QyukiMusic/about (accessed 9 October 2019).

Raghuram, P., A. K. Sahoo, B. Maharaj and D. Sangha (eds) (2008), *Tracing an Indian Diaspora: Contexts, Memories, Representations*, New Delhi: Sage.

Rai, A. S. (2019), *Jugaad Time: Ecologies of Everyday Hacking in India*, Durham, NC: Duke University Press.

Raina, P. (2018), Writer, in interview, 31 March, India.

Rajesh, S. (2018), 'TVF's Cannes Acclaimed Series, *ImMature* to Stream on Times Internet's OTT', *IWMBuzz*, 8 October. Available online: https://www.iwmbuzz.com/digital/news-digital/immature-tvfs-web-series-that-was-screened-in-cannes-this-year-will-now-stream-on-times-internets-to-be-launched-platform/2018/10/08 (accessed 13 April 2020).

Ramachandran, N. (2022), 'Zee5 Global Plots U.S. Expansion with Local Productions, Grassroots Penetration (Exclusive)', *Variety*, 29 July. Available online: https://variety.com/2022/tv/asia/zee5-global-us-expansion-1235329051/ (accessed 8 August 2022).

Ramnani, D. (2019), 'All India Bakchod Shuts Down as a Consequence of the #MeToo Movement'. Available online: https://www.in.com/entertainment/all-india-bakchod-shuts-down-as-a-consequence-of-the-metoo-movement-417839.htm (accessed 9 October 2019).

Rana, M. (2022), 'Top 10 Regional OTT Platforms', *The Mobile Indian*, 15 February. Available online: https://www.themobileindian.com/picture-story/top-10-regional-ott-platforms (accessed 10 August 2022).

Ranipeta, S. (2018), 'Why this Hyd-Based Digital Entertainment Startup has Hit the Goldmine with Its IPO'. Available online: https://www.thenewsminute.com/article/why-hyd-based-digital-entertainment-startup-has-hit-goldmine-its-ipo-75188 (accesseds 9 October 2019).

Ranjan, S. (2019), 'Hindi Row: Nationalism vs Linguistic Federalism', *Tribune India*. Available online: https://www.tribuneindia.com/news/comment/hindi-row-nationalism-vs-linguistic-federalism/788073.html (accessed 4 July and 9 October 2019).

Rao, L. (2001), 'Facets of Media and Gender Studies in India', *Feminist Media Studies*, 1 (1): 45–8.

Rath (2008), Home page, YouTube channel. Available online: https://www.youtube.com/user/yokalyanyo (accessed 9 October 2019).

Ravindran, S. (2018), Marketing manager, Netflix portal, in interview, 29 March, India.

'Reliance Jio Crosses 50 Million Subscriber Mark in 83 Days' (2016). Available online: https://indianexpress.com/article/technology/tech-news-technology/reliance-jio-crosses-50-million-subscriber-mark-in-83-days-4400972 (accessed 24 March 2020).

Rishi, B., A. Kacker and S. Gupta (2018), 'Entry of Reliance Jio in the Telecom Industry: A Ripple in the Ocean', *Emerald Emerging Markets Case Studies*, 8 (3). Doi: 10.1108/EEMCS-07-2017-0167.

Rosario, K. (2018), '#MeToo: Founder of Kwan Agency Anirban Blah Fired; Reliance Content Studio Head Ajit Thakur Accused'. https://www.thehindu.com/entertainment/movies/metoo-founder-of-kwan-agency-anirban-blah-fired-reliance-content-studio-head-ajit-thakur-accused/article25240758.ece (accessed 9 October 2019).

Ross, A. (2013), 'In Search of the Lost Paycheck', in T. Scholz (ed.), *Digital Labor: The Internet as Playground and Factory*, 13–32, New York: Routledge.

Roussel, V. (2016), 'Talent Agenting in the Age of Conglomerates', in M. Curtin and K. Sanson (eds), *Precarious Creativity: Global Media, Local Labor*, 74–87, Oakland, CA: University of California Press.

Roy, P. (2019), 'Why India has World's Cheapest Mobile Data', BBC News, 18 March. Available online: https://www.bbc.com/news/world-asia-india-47537201?fbclid=IwAR1Ef6j0lZi_qfmGS1o09SZ0SIMOEksvTEo35XTp6qj8jX9CeP-c0UZ1Z4w (accessed 24 March 2020 and 17 April 2021).

Roy, T. L. (2014), 'Meet the Duo Behind Shree Ventakesh Films Who Helped Turn around Bengali Cinema', *Economic Times*, 4 January. Available online: https://economictimes.indiatimes.com/industry/media/entertainment/meet-the-duo-behind-shree-ventakesh-films-who-helped-turn-around-bengali-cinema/articleshow/28355473.cms (accessed 1 March 2019).

Rudra, T. (2022), 'It Rules Amendments: Asia Internet Coalition Raises Concerns on Grievance Appellate Committee, Other Clauses', Inc42 Media, 4 August. Available online: https://inc42.com/buzz/it-rules-amendments-asia-internet-coalition-raises-concerns-on-grievance-appellate-committee-other-clauses/ (accessed 25 August 2022).

Russell, J. (2019), 'Chinese App Developers have Invaded India', *TechCrunch*, 2 January. Available online: https://techcrunch.com/2019/01/02/chinese-app-developers-have-invaded-india (accessed 9 October 2019).

S, V. (2021), 'Bengali Ott Player Hoichoi Woos Viewers in Bangladesh, Middle East Lines Up 20 New Shows for 2022', *Business Today*. https://www.businesstoday.in/latest/corporate/story/bengali-ott-player-hoichoi-woos-viewers-in-bangladesh-middle-east-lines-up-20-new-shows-for-2022-307580-2021-09-24 (accessed 10 August 2022).

S, V. (2022), 'Why Netflix's Content is Still Missing the Mark in India', *Business Today*. Available online: https://www.businesstoday.in/latest/corporate/story/why-netflixs-content-is-still-missing-the-mark-in-india-336337-2022-06-04 (accessed 9 August 2022).

Samtani, P. (2017), 'On the Record: Vijay Nair, Only Much Louder Founder and CEO, on His Journey so Far'. Available online: http://thepunchmagazine.com/arts/music/on-the-record-vijay-nair-only-much-louder-founder-and-ceo-on-his-journey-so-far (accessed 24 March 2020).

Sanjai, P. R. (2022), 'IPL media rights: Mukesh Ambani opted out of TV rights chase in Battle for Cricket deal', *The Economic Times*. Available online: https://economictimes.indiatimes.com/industry/media/entertainment/media/ipl-media-rights-mukesh-ambani-opted-out-of-tv-rights-chase-in-battle-for-cricket-deal/articleshow/92283860.cms (accessed 8 August 2022).

Sanson, K. (2021), 'Global Configurations: Re-spatializing Labor in Contemporary Film and Television Production', in Paul McDonald (ed.), *The Routledge Companion to Media Industries*, 182–91, London: Routledge.

Sarkar, G. (2020), '2020: The Tipping Point for the Indian OTT Ecosystem'. https://www.indiantelevision.com/specials/year-enders/2020-the-tipping-point-for-the-indian-ott-ecosystem-201230 (accessed 21 January 2021).

Sarkar, T. (2018), Co-founder, Indian Casting Company, in interview, 18 April, India.

Sathaye, S. (2018), Co-founder, Bhartiya Digital Party, in interview, 6 June, India.

ScoopWhoop (2014), Home page, YouTube channel. https://www.youtube.com/channel/UC2O-N1R4x56XhndL4qqfKcw (accessed 24 March 2020).

ScoopWhoop (2020), 'ScoopWhoop: 20 Years of Love Songs'. Available online: https://www.youtube.com/channel/UCx2HcmpB-UZGkMXOCJ4QIVA (accessed 1 June 2020).

ScoopWhoop Unscripted (2017), Home page, YouTube channel. Available online: https://www.youtube.com/channel/UC6JEz6BKg7hX7idKecN7QYA/about (accessed 24 March 2020).

Sehgal, D. (2018), Creative director/writer/actor, Pocket Aces Pvt. Ltd., in interview, 20 April, India.

Senft, T. M. (2013), *Camgirls: Celebrity and Community in the Age of Social Networks*, New York: Peter Lang.

Sethia, V. (2017), Stand-up comedian, in interview, 25 October, India.

Sethia, V. (2018), In-person interview, 25 October, email.

Shah, S. (2018), 'Facebook Renews *Sorry for Your Loss* and Three More Watch Originals'. Available online: https://www.engadget.com/2018/12/13/facebook-watch-sorry-for-your-loss/ (accessed 24 March 2020).

Shaikh, S. (2018), 'Helo: A Chinese App is Saying Ni Hao and a Lot More in India', *FactorDaily*. Available online: https://factordaily.com/helo-a-chinese-app-is-saying-ni-hao-and-a-lot-more-in-india (accessed 12 October 2019).

Sharma, D. (2019), 'Offline with an Internet Star: Mithila Palkar on Films, Life, Chai', *The Quint*. Available online: https://www.thequint.com/neon/girl-in-the-city-actor-and-Internet-star-mithila-palkar-interview (20 August 2019).

Sharma, G. and H. Kumar (2019), 'Commercialising Innovations from the Informal Economy', *South Asian Journal of Business Studies*, 8 (1): 40–61.

Sharma, N. (2018), 'Tracking #MeToo: These Powerful Indian Men Have Been Accused of Sexual Harassment by Women. So Far', *The Leaflet*. https://theleaflet.in/tracking-metoo-these-powerful-indian-men-have-been-accused-of-sexual-harassment-by-women-so-far/?fbclid=IwAR3T1kmxoes16ipkerYODw3ULrgPjqjpARXI3MOyZUOspcVLzBdJPC1wGlg (accessed 9 October 2019).

Sharma, S. (2020), 'Cheapest DTH Service in India'. Available online: https://techivian.com/cheapest-dth-service-in-india (accessed 27 March 2020).

Shinde, S. (2022), 'YouTube's Creator Ecosystem Contributed rs 6,800 Cr to Indian GDP', *Business Standard News*, 3 March. Available online: https://www.business-standard.com/article/companies/youtube-s-creator-ecosystem-contributed-rs-6-800-cr-to-indian-gdp-122030300588_1.html (accessed 4 August 2022).

Siddharth, A. (2018), Vice President, Saregama India Ltd., Film and Events, in interview, India, 15 March.

'Silly Monks Entertainment History | Silly Monks Entertainment Information' (2017), *The Economic Times*. Available online: https://economictimes.indiatimes.com/silly-monks-entertainment-ltd/infocompanyhistory/companyid-67378.cms (accessed 27 March 2020).

'Silly Monks Plans to Buy, Create Content in More Local Languages' (2018), *Financial Express*, 19 January. Available online: https://www.financialexpress.com/india-news/silly-monks-plans-to-buy-create-content-in-more-local-languages/1020869/ (accessed 27 March 2020).

'Sillymonks Ties Up with Aurous Avatar to Make Telugu Movies' (2019), *The Hindu BusinessLine*, 18 July. Available online: https://www.thehindubusinessline.com/news/sillymonks-ties-up-with-aurous-avatar-to-make -telugu-movies/article28564799.ece (accessed 17 December 2019).

Singh, A. (2018), Executive producer, Times Internet, in interview, 15 March.

Singh, A. N. and P. V. Ilavarasan (2016), 'Information and Communication Technologies (ICTs) are Important in Bringing Transparency in Governance. They Control Corruption', in S. S. Narayan and S. Narayanan (eds), *India Connected: Mapping the Impact of New Media*, 122, New Delhi: Sage.

Singh, G. (2018), Co-founder, One Digital Pvt. Ltd., in interview, 20 March, India.

Singh, R. (2022), 'Explained: The Frequency, Reasons, and Controversy over Internet Suspensions by the Government', *Indian Express*. Available online: https://indianexpress.com/article/explained/explained-the-frequency-reasons-and-controversy-over-internet-suspensions-by-the-government-8005450/ (accessed 13 August 2022).

Singh, S. (2019), 'TikTok Ban: ByteDance Planning to Invest $1 Bn in India, Says Zhen Liu, SVP'. Available online: https://economictimes.indiatimes.com/tech/Internet/tiktok-ban-bytedance-planning-to-invest-1-bn-in-india-says-zhen-liu-svp/articleshow/68948323.cms (accessed 9 October 2019).

Singh, S. and V. Ananth (2019), 'TikTok's Relentless Growth in India is Hitting Facebook'. Available online: https://economictimes.indiatimes.com/small-biz/startups/features/bytedance-bets-big-on-short-videos-to-engage-indian-market-takes-on-facebook/articleshow/69422493.cms?fbclid=IwAR1EJN4iZrk-knapaggpiK31I1SEHQlqtQ30FeDOMoBM7Hcj4T-q2HuK-zA (accessed 9 October 2019).

Singh, S. and A. Kumar (2019), 'Sexual Violence in the Indian Public Sphere: Counter-Public Creation and Deferral', *Space and Culture, India*, 6 (5): 8–28.

Skutnabb-Kangas, T. (2000), *Linguistic Genocide in Education – Or Worldwide Diversity and Human Rights?*, London: Routledge.

SN, V. (2018), 'Netflix May Launch Lower Priced Plans in India and Other Markets – ETtech'. Available online: https://tech.economictimes.indiatimes.com/news/Internet/netflix-plans-lower-priced-plans-in-india-other-markets/66267235 (accessed 27 March 2020).

Sorrells, M. (2019), 'India's Paytm Invests $35M to Expand Its Travel Business', *PhocusWire*. Available online: https://www.phocuswire.com/India-Paytm-35m-travel-investment (accessed 9 October 2019).

Srinivas, S. V., V. M. Shyam, R. Nanduri, V. Singhal and V. Dath (2018), 'From Single Screen to YouTube: Tracking the Regional Blockbuster', *BioScope: South Asian Screen Studies*, 9 (2): 233–50.

Srivastava, J. and E. Roy (2016), 'Theoretical Perspectives: Issues in the Indian New Media Environment', in S. S. Narayan and S. Narayanan (eds), *India Connected: Mapping the Impact of New Media*, 20–46, New Delhi: Sage.

Srivastava, P. (2015), 'A Dummy's Guide to NCCS'. http://www.afaqs.com/news/story/42980_A-Dummys-Guide-to-NCCS (accessed 27 March 2020).

Sundaram, R. (2009), *Pirate Modernity: Delhi's Media Urbanism*, London and New York: Routledge.

'Supernatural Genre is Fading Away from Indian Television Industry; *daayans, tantriks* to Say Goodbye' (2019), Dainik bhaskar. Available online: https://dbpost.com/supernatural-genre-is-fading-away-from-indian-television-industry-daayans-tantriks-to-say-goodbye (1 April 2020).

Suthar, M. (2018), 'Poulomi Das, Gagan Anand and Sahil Shroff in ALTBalaji's *Baarish*', *IWMBuzz*. Available online: https://www.iwmbuzz.com/digital/news-digital/poulomi-das-gagan-anand-sahil-shroff-altbalajis-baarish/2018/12/11 (1 April 2020).

'Take Ten: Seeking India's Next Generation of Storytellers. About Netflix' (2022), Netflix, 24 January. Available online: https://about.netflix.com/en/news/take-ten-seeking-indias-next-generation-of-storytellers (accessed 15 August 2022).

Taneja, N. (2017), Head – Development of Y-Films, Yash Raj Films, in interview, 19 December, India.

Tantra (2018–19), Viacom18 Media Pvt. Ltd. Produced by Swastik Productions.

Tejwani, R. (2017), Founder, Green Chutney Films, in interview, 21 December, India.

Tewari, S. (2017), 'Celebrity Management Firm Kwan Launches Marketplace for Digital Entertainment'. Available online: https://www.livemint.com/Consumer/Ugl0j5eORi5SSz6ucbS61N/Celebrity-management-firm-Kwan-launches-marketplace-for-digi.html (accessed 1 April 2020).

Tewari, S. (2018), 'Kwan Entertainment Launches Sports, Media and Consumer Unit Kwanabler'. https://www.livemint.com/Consumer/qk0uZsGSpFmiagZgdrTiXO/Kwan-Entertainment-launches-sports-media-and-consumer-unit.html (accessed 1 April 2020).

Tewari, S. (2020), 'Local Tongues Lure Viewers', *mint*, 18 December. Available online: https://www.livemint.com/companies/news/youtube-says-more-indians-are-watching-ads-in-local-languages-online-11608266318320.html (accessed 7 March 2021).

Tewathia, N., A. Kamath and P. V. Ilavarasan (2020), 'Social Inequalities, Fundamental Inequities, and Recurring of the Digital Divide: Insights from India', *Technology in Society*, 61 (3): 101251.

Thakur, N. (2022), 'Is Woke Content Harming Netflix's India Business?', Outlook. Available online: https://www.outlookindia.com/business/is-woke-content-harming-netflix-s-india-business--news-46653 (accessed 9 August 2022).

The Bong Guy (n.d.), Home page, YouTube channel. Available online: https://www.youtube.com/channel/UCh5bICCatQ70Fx4-jwAmWKQ (accessed 1 April 2020).

The Bong Guy (2018), 'The Bong Guy v/s Dev Hoichoi Unlimited'. Available online: https://www.youtube.com/watch?v=U69bIptV_Gw (accessed 1 April 2020).

Thomas, M. (2018), 'India's Deep Class Divides Extend to How Its Youth Use the Internet'. Available online: https://qz.com/india/1227749/study-shows-stark-differences-in-how-rich-and-poor-indian-youths-use-the-Internet (accessed 16 September 2019).

Thomas, P. (2019). *The Politics of Digital India: Between Local Compulsions and Transnational Pressures*, 1st edn. Oxford University Press.

Thussu, D. K. (1999), 'Privatizing the Airwaves: The Impact of Globalization on Broadcasting in India', *Media, Culture and Society* 21 (1): 125–31.

Timothy, H. and A. Lotz (2017), *Understanding Media Industries*, Oxford: Oxford University Press.

Tinic, S. (2005), *On Location: Canada's Television Industry in a Global Market*, Toronto: University of Toronto Press.

Tiwary, I. (2020), 'Amazon Prime Video: A Platform Ecosphere', in A. Athique and V. Parthasarathi (eds), *Platform Capitalism in India*, 87–106, Cham: Palgrave Macmillan.

TRAI (2015), Press release. Available online: http://trai.gov.in/WriteReadData/PressRealease/Document/PR-32-TSD-May-15_10072015.pdf (accessed 1 April 2020).

'TRAI Chief Sees New Govt Pushing Reforms in Telecom, 5G Roll-Out' (2019). Available online: https://www.businesstoday.in/sectors/telecom/trai-chief-sees-new-govt-pushing-reforms-in-telecom-5g-roll-out/story/352358.html (accessed 1 April 2020).

Tripathy, R. (2013), 'Mapping the Invisible World of Bhojpuri Cinema and Its Changing Audience', in K. Moti Gokulsing and Wimal Dissanayake (eds), *Routledge Handbook of Indian Cinemas*, 150–61, New York: Routledge.

Tripling (2016), TVFPlay, produced by Contagious Online Media Network Pvt. Ltd., Mumbai.

Tripling (2019), SonyLIV (Season 2), produced by Contagious Online Media Network Pvt. Ltd., Mumbai.

'Twitter Debuts in India with Bengaluru-Based Social Networking Sharechat' (2019). Available online: https://www.vantageasia.com/twitter-debuts-sharechat-india (accessed 9 October 2019).

UDigital (n.d.), Home page, Facebook page. Available online: https://www.facebook.com/ArréIndia/ (accessed 1 April 2020).

UDigital (2015), Home page, YouTube channel. Available online: https://www.youtube.com/channel/UC2O-N1R4x56XhndL4qqfKcw (accessed 1 April 2020).

UDigital (2021), Home page, YouTube channel. Available online: https://www.youtube.com/channel/UC2O-N1R4x56XhndL4qqfKcw (accessed 1 April 2021).

Upadhya, C. (2008), 'Management of Culture and Management through Culture in the Indian Software Outsourcing Industry', in C. Upadhya and A. R. Vasavi (eds), *In an Outpost of the Global Economy: Work and Workers in India's Information Technology Industry*, 101–35, New Delhi: Routledge.

van Dijck, J. (2009), 'Users Like You? TheorizingAgency in User-Generated Content', *Media, Culture & Society*, 31 (1): 41–58.

Varshney, R. (2018), 'Facebook Adds More Indic Languages to Its Transliteration Tool on Android – MediaNama', *MediaNama*. Available online: https://www.medianama.com/2017/09/223-facebook-adds-more-indic-languages-to-its-transliteration-tool-on-android-app (accessed 1 April 2020).

Venegas, C. (2009), 'Thinking Regionally: Singular in Diversity and Diverse in Unity', in J. Holt and A. Perren (eds), *Media Industries: History, Theory, and Method*, 120–31, Oxford: Wiley Blackwell.

Venkatesh, S. (2017), 'Netflix Announces Partnership with Airtel, Vodafone and Videocon D2h', *Forbes India*. Available online: https://www.forbesindia.com/article/special/netflix-announces-partnership-with-airtel-vodafone-and-videocon-d2h/46195/1 (accessed 27 March 2020).

Venugopal, V. (2019), 'RSS Wants Streaming Platforms to Nix "Anti-India", "Anti-Hindu" Content'. Available online: https://economictimes.indiatimes.com/news/politics-and-nation/rss-wants-streaming-platforms-to-nix-anti-india-anti-hindu-content/articleshow/71485819.cms?fbclid=IwAR0U3PvXLJwQpupv36fW5ttWepLvtlA7xfFuv0QYkxtXpP-v4mhppAdy4s8andfrom=mdr (accessed 9 October 2019).

Vikas, S. N. (2018), 'Netflix Partners Pocket Aces' Dice Media to Create Scripted Shows', *Economic Times*. Available online: https://tech.economictimes.indiatimes.com/news/Internet/netflix-partners-pocket-aces-dice-media-to-create-scripted-shows/65122089 (accessed 9 October 2019).

Vish ya Amrit (2018–19), Viacom18 Media Pvt. Ltd. Produced by Rashmi Sharma Telefilms.

'Vodafone India Partners HOOQ to Strengthen Vodafone Play's Content Catalogue' (2020), *ETtech*. Available online: https://tech.economictimes.indiatimes.com/news/mobile/vodafone-india-partners-hooq-to-strengthen-vodafone-plays-content-catalogue/60408016 (accessed 27 March 2020).

'Voot to Launch 18 Originals in the Coming Months' (2018), afaqs. Available online: https://www.afaqs.com/news/marketing/53540_Voot-to-launch-18-originals-in-the-coming-months (accessed 24 March 2020).

Wonder Munna (n.d.a), Home page, Facebook page. Available online: https://www.facebook.com/WonderMunnaa (accessed 1 May 2020).

Wonder Munna (n.d.b), Home page, YouTube channel. Available online: https://www.youtube.com/channel/UCRVSux9mnpTPYHs1yp8SIPA (accessed 1 May 2020).

Yeh Meri Family (2019), Netflix/TVFPlay, produced by Contagious Online Media Network Pvt. Ltd., Mumbai.

YouTube launched in India (2008), *Economic Times*. Available online: https://economictimes.indiatimes.com/tech/Internet/youtube-launched-in-india/articleshow/3017907.cms (accessed 16 September 2019).

Zafirau, S. (2008), 'Reputation Work in Selling Film and Television: Life in the Hollywood Talent Industry', *Qualitative Sociology*, 31 (2): 99–127.

'Zee5 Announces First Bengali Web Series, *Kaali*' (2018), *The Digital Hash*, 13 November. Available online: https://www.thedigitalhash.com/zee5-announces-first-bengali-web series-kaali (accessed 1 May 2020).

'Zee5 Launches Its Third Telugu Original' (2018), Media news 4u-Written by *MN4U Bureau*, 16 November. Available online: https://www.medianews4u.com/zee5-launches-its-third-telugu-original-b-tech-on-nov-15/- (accessed 3 March 2019).

'ZEE5's Tejkaran Singh Bajaj Moves to Jio' (2018), afaqs, 12 December. Available online: https://www.afaqs.com/people-spotting/258_ZEE5s-Tejkaran-Singh-Bajaj-moves-to-Jio (accessed 24 March 2020).

Zelenski, D. (2002), 'Talent Agents, Personal Managers, and Their Conflicts in the New Hollywood', *Southern California Law Review*, 76: 979.

Index

Bold numbers denote illustrations or tables.

Aalambayan, Siddharth, 71–2
actors, 41–2
    career trajectories, 30–1
    social and cultural capital, 41
adaptation rights, 116
Addatimes, 5, 44, 58–9, 85–6, 91
advertising, 34, 48, 61
Advertising video-on-demand (AVoD), 6, 126
agency, lack of, 94
Ahsan, Farid, 127
Ahuja, Anmol, 32–3
Airtel, 5
All India Bakchod (AIB), 78–9, 124
Altbalaji, 5, 45, 52–3, 90
Amazon Prime, 5, 7, 11, 49, 59, 66–7, 89–90, 101, 110, 123, 127, 131, 132
    censorship, 75
    investment in stand-up comedians, 105–6
    local strategies, 54–6, 59, 122
    subscription rates, 54
analytics, 90–1
Anand, Sidharth, 42
Anderson, J. D., 92
Apple TV, 55
Arré, 68–9, **69**, 127
Athique, A., 5, 10, 20, 45, 85, 88, 90, 103
audience
    multilingual, 9
    price-sensitive nature of, 43
    television, 34–5
    understanding, 68
audience fragmentation, 85
audience migration, 42
autonomy, 26

Balaji Telefilms Pvt. Ltd., 45, 52–3
Baltruschat, D., 19
Bam, Bhuvan, 49, 69–71

Banerjee, Abhishek, 32–3, 131
Baym, N., 72
BB ki Vines, 70
Bengali diaspora, 88–9
Bengali language, 57–9, 90–1, 92, 123
BhaDiPa, 93, 95–6, 97
Bhaumik, Moinak, 58
Bisht, Nidhi, 36–7, 52, 67–8, 73
Biswa Kalyan, 2
Biswas, Indrani, 78, 91–2, 94
black money, 120
Bollywood, 14, 17, 59, 71, 73, 95, 120–1, 131–2
Bourdieu, P., 61
Boyle, Raymond, 9, 9–10, 99, 102, 111
branding, 59, 109–10
Brickell, K., 88–9
Broadcast Research Council of India, 35
broadcaster-owned portals, 49–51
Broadcasting Content Complaints Council (BCCC), 74
Burgess, J., 66–7
business models, 6, 10, 46–7, 126, 127
Bytedance, 128

Cable News Network's (CNN), 15
Cable Television Network (Regulation) Act (1995), 15
cable TV, 15
camgirls, 96
Caravan, 28–9
career building, 63–4, 69–72, 81, 130
career trajectories, 30–1, 101
caste-based politics, 17–18
casting agents, 32–3
catch-up content, 50
celebrity, 96–7
Censor Board of Film Certification (CBFC), 74

censorship, 74–6
Chacko, Ajay, 68
Chakraborty, Indranil, 28
Chaudhuri, Amitabh Reza, 58
China, 126, 127–8
Chitrapu, S., 9, 17
Chopra, Anupama, 77
cine-ecological approach, 19
cinema infrastructure, lack of, 95, 98
CMIS approach, 10, 16–17
code of best practices, 75
commercial capital, 61
commercialization, 129
commissioning, 26
common content strategies, 91
Computer-Generated Imagery, 53
connected viewing, 10
content around content, 50
content creation, 67
content distribution, 43–4
content strategies, 59
content strategy, 68
content-driven strategy, 111
controversial topics, 76
corporate structures, 64, 67–9
costs, 43
counter terrorism, 76
Craig, D., 6–7, 9, 10, 19, 64, 66, 91, 100, 111
creative vision, 40
creativity, 8, 28, 40–1, 93
  precarious, 62–4, 81
creator culture, 1, 61–82, 120, 130–2
  #MeToo movement, 78–81
  career building, 69–72, 81, 130
  censorship, 74–6
  corporate structures, 67–9
  entrepreneurial labour, 72–4
  future challenges, 74–81
  gender inequality, 76–8
  multitasking, 73–4
  new business practices, 64–74
  online, 39–40
  power dynamics, 129–30
  precarious creativity, 62–4, 81
  professional identity, 66–7

socio-technological transformations, 100
  strategic approaches to labour, 64–6
creator labour, marginalization of, 17
creator localization strategies, 91–6
creator mobilization strategies, 84, 123
creator networks, Multi-Channel Networks (MCN) as, 111–14
creator porosity, 131–2
crime, 14
cross-platform strategies, 66–7
cross-pollination, 16
cultural diversity, 44, 54, 88
cultural hierarchy, 63
cultural identities, 89
cultural intermediaries, 102
cultural logics, 26–38, 89
cultural politics, 44, 90
  language, 94–6
cultural production, behind the scenes, 102
cultural taboos, 76
Culture Machine, 10, 113–14
Cunningham, S., 6–7, 9, 10, 19, 64, 66, 91, 100, 111

Das, Jyoti Kapur, 70
Das, Prasanto, 114
Dasgupta, Partho, 35
data prices, 84
Datta, A., 88–9
Dave, Datta, 107–9
de Certeau, M., 89
death threats, 76
decision-making, 9
Dice Media, 73–4
digital calling cards, 66
digital divide, 84
digital environment, complexity, 119
Digital India initiative, 6
digital labour, 102
digital 'pure-play' native portals, 5
digital surveillance, 128
digital transformation, 2
direct access, 50
disenchantment, 29
Disney+, 49–50, 54
distribution network, 120–1

DittoTV, 50–1
Dua, Mallika, 77, 110
Dugal, Rasika, 28, 37, 77–8, 132
Dutta, Kiran, 92–3, 96–7, 131
Dutta, Tanushree, 78
Dwibhashyam, Girish, 56

ecological approach, 19
economic imperatives, television, 25
eco-sphere business model, 127
elitism, 124
Enam Holdings, 68
entrepreneurial labour, 72–4, 124
ethical markers, 93

Facebook, 1, 3, 5, 6, 7, 8, 11, 47–8, 64, 65–6, 82, 85, 90–1, 121, 124, 127
Facebook Reels Play Bonus Program, 48
fandom practices, 96, 123
Film and Television Institute of India (FTII), 77–8
film financing, 120
5G, 6
Flipkart, 126–7
fluidity, 71–2, 119
formal–informal exchanges, 8, 20
formal–informal media economy, 10, 13–15
free marketplace, 127–8
freedom, 117
Freemium model, 6, 46–7, 49
frugality, 64–5
Fuchs, C., 102
future, the, 125–32

Ganti, T., 131
gatekeeping, 26
gender, 18
gender inequality, 8, 76–8, 110, 125
General Entertainment Channel (GEC), 27, 29, 33
genre diversification, lack of, 31
geopolitics, 44
Ghose, Priyam, 48, 72, 90–1, 97
ghostwriting, 27–8
gig economy, 102
global online distribution networks, 5

global outreach, 131
global portals, local strategies of, 54–7
globalization, 19, 62
Google, 6
Gopal, Radhika, 107–8
Govil, N., 16–17, 22
Great Indian Laughter Challenge, 110
Green, J., 66–7
Guha, Pallavi, 80
Gulati, S., 28, 29
Gupta, Amrit, 27–8, 31, 131
Gupta, Nabh, 46, 55

Hardy, K. C., 89, 93
Hastings, Reed, 54
Hegde, Chaitanya, 107–9
hegemonic practices, 63
Helicopter view, 119–22
Helo, 128
Herbert, D., 16
hierarchies, 26, 63, 64, 67–9
Hindi film industry *see* Bollywood
Hindi language, 44, 57, 88, 90, 98, 123–4
Hindi-centric government policies, 88
Hobson, Dorothy, 30–1
Hoichoi, 5, 44, 57–8, 58, 72, 85–6, 91, 96–7
Holt, J., 10
HOOQ, 126
Hotstar, 5, 6, 49–50, 54, 57–8, 59, 82, 101, 123
human-led approach, 112
Hussein, Mohit, 41

identity, 91–2
Iflix, 126
Indian Government, 128, 129
Indian Language Internet Alliance, 6
Indian Premier League, 50
industrial logics, television, 26–38
industrial practices, 122
inequalities, 63 *see also* gender inequality
influencers, 101
informal economy, 13–15
informality, 13–15, 62, 133
'Information Technology (Intermediary Guidelines and Digital Media Ethics Code) Rules 2021, 75

innovation, 30
interdependencies, 20, 120, 132–3
international diaspora, 51
internet, 5, 25, 39, 43, 123
Internet and Mobile Association of India (IAMAI), 75
internet penetration, 42, 123–4
internet-based content distribution services, 1, 2, 3
internet-distribution television, 11
interviewees, 20–1
interviews, 21–2

Jagad, Aayushi, 77
Jaggi, Ruchi, 36
Jain, Sidharth, 116
Jassal, Karandeep, 97
JioOnDemand, 44–5
job insecurities, 102
Joshi, Rohan, 27, 104
jugaad culture, 13

Kamra, Kunal, 67
Kapoor, Ekta, 39, 52–3
Kapur Das, Jyoti, 33
Kar, Saurav, 92
Kasturia, Naveen, 40, 72
Kay, K., 26, 63, 67, 77
Khan, Shah Rukh, 71
Khan, Zakir, 2, 77
Khanna, Kopal, 105
Khatri, Atul, 66
Kohli-Khandekar, V., 15
Koli, Prajakta, 113
KPMG, 27
Kripal, Arunesh, 113
Kuiper, 102
Kumar, A., 26, 35, 40, 89
Kumar, B Sai, 68
Kumar, Sangeet, 62, 63
Kwan, 1–2, 106–7
Kwanabler, 107

labour, strategic approaches to, 64–6
labour practices, 108–9
languages, 44, 51, 54, 83, 84, 86–8, **87**, 89–90, 94–6, 98, 123, 123–4, 127

language-specific portals, 5, 44, 57–9
LGBTQ+ community, 80
liberalization, 88
linguistic organization, 9
Little Things, 39
lived experiences, 38
Lobato, Ramon, 10, 13, 54, 100, 111
local identities, 46–7
localization, 88–9, 103, 106
localization practices, 48, 54–6, 59, 86, 107–9, 122, 123
    Multi-Channel Networks (MCN), 114, 115–6
    talent agents, 107–9
    creator, 91–6
    platform/portal, 89–91
Lorenzen, M., 14, 17
Lotz, Amanda, 7, 10, 11, 16

McGlynn, Paula, 93
Madhavan, Ranganathan, 30–1, 41
Maguire, J. S., 102
Makhija, D., 132
Malhotra, V., 36
Mandal, Pankaj, 109–10
Marathi films and television, 94, 94–5
Marathi language, 94–6, 123
market instability, 126
market intelligence, 101
Mathews, Raica, 104
Matthews, J., 102
meaning-making practices, 20
Media and Entertainment industry, growth, 2–3
media economy, 20
media personnel, exchange, 52
media production ecology, 19
medium-agnostic approach, 122
Mehra, Rajiv, 58
Mehta, B., 26, 34
Mehta, Nalin, 27, 30
memes, 65
Merchant, Niyati, 68
methodology, 20–2
#MeToo movement, 78–81, 125
micro-celebrities, 96
migration, 89

Mistry, Jigisha, 46
Mitra, A., 84–5
Mittal, Aditi, 66, 76, 77
Mittal, Chhavi, 40–1
mobile phones, 43
Mohan, S., 9, 86, 88, 114
Mohta, V., 91
monetization, 61, 65–6, 121, 123, 128–9
money-laundering, 14
Moorti, S., 36
MTV, 40
Mukherjee, Debashree, 19, 44
Mukherjee, Joy, 95
Mukherjee, Rahul, 19, 89
Multi-Channel Networks (MCN), 2, 9–10, 99–100, 100–2, 111–16, 122
    content-driven strategy, 111
    as creator networks, 111–14
    diversification, 114–16
    localization practices, 114, 115–16
    over-dependence on YouTube, 111–12
    role, 111
    services, 113
    talent-driven strategy, 111
multimodal practices, 64
multiple talents, managing, 109–11
multiscalar approach, 16
multitasking, 73–4
Munshi, S., 30, 36
Murmu, Korok, 58–9
MxPlayer, 1, 126

Nair, Sunil, 53, 90
naming conventions, 91–3
Nanda, Vinta, 79–80
Nandakumar, Anusha, 93
Nath, Alok, 79
National Digital Communication Policy, 6
National Optical Fiber Network, 6
nationalism, 35
nation-building, 44
Natu, Sumedh, 77
Neff, G., 74
Netflix, 1, 5, 7, 11, 43, 49, 59, 82, 101, 123, 131, 132
    AVoD service, 126
    censorship, 74–5
    local strategies, 54, 59, 107–9, 122
    Respect workshop, 79
    revenue model, 126
    subscriber numbers, 54
Network18, 45
networking, 63
new business practices, 64–74
    career building, 69–72
    corporate structures, 67–9
    entrepreneurial labour, 72–4
    professional identity, 66–7
    strategic approaches to labour, 64–6
new screen ecology, definition, 18–20
New Telecom Policy (NTP), 15
niche portals, 126
non-hierarchical corporate structures, 64, 67–9
non-linear programming, 26

OML, 55
One Digital Entertainment, 10, 112
online content practices, 83–98
    creator localization strategies, 91–6
    platform/portal localization strategies, 89–91
    regional, 85–9
    regional online creators, 96–7
online creator cultures, 39–40
Only Much Louder, 1–2, 77, 80, 103–6, 107, 109–10
'on-the-ground' view, 123–5
Over-the-top (OTT), 3
OZEE, 50–1

Pandita, Anirudh, 64–5, 68, 73–4
Pant, Sorabh, 64, 74
Paramount Pictures Pvt. Ltd., 45
Parkar, Mithila, 74
Parthasarathi, V., 5, 9, 20, 103
participatory culture, 26, 41
participatory framework. 3, 65
partnerships, 101
patriarchy, 37
Paytm, 127
Permanent Roommates, 38
piracy, 6, 120

platform economy, 5
platform/portal, localization strategies, 89–91
platform–portal interdependencies, 7–8
platform–portal–creator axis, 9
platform–portal–film divide, 11
platforms/portals, 3, **4–5**, 5, 10–12, 43–59, 100, 120, 121, 121–2, 131, 133
    broadcaster-owned portals, 49–51
    content strategies, 125
    diversification, 126–7
    the future, 125–9
    language-specific portals, 44, 57–9
    local strategies of global portals, 54–7
    market instability, 126
    new features, 64
    niche, 126
    production costs, 124
    pure play local portals, 51–6
    reach, 65
    social media platforms, 45–8, **47**
    telecom-led portal, 44–5
    transition from, 124
Pocket Aces Pvt. Ltd., 38, 64–5, 68, 73–4, 124, 127
political economy, 62–4, 131
porosity, 16
portals *see* platforms/portals
Powder, 37
power dynamics, 129–30
precarious creativity, 62–4, 81
precarious labour, 8
precarity, 124–5, 130–2
privacy, 48
production costs, 124
production culture, 1, 2, 25
production schedules, 28
professional identity, 66–7
professional standards, 31
professionally generated content (PGC), 10–11
profitability, 14
public interest litigation (PIL), 74
Punathambekar, A., 9, 84, 86, 88, 114
pure play local portals, 51–6
Put Chutney, 86

Qyuki Digital Media, 10, 113, 114

Rahman, A. R., 84
Rai, Amit, 13
Rao, Rajkumar, 41
Rashtriya Swayam Sevak, 75
Rath, Biswa Kalyan, 105
ratings, 34, 35, 53, 58
Ravichandran, 51
Ravindran, Sidharth, 34, 86–8
reach, 65
reality shows, 27
regional content, 83–4, 85–9
regional creators, 44, 96–7, 124
regional film industry, 97
regional landscape, 86–8, **87**
regionalization, 88–9
regulation, lack of, 63
Reliance Industries Limited (RIL), 5, 52–3
Reliance Jio, 44–5, 94–5, 119–20
Reliance Jio Infocomm, 50
Reliance JioOnDemand, 5–6
remuneration, 65
representation, techniques of, 30
research objectives, 10–11
revenue streams, 6, 65–6
right-wing extremist forces, 75–6
Rishi, B., 44
risk, minimizing, 65, 72
risk-taking, 62
roles, innovating, 70
Roussel, V., 103

Sachdeva, Ankush, 127
safety, 48
sampling, 21
Sanson, K., 10
Saregama, 48
Sarkar, Priyanka, 58
Sarkar, Trishaan, 32
Sathaye, Sarang, 93, 94, 94–5
screen infrastructure, lack of, 95, 98
Screwvala, Ronnie, 68
scriptwriting, 108
Sehgal, Dhruv, 38–9, 39–40, 41, 73–4
self-branding, 65
self-employment, 65
self-imposed censorship, 76

Sena, Shiv, 74–5
Senft, T. M., 96
Sethia, Vaibhav, 66–7
sexual harassment, 78–81
Sexual Harassment Act, 79
Sharechat, 127
Shitty Ideas Trending, 40–1
short-form content, strategic use of, 65
Silly Monks Entertainment Pvt. Ltd., 114–16
Sillymonks, 10
Simon Fraser University, 93
Singh, Bhanu, 127
Singh, Gurpreet, 112, 113
soap operas
  audience, 34–5
  cinematic techniques, 38
  critique, 28–9
  distinctiveness, 29
  failure of, 29–30
  gendered perception of, 36–8
  melodramatic overtones, 30–1
  over-reliance on, 25, 26–7, 121
  production practices, 37–8
  techniques of representation, 30
social capital, 2, 41, 52, 61
  monetization, 65–6
social media
  career building through, 62, 63–4, 69–72, 81
  lack of transparency, 72
  multitasking characteristic of, 62
social media affordances, 72
social media creator labour, 59
social media platforms, 2, 45–8, **47**, 100
  close-ended, 7
  open-ended, 7
  US-centred, 6–7
social relations, 8
socioeconomic growth, 18
Sony, 5, 51
Sony Pictures Network India, 51
SonyLIV, 11, 59, 101, 123
spatial communities, 86
spatial stories, 89
specificity, 59

sponsorships, 124
sports programming, 49, 50, 58–9
Spuul, 5, 56–7
Srinivas, S. V., 20, 84
stand-up comedians, 66, 95, 103–6, 110, 122, 124
Star India Network, 49
Story Ink, 116
strategic approaches to labour, 64–6
Strauss, A., 22
streaming services, 1, 3, 5, 17
subscriber base, 49
subscription rates, 54
Subscription Video-on-Demand (SVoD), 6, 17, 55, 56–7, 58–9, 91
Sundaram, R., 10
Suresh, Sumukhi, 105
sustainability, 64–5
SVF Entertainment Pvt. Ltd., 57

Taeube, F. A., 14, 17
talent, lack of, 30
talent agents, 1–2, 99, 100–2, 103, 103–11, 122
  capitalistic tendencies, 130
  diversification, 106–7, 129–30
  influence, 106
  localization practices, 107–9
  multiple talents, 109–11
  power dynamics, 129–30
  role, 103–6
  tensions with, 110
  transnational ambitions, 107
talent development, lack of, 27
talent industry, 9–10
talent management companies, 102–3
talent metrics, 104
talent-driven strategy, 111
telecom company-led portal, 5, 44–5
telecom competitors, 5
television, 15, 25–42, 30–3, 94
  audience, 34–5
  audience migration, 42
  casting practices, 32–3
  channels, 27
  content library, 120

dependence on advertisements, 34
dominance, 125
economic base, 34–5
economic imperatives, 25
economies of scale, 34
fundamental challenges, 27
gatekeeping, 26
gendered perception of, 36–8
hegemonic practices, 63
hypersensitive approach, 30
industrial and cultural logics, 26–38
lack of enthusiasm, 40
lack of genre diversification, 31
liberalization, 88
new screen ecology, 38–41
over-reliance on soap operas, 25, 26–7, 121
ownership structures, 119–20
post-liberalization, 27
production culture, 25
regressive programming practices, 8
viewership, 3, 25
textual evidence, 22
The Viral Fever (TVF), 7
Thomas, Julian, 13
Thomas, M., 6, 10
TikTok, 128
Times Internet Ltd., 1, 71
Tiwary, Ishita, 55
Tollywood, 57–8
top of the building view, 122
trade magazines, 22
traditional broadcasters-led portals, 5
Transaction Video on Demand (TVoD), 6
translocality, 88–9
transnational exchanges, 89, 123
Tulsea, 1–2, 107–9, 110
TV18 Broadcast, 50
TVF, 1, 55, 67–8, 73, 124
TVF Pitchers, 40
TVFPlay, 5, 51–2, 101

United Kingdom, talent industry, 9–10
urban–rural divide, 34

user-generated content (UGC), 10–11, 45–7, 124, 126

value-generation, 102
van Dijck, J., 11
Viacom18 Media Pvt. Ltd., 21, 50, 62
Viacom18 Motion Pictures, 50
video cassette distribution, 85
viewership
　female, 53
　habits, 43
　male, 53
　streaming services, 3
　television, 3, 25
viewership metrics, 8, 18
viewing habits, 43
Vishwa Hindu Parishad, 75
Vodafone, 5
Voot, 5, 6, 50, 59, 62
Vyas, Original, 30–1

Walmart, 126–7
web series, 38–9
Whistling Woods International, 45
women, 18, 29–30, 36–8
writers, 108–9

Yashraj Films, 57
YouTube, 1, 2, 3, 5, 6, 7, 8, 39, 40, 45–7, **47**, 51, 52, 64, 65, 66–7, 70–1, 82, 100, 121, 124
　algorithms, 62
　gender inequality, 77
　localization practices, 86
　over-dependence on, 111–12
　participatory culture, 26, 41
　PGC content, 11
　regional online content, 83–4, 85
YouTube Space, 45–6

Zafirau, Stephen, 102–3
ZEE5, 5, 50–1, 58–9, 59, 126
Zelenski, D., 99
Zuckerberg, Mark, 48